THE PURPOSE OF THIS BOOK

THE PURPOSE OF THIS BOOK is to awaken from the dream of mortality (birth-death), that is, the illusion of the body-mind and world as being the basis of reality, which is the single cause of all suffering; to realize the truth of the One Reality without a second, ever-present as the Heart of Being, and remain in and as this absolute, pure Universal Awareness.

This means recognizing and ceasing the perpetual meditation of a separate-self identity, or ego — the false notion of individuality and self-conceit of being a separate "entity" or believed "person" living in time and space, habitually misidentified with the body-mind as being the Self. It is realizing Self as simple, pure, non-dual, Universal Awareness — the faceless, formless expression of pure Being living always, already in this eternal now, this one infinite presence — the nature of which is contentment, or peace, freedom, love and joy.

– A. Ramana

THERE IS NEITHER I,
NOR OTHER THAN I,
THERE IS ONLY. . .

by
A. Ramana

Published by

ähäm

AHAM Publications
Asheboro, NC 27205
U.S.A.

(Printed in India)

By this author:

Consciousness Being Itself
The Handbook to Perpetual Happiness
Discover Meditation™ Booklet & Tape
Radical Realizations and Frequently Used AHAM Terms
Living Free
Living Free While Incarcerated
Freeing Yourself From the Prison of Your Mind

This book was originally published in 1979 as a training manual.
The first revised edition copyrighted © 1989
as *AHAM's Freeborne Training Manual*.

First bound edition © 1999

Revised bound edition © 2006

AHAM Publications
Asheboro, North Carolina 27205

Cover: photo is the holy hill, Arunachala, South India,
Jim Dillinger, photographer; touchup by Julie Peters;
Layout by Atma Christiansen.

AHAM Publications, 4368 NC Hwy. 134,
Asheboro, North Carolina 27205 USA
Phone: (336) 381-3988 Fax: (336) 381-3881
E-mail: ahamcntr@asheboro.com
Web site: www.aham.com

AHAM Publications is a division of the ASSOCIATION OF HAPPI-
NESS FOR ALL MANKIND (AHAM) INC., a nonprofit spiritual education organization. AHAM, at its Meditation Retreat and Spiritual
Training Center in North Carolina, and at its ashram in South India,
conducts various Consciousness Transforming Seminars based on
the pure Teachings of the great 20th century sage, Bhagavan Sri Ramana Maharshi. Particular emphasis is given to non-duality, to the
process of Self-Inquiry, his special "*method*" for Spiritual Enlightenment, or perpetual abidance in the pure Awareness of the true Self.

ISBN: 1-888599-34-0 (Soft cover)

Bhagavan Sri Ramana Maharshi

A. Ramana

TABLE OF CONTENTS

TABLE OF CONTENTS

TABLE OF CONTENTS

SECTION III
Traditional Techniques

SECTION ONE

PRELUDE:

ACKNOWLEDGMENTS,

DEDICATION,

PREFACES,

AUTHORSHIP,

APPRECIATION

JUST FOR THE RECORD

ORIGINALLY, THIS BOOK was written for readers not yet ready to hear and embrace the Highest Truth of Advaita (non-duality), but only beginning to consider it, who embrace basic New Thought or similar metaphysical teachings. The text requires you to stretch your beliefs a step beyond where you may presently feel easy or comfortable.

In those days, some were dealing with what to them were "new" spiritual truths, principles, and concepts to be assimilated by the mind, or into their systems of belief. Many had lived their lives in the heart of "the Bible belt" of North America, and their minds had been conditioned by the fear, superstition, and narrow beliefs of fundamentalist religion.

Admittedly, statements and references in some parts of the text, written years ago and not here revised, appears to come from duality (Dvaita), and as either being what's so or as the writer's level of realization and teaching. Its wording may seem to support the false assumption (though incorrectly) of there being believed individuals or separate persons living in time and space – even though this is consistently refuted and contested throughout the text, as being *not* the highest truth.

The Ultimate Truth is always, already the One Reality of the Supreme Absolute Being, ever appearing here and now *as* all apparent persons, places, things, and events, with there being *no separate individual* anywhere to know this. Truth is the very Seeing/Knowing Itself, being infinite and eternal and yet itself incapable of being seen or known. All *is* IT.

Everyone understands the importance and benefit of words for conveying knowledge and clear, intelligent understanding between people. A basic problem however is words often have different meanings to different people. What is more, words arise in the present, while the information they convey or facts they describe often occurred in the past and is no longer so, for the past does not exist, only the present exists.

The problem with using words to convey meaning to spiritual truth is they are manifestations in duality, or the mind, which is *not* where the true Self abides – at least not in its pure essence. It permeates time and space, but does not live there.

Since words are products of thought that is only from the past though rising in the present, words cannot "get at" the true Self, cannot adequately describe or state what It *actually is*, or even its true nature, since It is occurring in the eternal present prior to thought or words. We can *be* the Self; we cannot in Truth adequately *describe* or *explain* or even "know" the Self. There is no "other" to know the one Self. The Self, being the pure Awareness that "lights up" (gives its light to) the mind and apparent thinker, it cannot be seen with the mind, because It (the Self) is *prior to* the mind. The eyes cannot see themselves, nor can the pointing finger point to itself.

This means, therefore, that all that you are reading here is in fact *not itself* the truth; it is merely "pointing to" the truth, the true Self, which *ever-abides* prior to time and space. Realization "discloses" the Truth: there is not now, nor has there ever been, nor will there ever be an individual being, a separate self, or "person" living "outside" the One Reality. All in Truth "is" the Absolute Being – (poor English, but rich truth). *We all are That* which presently emanates as this One Universal Awareness.

So, please accept this explanation of the "necessity" of using these limited words to try and communicate what can never be correctly stated or said – particularly the first person words like "I," "me," and "my," and/or the second and third person words: "you," "he," "him," "she," "her," "they," "them," "their," etc. These are mere grammatical conveniences, *not the truth* as has been realized and is being shared in this very wordy series of discourses. Silence, or silently *being* the pure Awareness that *is* the Truth, is itself the one *true* "language" that actually "says" the truth. Everything else is clatter.

There is really "no one here," there is "nobody home," nor am "I" seeing "you" as an individual; for in truth there is *no one*. Only the infinite, eternal Being *is*, and we are all That.

Please try to remember this, throughout this text: that there is in fact no separate, individual being to whom or for whom this book is written or intended, that "such a one" (anyone being addressed as such) is *only* a concept, like everything else presently appearing in consciousness, or in this apparent world of time and space.

DEDICATION

THIS REVELATION OF TRUTH is gratefully dedicated to all the Teachers of Spiritual Knowledge whose writings, teachings, talks, and physical or subtle Presence has contributed to completing and stabilizing this writer's spiritual awakening and abidance in the Self. In particular is Jesus Christ.

To name just a few of these, prior to Realization, are Emmet Fox, Charles and Myrtle Fillmore (the cofounders of Unity), Emilie Cady (a very special writer in the early New Thought movement), Joel Goldsmith, Neville Goddard, Walter Russell, Paramahansa Yogananda, Roy Eugene Davis, Ram Das (formerly Mr. Richard Alpert), Bubba Free John (before he started changing his name and whose present name is not certain or important), Sri Ramakrishna and J. Krishnamurti. There have also been many others too numerous to mention, but all of them are held in very high esteem.

Not long after the initial "transforming event," the opportunity occurred to have Conscious Company (*Sat Sanga*) with Swami Muktananda (Baba), a Siddha Yogi. This included the direct physical meeting with him and imbibing of his direct spiritual presence (*darshan*) and his profound grace. This served to confirm the authenticity of the earlier Awakening, and to stabilize it. It was Baba who gave me the spiritual name "Ramana," after my beloved Guru. The writings of Bhagwan Sri Rajneesh (Osho) also served as verification of the completed transcendental state that now and always remains.

But, most highly revered and with gratitude is Bhagavan Sri Ramana Maharshi, whose infinite and eternal grace itself brought about "my" spiritual Awakening. To him there is unending gratitude for being totally consumed in what can only be described as present-moment eternal Bliss – or Pure Happiness, Freedom, Peace and Love ... NOW.

It was Sri Bhagavan's great grandnephew, V. Ganesan, who gave "me" the other name, "Arunachala," about 25 years later.

– A. (Arunachala) Ramana

PREFACE TO FIRST REVISED EDITION

THE FIRST BOUND EDITION of this book, printed in early 1999, unfortunately contained many typographical errors despite several proof readings.

In spite of its errors, there have been gracious responses from readers the world over expressing their appreciation and joy in reading it, and the way it has clarified many of their doubts, and answered many long-held questions.

This writer is happy to have more people benefit from what is often reported to be its simple, direct message of "the way *'it all is,'* and *works."* The book is now used as a text in the home study follow-up for students who have attended the third phase of AHAM's entry-level programs, and is a prerequuisite to attending all other later AHAM programs.

Since its first printing, AHAM's "campus/retreat facility" has grown substantially, having added a large modular 6-bedroom house on its existing property. We have also purchased the property (2.5 acres with house) next to us to the south, converting it into what we call "The Awareness Center," our main training room. One of our members has purchased the house next to us on the north with its 10 acres of property. She converted the house's garage into a large activity room, held for AHAM's use as an extra training room. In addition, next to it is a small bunkhouse used mainly for AHAM's young people and occasionally for the "spill-over" when larger numbers attend programs.

AHAM also now owns and operates a beautiful, new modern 26-guest capacity ashram in Tiruvannamalai, South India, near the foot of the holy mountain, Arunachala. It is located about 3.5 miles around the hill from Sri Ramanasramam, the ashram (hermitage) and shrine of Bhagavan Sri Ramana Maharshi. This writer stays at our India Ashram about four months each winter and offers *Sat Sanga* (Conscious Company) sessions for spiritual seekers from around the world. In addition, AHAM's entry-level programs are conducted there every year during that time.

PREFACE TO THE FIRST BOUND EDITION

THIS BOOK was written in 1979 in Greensboro, North Carolina. The text was then used as the training manual in what was one of AHAM's first workshops, "The Freeborne Seminar." Many people studied it in its 3-ring binder format in those days, knowing it by the workshop name, "The Freeborne Manual."

This was before AHAM – the Association of Happiness for All Mankind – had a facility of its own. In those days, I conducted consciousness transforming workshops in and around Greensboro, in various facilities, such as the Founder's Hall at Guilford College, borrowed conference rooms at the Gate City Savings and Loan bank, and various community colleges. The primary location was in the townhouse of Patricia Thompson, which she also provided to me as my home for almost 15 years, and to AHAM as its first official, permanent address.

These seminars were usually attended by spiritual seekers, most of whom were introduced through the diligent efforts of Elizabeth MacDonald, my first student in Greensboro, who is now AHAM's executive director and senior trainer.

In 1980, a small group of dedicated, regular participants had formed. They requested that I give weekly talks on Sunday mornings. These talks began in the Janus Theater in Greensboro. A year later, AHAM rented a building on West Market Street in Greensboro where a small bookstore was started. In the back of the storefront building, separated only by a ceiling-to-floor divider curtain that we put up, weekly "Sunday Morning Interludes" were held. These sessions were an alternative to traditional church services for those who no longer felt compatible with their professed religion, but were still earnestly pursuing God, or Self-realization. On other occasions, which became more frequent over time, this area served as a training room for the ongoing workshops and programs and as a meeting room for other group functions for the increasing numbers of active AHAM participants. Some drove in regularly from other cities, like Winston-Salem, Charlotte and Statesville, North Carolina, and others from even greater distances like Asheville, North Carolina, Atlanta, Georgia, Virginia Beach, Virginia, etc., to attend the weekend programs, talks and other activities.

West Market Street soon became a very busy and noisy street for a facility dedicated to meditation. But, we all came to love "our little center" and to respect the quality of Conscious Energy felt by just walking into the building.

Most people who visited our bookstore to browse or buy books could not understand the Presence of extreme Stillness and intense Peace they felt from just being in the store. Being as we were (and still are) in the middle of what is commonly known as "the Bible belt," this quality of extreme Stillness was *very* intense for some of our visitors. The subject matter of our free literature was also radically different from what they were accustomed. Since our book selections were primarily about spiritual enlightenment, God-realization, higher states of consciousness, transformation, comparative religions, etc., and often were either by or about Self-realized teachers (some with strange or foreign names they could not pronounce) some of the local people became immediately disinterested, and even uncomfortable, and left quickly. Rumors began to spread, warning those in this very conservative traditionally Christian community, that we were "a religious cult." This was also because we presented Jesus Christ in a more open and liberal manner, according to the doctrine and teachings of *Advaita* (non-dual) Vedanta. Or, more like the spiritual philosophy of the less known and accepted New Thought Movement embraced by liberal thinking churches such as Unity, Religious Science and Divine Science. Spiritually, these movements offer a refreshing reprieve from the often fear-based teaching of some modes of fundamentalist Christianity.

Today, AHAM owns and operates a beautiful, peaceful meditation retreat and spiritual training center or ashram located about 45 miles south of Greensboro. Here we conduct a full curriculum of Consciousness Transforming Programs for beginning and advanced students.

Each year hundreds attend our programs from all over the world, from Europe to Australia, from Canada and Central America to India. They come for special spiritual training and guidance, or simply to rest and relax or "hang out" in Conscious Company. Many come for weeks and months at a time to enjoy living and working in the transformational spiritual energy and the underlying silence, stillness and peace of our facility. Some have even moved nearby, to permanently live and work close to our center.

AUTHORSHIP

THIS IS "YOUR BOOK." It is or has been written by *you*, *for* you. It is your own message to you about the Ultimate Truth of Who and What *You* Really Are. Therefore, much of it is written in FIRST PERSON, as a present moment affirmation to yourself, by yourself, about the Self you *really* are. When you read the portions written in first person, do not think they are just the words of this author whose name appears on the cover of the book. Read these words as *your own words to yourself!*

When you read them, it will be the present moment, just as it is now the present moment in which they are being written. As you read, you may awaken to, realize and verify the Truth they convey: that there is in fact *no* entity or "person" – i.e., no separate self or individual as "I," or "me," or "you," or "your," or "him," or "her," or "us," or "them" actually existing separate and apart from the One Reality. There is only the Universal Self, or pure Awareness in which all concepts of "I" and "not-I" appear, remain for an interval, and subside.

Almost every paragraph herein is a Conscious Process in itself. In many instances, each paragraph is a complete and self-contained message, even though it is also part of a larger all-inclusive message, which is likewise a whole message.

Thus, it is suggested you read "Your Book" from beginning to end, and then again and again. Then, in any moment when there is felt the need for spiritual or emotional steadiness, or you just want to relax and meditate, open "Your Book" at random and read any portion that catches your eye.

A continuous, repeated reading of this book – Your Book – over time will ultimately, spontaneously awaken you to the prior state of the true Self, which is the true and natural state, being the Location of Eternal Happiness in the Heart, known in the East as *Sahaja Samadhi*, and in the West as Christ Consciousness, Transformation, Enlightenment or Self-Realization.

A NOTE OF APPRECIATION

THIS WRITER wishes to express appreciation and heart-felt gratitude to Virginia Rhodes for her generosity of time and energy in the exhausting effort of typing and then correcting, and again retyping the original manuscript of this book in 1979 – *without the benefit of a word processor*. It took countless hours to accomplish, for she had only her ordinary yet reliable electric typewriter.

Thank you, Virginia. Your selfless dedication is appreciated not only by this writer, but also by the many early participants in AHAM's Freeborne Seminar where the first edition of the book, which you typed, was used as our training manual.

Also, sincere thanks go to both Linda Swanson and Richard Fletcher for their long and tireless work in editing the revised manuscript for the first bound-edition of this book.

Linda, your overall editing and suggestion to rearrange various ideas and themes from the original into a better, more efficient thematic order, including the creation of new sections, etc., and Richard, your extensive editing, and your suggestions urging the use of different, clearer wording throughout the text to express the main ideas, have combined to make the book easier to read and understand.

My warm thanks goes to you both.

And, in addition, my sincere appreciation is now extended to Charlotte Twardokus, Jan Sundell, Anne DeLaVergne and Doug High for their contribution in reading and editing this first revised edition, and also to Linda Swanson for her additional proof-reading of it as well. Also, to Vivian Zelig for her help in laying out its new cover.

INTRODUCTION:
REALIZING A "CONSCIOUS MIRACLE": THE WAY OF HAPPINESS-NOW

TO BEGIN WITH:

UNDERSTANDING TRUE RELATIONSHIP

or

HAPPINESS IS IN NO "OTHER"; TRUE HAPPINESS IS ONLY IN THE SELF

REALIZING A "CONSCIOUS MIRACLE":
THE WAY OF HAPPINESS-NOW

TOTAL HAPPINESS-NOW IS NO MERE WISH. It is not only possible, it is the *natural state* – prior to body-mind identification, prior to the formation of the mind and its content of conditioned memories of the past, its many patterns and forms (subjective or objective) in apparent time and space.

The Purpose of AHAM – THE ASSOCIATION OF HAPPINESS FOR ALL MANKIND is to share *The Enlightened Way of Happiness-NOW!* It is for everyone ready to discover and realize the true nature of the Self as the actual Location of Real Happiness and the immediately present, natural state. It is to consciously transform one's ability to experience life, so that the usually seen abuses and disturbances of apparent ordinary daily life are no longer seen, felt or considered upsetting, but that one's true nature – which is always, already present happiness – is freely lived and expressed *here and now*, in every moment and experience!

Therefore, the purpose of AHAM, and this book, is to awaken to the true Self. It is to discover living *prior to* all dualities and opposing patterns – to transform all your anger into compassion; upset, restriction and limitation into freedom and humor; confusion into certainty, peace and order; hatred into forgiveness, compassion and love; dis-ease and illness into ease and health; lack into abundance – or, in short, *all* unhappiness into Happiness-NOW.

In all the programs presented at AHAM in its Conscious Curriculum, it is seen how sorrow and suffering, impairment and limitation are unconsciously inflicted on "ourselves" by identifying with the body-mind and the constant sense of being separate from the Source (God) and the apparent world, and the mind's ordinary, ever-compulsive resistance to the experiences of life. We then paradoxically *seek* security and happiness *in* and *from* the world in the form of pleasure, which we believe comes *only* from more, better and different experiences *in* the world, i.e., from objective persons, places and things, or subjective personal experiences. As Bhagavan Sri Ramana Maharshi, the great 20th century Sage of South India, said, *"Without knowing the real nature of one's Self, and being identified with the body-mind as being the Self, and trying to find happiness in the world from the pleasures of the world, is like grabbing hold of a hungry crocodile, thinking it to be a log, and trying to use it to cross a river."*

The Self is consciousness or pure Awareness. Consciousness is the only existence or reality. Absolutely, Self is the "nothing-ness" of timeless, space-like pure Awareness in which everything appears and disappears. The true Self is God expressing as the one and only Reality, the source and substance of all that is, the Self of all selves, the very Being of all beings.

When "I" think I am separate from "you" – when "I" feel "other" than "you" – I am creating a gap between us, a separation, a division in our sameness or true oneness. This is avoiding Relationship, rejecting "this aspect" of Self or not acknowledging you as the one Self. I am avoiding or rejecting the truth; for *all* is Self. This even happens when I believe, affirm, and feel that "I" love "you" as an "other." It bifurcates Consciousness. It divides the one Consciousness into two, making love the opposing counterpart of non-love, or hate.

This very activity, or "separativeness," is "sin," the primary activity of ordinary individual consciousness (or "man"). Sin is the ongoing activity of dividing the one Consciousness into the appearance of many (which is duality). It is meditating a "separate self" identity and thinking this is "you." This creates fear, threat, suspicion, anger, sorrow and unhappiness in life. It also motivates seeking happiness and security in and from the world. It causes the continual striving in the world for pleasure. It causes greed, the acquiring and accumulation of more, better and different experiences in the world (persons, places and things) all erroneously believed to provide happiness. This brings a false sense of security, pleasure, control, power, and avoidance of pain and suffering, which are always only short-lived and unfulfilling.

Already suffering from this primary ignorance of separateness itself, by being identified with the body-mind as the Self and living from this false sense, feeling ourselves to be separate from the Source, then *all* actions arising from this separated sense are *already destined* to failure, frustration or further conflict. No matter what we believe, think, say or do, it results in reactions or opposition from the world. Such opposition is in exact proportion and degree to the original force with which all so-called "personal" actions are initiated, sent forth, sustained, continued, enforced, or defended by us. This is the very principle and basis of all worldly conflict, contradiction, and confusion. It is the cause of all one's suffering.

When we spiritually Awaken, and live life *as* and *from* the Source, pure Awareness, the very Self, or the Heart of being – *as* the Source, the Heart, the very Self – all sense of "I" and "not-I" dissolves. Oneness, sameness or non-difference from the Source and all that is – which is unconditional love, acceptance, and approval – is experienced and lived NOW, in this instant ever-present moment, which is *always* NOW.

This is *Living Free!* It is *being* love, peace, freedom, and happiness – not dependent on anything or anyone outside *for* love and happiness, and not being "someone" who is living free. The One Self is naturally radiating, sharing, expressing love and happiness. This is occurring with regard to everyone and everything *appearing in and as the world*. This lived principle and process manifests its own nature and its own counterpart: the corresponding subjective and objective experiences of *living* prosperity, *living* joy, *living* health and *living* happiness in true relationship with all life. The experiences felt are primarily of these qualities and states, regardless of all the outer or objective events and circumstances *appearing* to be going on in the world to the contrary.

This has been the direct experience and expressed teaching of the world's Great Beings or Master Teachers throughout history. This is what Jesus Christ shared with his disciples, and is available to his present devotees, or to those who can "hear" his True Message. Nor is it different from the teachings *even earlier* of Lord Buddha. It is not any different from the Sufi sect of Islam. It has also been verified and demonstrated in modern times by the lives and living examples of Sri Ramakrishna and Bhagavan Sri Ramana Maharshi.

Those identified with the body-mind as being their "self" see life divided as "I" and "other," or "I" and "not-I." A Sage, Buddha, or "Christed-being" (anyone enlightened, living free from body-mind identification in the Awakened realization of pure Truth, perfect Understanding and Real Happiness) sees life and all in it as merely an expression or out-picturing of the One Being that always, already is. They see everything occurring *in* the Self, *as* the Self. The world is seen, including everyone and everything in it, as an expression of the One Being, or Self, the One Reality – not separate, not different – and with no compulsion or desire to compare, judge, resist, reform or change what is now present, or currently so.

What is *so*, in any given moment, is the truth in that moment. When not separate from life, there is no conflict with what's so in any moment. Life is always, already perfect, and is seen with compassion and humor. There is true acceptance of what otherwise appears as opposing, ugly, unfriendly or unpleasant to the perception of bystanders. We may even see it being uplifted or improved. If pain arises or appears in our experience, it is seen in the moment as only appropriate, or for what it is without judgment or rejection. We accept it and see it eventually disappear or transformed into pleasure, compassion or humor. We see anger for what it is, accept it, and watch it transform into compassion and humor. We see fear of death for what it is, accept it, and see it transformed into the awareness of eternal life.

Ordinary Self-abidance when realized, is one's direct or immediate *now*-awareness and experience; it is *not* a belief or concept. This is living *as* the Awakened Heart, or Self. Abiding in and *as* the Self, this pure Awareness or Source dissolves the mind, the believed to be conditioned individual and the total accumulated content of its patterned tendencies (the past), leaving a clear space of steady, ceaseless happiness *always* remaining here and now as pure natural Self expression.

AHAM is a Fellowship, a Conscious Community, a mutual Association dedicated to living here and now present as the Awakened Heart, in now-Happiness. Participants live free of concern, participating in interactive relationships, serving the remembered expression of Truth, ever removing, releasing and transcending any conditioned tendencies or habits of limitation, all separateness and separativeness, all "doing" and tendencies "to do," all "seeking" and tendencies "to seek." This conscious fellowship is made possible by AHAM's special programs, spiritual training, consciousness-clearing workshops, and other regular association functions. However, it is sustained principally by the presence and grace of Conscious Company (*Sat Sanga*) and Fellowship, a transformed spiritual environment of non-seeking and non-separativeness, or *pure living love.*

It is the false assumption of separateness and the assumed

and lived sense of "past and future time" that give rise to these illusions as apparent "realities." In Absolute Truth, *there is no separate one.* There is no reality in either the past or the future. *They do not of themselves exist!* Time is a concept maintained entirely by agreement. The only reality is the ever-present (eternal) now, the ever-present (infinite) here, or the infinite and eternal Self, which lives only in and as this eternal and infinite state of uncaused, unqualified Awareness.

Time and space are merely concepts that together make possible our usual perception of an ordinary three-dimensional world filled with objects, including our own body, and the bodies of seeming "others." Without apparent space (volume), there could be no room or area in which objects of mass could exist or appear, and without apparent time (the period, interval or duration for perceiving), no way for their perception to occur. Thus, *these two primary concepts* – time and space – provide the way and means for all phenomenal objects (even the sense of objectivity itself) to occur. Since all objects are themselves entirely dependent on concepts for their very existence, this means the phenomenal world of objects (including all persons, places and things) is in fact *totally conceptual!* It does not exist, as such. The phenomenal world only exists conceptually or perceptually, or only in our consciousness of it. It is *entirely* mental, an illusion. It exists *only* in the mind!

The body and the sense of separateness, which give rise to the ego or the seeming separate-self when identified with, appear to occur in the realm of all these seeming phenomena, but actually occur only in the mind. Truth, reality, oneness and wholeness are eternal, and abide in the Absolute Realm of pure Being, the Self. This is the Realm of God, the Source, the Heart, and the Holy Spirit. This was (is) the Realization of Buddha, it is enlightenment, and is not different from Christ's Consciousness, but there is no "one" knowing this, it is the pure Knowing itself.

Exclusive meditation or contemplation of the Source, the Heart (which is no-Thing and is no-Where), is *inclusive* of everything and is everywhere. This "no-thing-ness" and "no-where-ness" of the Source (Heart) is paradoxically experienced everywhere and in everything. When considered, or contemplated in relation to the body, it is felt as the primal psychic center (Center of consciousness, or the Spiritual Heart) experienced on the *right* side of the chest. This is where *everyone* always naturally and innocently indicates or gestures when pointing to "him" or "her" self. This primal Heart-center (in Sanskrit called, *Hridayam*), when discovered, is realized as a direct reflection of the Source, Real God, the Holy Spirit, the living energy of the Divine, the Absolute Supreme Being, the very Self of all selves. It shines or radiates in this location or area like direct sunlight is reflected in a mirror.

Those to whom this discovery and Awakening occur realize it as being alive and present as the very Self. This was Moses' realization as taught directly by God that, "*I AM THAT I AM.*" (Exodus 3:14) I AM is the Self, it is Jehovah, Buddha, Christ. With this Awakening, all the Great Beings around Whom all the world's major religions were formed – such as Buddha, Jesus Christ, and Mohammed – or were reinforced, magnified, or intensified – such as Rama or Krishna or Bhagavan Sri Ramana Maharshi, etc. – are the very same. They are not different from God. Thus, they are eternally alive in the Heart or inner being of everyone, as the Source of every being. Being always one with (or not different from) the Source, they are in fact alive in the Heart of each of their true devotees. They are not different from the true living Heart of all humankind, whether humankind as a whole is aware of this Truth or not. This becomes the *living* Truth or Reality for *all* when discovered and awakened. This is the Location of Real Happiness.

When this Truth is Awakened, it is the true "second coming" all of Christendom is awaiting; it is the coming of the true Messiah, Judaism is awaiting; it is Enlightenment that Buddhists are seeking; and, it is the all-encompassing and compassionate Allah the Merciful the Moslems are worshipping.

Referring to this Awakening, the Bible says, "*You will know the truth and the truth will make you free*" (John 8:32), which refers directly to this Realization of Self.

AHAM's ongoing purpose is to provide and preserve the Conscious Transformational Process of Self-Inquiry, which is the most direct process for this Self-discovery and Awakening to occur. Spiritual Enlightenment, with Self-Inquiry, is available for *anyone* open and receptive to It. However, a certain degree of spiritual maturity or readiness is required to see this, accept it, and diligently apply it in one's life.

AHAM's Sponsorship Program, developed in June 2004, is a recognized active society with many living free of body-mind addiction. Much like with Alcoholics Anonymous (AA) or Narcotics Anonymous (NA), or releasing addiction to substance abuse, AHAM's Sponsorship Program is dedicated to releasing the addiction to body-mind identification and compulsive thinking – the *primal addiction* that gives rise to *all other addictions*. This *can* occur by living the AHAM Teaching and having the guidance and assistance of an AHAM Sponsor in mutual support during this final or terminating endeavor.

AHAM also provides both the environment and the "place" for this Conscious Transformation to occur, at two locations our Spiritual Retreat and Training Center located 10 miles south of the city of Asheboro, North Carolina, and our ashram in South India. These are both very peaceful, yet high-energy facilities, and conscious environments for *daily living* the Truth *from* the transcendental state of present Peace and Happiness. Each support those ready to live "here and now" in direct realization and awareness *as* the one Self, free of all suffering and self-imposed limitation – including all sense of separateness and seeking, all sensed anger, fear, guilt, frustration, burden and unhappiness! From the Awakened Heart, the true Self, this is the natural state. From the point of view of the world, it appears to be a conscious miracle!

Many have discovered and are now *living* this realization, and themselves *already know* that AHAM is *an idea whose time has come!* Our two existing AHAM facilities are only the beginning of many planned AHAM communities to further fulfill AHAM's ongoing mission and purpose.

You see, **"Our Name Is Our Purpose!"** – i.e., the Association of Happiness for *All* Mankind.

With AHAM's growth, dedicated to expressing this highest purpose of life, there is always the need for those wishing to truly live free and see it happen, not only for them but also in the world-community. More who recognize this are now moving near to the AHAM Center to live and assist in this work. They are performing their personal skills, professions or vocations in the community, or nearby cities, and are assisting at the center as their time permits. We invite you to help. Or, join us in *living* this simple, pure teaching *wherever* you work or reside, in whatever community or country.

THE PARADOX OF OUR NEED FOR SELF-CONFIRMATION

WE ORDINARILY look for confirmation of our being outside ourselves. We are always looking to others to approve of and accept us, to confirm that we are worthwhile, that our existence is important and certain. It's as if we feel we don't even exist, or "matter," unless someone or something outside of us points to us and says that we are real, or are OK, and that we *do* "really matter." "Really mattering" is felt to mean having existence. "Matter" is that which lives in time and occupies space; it is something having form and dimension. To "really matter" then, means we are considered to be significant, or to have true being or real existence.

Now, the paradox is, we cannot deny our own existence. In fact, we don't even have to think to know that we exist. This is self-evident, and not as a body-mind, but as pure Awareness. But for most, that is not enough. We are always looking for confirmation of our "self" as though we do not exist. It is as if we are denying our existence, and while doing so, we are forever needing, craving and efforting for self-confirmation.

No one has to have a mirror to know that he or she *is*. You can know that you exist by your mere presence, your existence *as consciousness*. Descartes said, *"I think, therefore I am."* This means, the proof of existence is self-evident. But, the fact is, Descartes had it backwards. It is "I am, therefore I think"... that is, being is even *before* thinking occurs. It appears, then, that Descartes was not fully enlightened, at least not when he made this historically famous assertion.

Imagine entering a totally dark room, with no light to even see your own body, and a draft immediately slams the door shut behind you and it locks. Then suppose, right away, someone outside the room asks through the door, "Is my book or my coat in there?" Being in the dark, you would have to say, "I don't know." However, if they ask if *you* are in the room, even though you cannot see any limb of your body, you can easily and immediately know and reply, "Yes, I am in here." Your existence is not dependent on your body, your thoughts, or your sense perceptions, or anyone else's thoughts or physical senses or perception of you. You *are* existence, *itself!* You do not have to *think* you exist, to *know* that you exist!

Existence must exist, for there to be even the idea or notion of existence. Reality must be, in order for the sense of reality to be. Existence is the *only* reality. Existence exists eternally as Being itself, in the timeless awareness of I AM – to infinity.

Reality is always real. True reality cannot change and also (then) be real. That which changes is not real. That which changes has only the *appearance* of reality. Jesus said, *"Judge not by appearances* (that which is not real) *but judge by righteousness"* (that which is real or does not change). (John 7:24)

Thought changes. With the continual change of thought, the world of size, shape, and form is continually changing. The world of form is therefore not intrinsically real, but rather only apparently real. It is more of the quality of a dream. And, like the dream we have in our sleep, it is not of itself real.

That which *never changes* is Real. Primal consciousness (Pure Awareness itself) never changes, even though the *content* of consciousness changes constantly. Primal consciousness is the source and support of mind, which is the source and support of thought, which is the source and support of the world and the objects comprising the world. Thus, primal consciousness is the only reality. Mind and thought are its content.

The world is the content, expression, or manifestation of consciousness, or thought, appearing as a reflection on the one pure Awareness I AM, which is the prior supportive context of all that is. Conscious Awareness (as pure Being, or Context) does not change, even though that which I AM conscious *of* is in constant flux, is continually changing.

Before there is consciousness of any thing, or of expressing *as* any particular thing, *I am conscious!* But, there is no such entity as such who is doing the expressing. The pure Consciousness I AM is the true Self, not the sense of "I," or the "I"-thought I *think* I am. The pure Consciousness I AM, *prior* to the "I"-thought, is what is real. But the "I"-thought and that which I am conscious *of* (or conscious of being) is not real; it ever changes. What I am conscious of being is only a conceptual state, the ego, with which the pure I AM (pure Awareness) is possibly, momentarily identified. But it ceases as *my* state the moment I release identification, attachment or association with it. Yet, with the release of states I don't cease to be, for I AM real. I AM is pure, infinite, eternal Awareness.

Thus, I (the very Self) doesn't change, but my states do. I am not my states. All states are like garments I wear momentarily. It is the mind that fashions conscious energy in the form of the identified or chosen state, but I AM (the true Self) is not any state. I AM *is*, eternally, prior to all states, beyond all states, and untouched or unchanged by any state.

People and events appearing in the world disclose the states with which "I" (as mind) have become identified, by actively awakening or triggering these states. They are thoughts, or past experiences that, like images reflected in a mirror, are projected on the screen of pure Awareness, the true Self that I AM.

I, looking "outside" at the world-mirror, the movie of ordinary life, see these states projected there in the form of the people, places and things making up the world. I perceive them like holograms, physically appearing as the persons, places and events reflected in the mind, and seen by the awareness I AM. If what I see in the world is what I call "beautiful," it is actually a beautiful state awake and alive in mind, seen by the awareness I AM. If what I see in the world is seen as "ugly," it is actually an ugly state that is alive or awake in the mind. By looking for what is good, true and beautiful *from* the world, or from *life in the world*, without understanding the true nature or mechanism of the mind's perception, then I am looking amiss and will not find the *real* thing, quality, or experience I actually want or am looking for.

Goodness, truth, and beauty originate only within *Myself* (the Self) as their Source. These qualities or types of events will occur in "my" world only when I bring them into the world myself. If I expect them *from* the world, I am opposing the very process by which I can find and experience them. Even when I *think* they were given to me by someone or something outside myself or from the world, the truth is I was only experiencing them in myself. I was feeling their joy in *me*, not in the person, place or thing which seemed to bring them.

Our ignorance of this process is the cause of all suffering, limitation, and unhappiness! It is why we fail in our pursuit of happiness. When we habitually seek happiness *in the world*, from the persons, places and things seen in the world that we desire (which is ordinary man's ongoing pursuit), this is the *very cause of man's misery*, and his *continuing* in misery.

We cannot find happiness in the world. It is not there, not even the least trace or slightest bit. There is no happiness in *any* person, place, thing or experience in the world – *none whatsoever!* Even when we believe we are happy because of someone, or something happening to us or for us, that experience of joy is *not* in the person or thing itself. The truth is, that as happiness is occurring in our experience, as if from some apparent outer cause, our attention has actually pivoted and partaken of the *inner* quality of happiness that is *already there* as *our very nature.* The experience is *in us*, and *from us*, not in or from the world, not in the object or event itself. Real and true happiness is *always, already within us*, as the very nature of our being, in the interior of the heart-core of our very being.

When we spiritually awaken and rediscover this inner source (the Self) and live *only* from It (rather than from the ego and its compulsion to seek happiness in the world), we realize *"the truth that sets us free"* from all unhappiness, bondage and limitation. With this discovery, taught by the Master Jesus (John 8:32), we are reestablished in the kingdom of God that is *within us*, just as Jesus said it is. (Luke 17:21)

To look for some other person or thing outside our self to confirm our being, or to give us a sense of life, is looking for happiness or salvation in or from the world. This is putting the Self at the effect of the world and making the world "cause" in our life. To be thus "at effect" in relation to the world violates the basic teachings of the scriptures of all the major world religions, particularly the Bible. Even common "horse sense" would say that it is backwards. *"You shall not make for yourself a graven image or any likeness of anything that is in heaven above, or that is in the world beneath, or that is in the water under the earth; neither shall you bow down to them or serve them..."* (Deuteronomy 5: 8-9)

This commandment of Moses, when spiritually understood, refers to living life at the effect of thoughts and desires and depending on the outer things of the world for happiness. For the world seldom conforms to our demands, to how *we* want our life to be. Ordinary life in the world is often very unreasonable and unreliable, as are most of the people on whom we would depend for happiness. They often fail or refuse to do what we wish or expect, and are frequently unable to live up to our expectations; or they may intentionally deceive us. Or, they may die, leaving us alone, lost, and in pain.

To look for happiness outside of Self *from* relationships, is to experience duality or separateness from the Source. This avoidance of Truth is the real meaning of "sin." The truth is that our real and true nature *is* happiness, and is only found *in* the Self as the quality of true Self-acceptance and Self-love.

Seeking happiness in *any* outer or worldly form means having to deal with one upset or disappointment after another, whereas, simply abiding as we are in the true Self is being always, already happy. The inner Source of being, which is not different from God (or "Father" as Jesus referred to It), is the Location of the only real and lasting happiness.

"Do not love the world, or the things in the world. If anyone loves the world, love of the Father (the true Source or happiness) *is not in him. For all that is in the world, the lust of the flesh, and the lust of the eyes, and the pride of life is not of the Father, but is of the world. And the world passes away, and the lust of it; but he who does the Will of God abides forever"* (in true happiness). (1 John 1:15-17) Here John, Jesus' illumined disciple, is explaining the very same principle: there is *no* happiness in the world!

No person can ever be our happiness or source of happiness. If we think so, we are courting unhappiness and tragedy. If you think your happiness comes from another person, or even you *as a person*, then you had better know the other half of it as well! Your *un*happiness is also just as available from that same person! In due season, it will come forth to make its presence known and felt in your experience, and just as intensely as your "believed" happiness from them. The "one" who "makes" us the happiest is also the one who can "make"

us the unhappiest, or is the most capable of doing so. Therefore, the element of fear is always present in *every* happy relationship. It is always waiting just behind the scenes, to be
brought about by some incident, action, or refusal to act on the
part of the one "depended upon" for our happiness.

It's very simple, and a fact, that the persons we care for the
most can hurt us the most. They may say something that is
hurtful, intentionally or unintentionally. They may reject us,
or withdraw or withhold their support of us. Or they may die,
leaving us alone without an adequate replacement for our
needful dependency.

Someone reading this may come to the incorrect conclusion
that I am against having personal relationships. I am *not*
against personal relationships. Rather, I simply advise everyone to be *knowledgeable* and *consciously alert* about the *true* Location of Happiness. I am only cautioning against the "sin" of
"needful" dependency, in particular depending on anything
or anyone outside the Self for happiness. I am not for or
against *anything*. Rather, I am conscious of the truth about
what is detrimental or beneficial to one's happiness or well being.

Understand, you must *give* happiness *to* your relationships,
not try to take, acquire, or get it *from* your relationships. Happiness is inherent in the Self, *not* in any relationship. I'm
warning you against being unconscious in your relationships,
those based on your dependency, or incorrect relationships
ignorantly based on "need," so often seen with most people.

Our real existence or true Being (and thus real happiness) is
independent of any "other" being. Consciousness is its own
light. Consciousness is the only Light of Being. The one and
only Light of Being is I AM. Only I can say "I am" with regard to myself or my own state of being, well-being or lack of
well-being. No other says "I am" on my behalf, nor speaks
"the Word" – meaning, being the true Self – for me. *"In Him* (I
AM), *was* (is) *life, and the life was* (is) *the light of men. The light
shines in the darkness* (in our ignorance of it) *and the darkness has
not overcome it"* (or has not yet realized it or known it directly
for one's self). (John 1:4-5) [Read the above sentence again,
but only the *italicized* words, for it is the actual scripture].

This means that we do not have to strive or make effort in order to BE. We don't have to *do* anything in order to BE. Being is what we always, already *are*. There is never a moment in which we are not. Even when we appear *not* to be (as in sleep, coma, swoon, etc.), our being is never interrupted by the absence or variation in our state. We are still present, bearing witness to the particular state, as "I slept well," "I was in a void," "I was in a state of nothingness," or "I was unconscious," thus indicating our *presence* even in the states of coma, unconsciousness, or dreamless sleep. When thinking stops, we do not cease being or existing. We are still present, bearing witness to the state or fact of no-thought, or unconsciousness. The lack of thought, due to the withdrawal of the mind, may give rise to the notion of unconsciousness. However, we are ever-present as pure Awareness, being aware even of our own unconsciousness. When consciously alert, we may stop thinking, but it does not mean we stop being, or existing.

There is no such thing as absolute unconsciousness, meaning absolute non-awareness or non-being. There is only relative unconsciousness. And relative unconsciousness is not actually true unconsciousness, or loss of Awareness. It is only the void, blackness, blank, or clear state resulting when thought ceases, as in deep sleep, coma, fainting, or swoon. This is because the mind is withdrawn. This is ignorance-bliss.

Through long continued spiritual discipline, or the practice of meditation, the conditioned tendencies of the mind may be neutralized, transformed, dissolved or totally erased from the mind. The mind is then left in its original pure state of uncontaminated, unconditioned light. The apparent unconsciousness of deep sleep, coma, fainting or swoon is transformed into the awakened awareness of the eternal and infinite, uncaused and unqualified I AM – the living, radiant Heart, the very Self – which is the Source or Supreme Self of all selves. This is Conscious-Bliss.

This Bliss is also known as Christ Consciousness. Other terms are Jehovah Consciousness, Buddha Consciousness, Krishna Consciousness, Enlightenment, Transformation, Self-Realization, God-Realization, etc. It is the quality of pure Being, prior to all states, in and from which some Old Testament prophets, Jesus, Buddha, Krishna, etc., naturally and continually lived, and were always, already conscious.

For example, Moses was among the first to consciously realize, and later Jesus was fully aware that his own I AMness was one with or not different from the very I AM of real God, the Supreme Being. Jesus called this pure Being, "Father" (meaning the Source). He knew that IT shines in the interior of the heart-core of *all* beings, as the very Self of all selves, as present-moment peace, joy, love, creativity and prosperity, and as the only real happiness!

When this direct, present-moment realization is re-cognized (again known), liberation or "salvation" occurs. It is the "second coming" of Christ awaited or sought by the Christians. It is the coming of the Messiah awaited by the Jews. It is not only freedom from fear, suffering, hatred and unhappiness, but the end of their having an effect on you. It is the awakening and realization of perpetual joy, deep peace – the fulfillment of all desires, as it dissolves the one that formerly had a sense of desire.

However, this is not coming to the world in a massive Revelation or Apocalypse, or to a special or qualified religious group or society, but must or will be directly *realized* and *lived* by those that are spiritually or fully Awakened to it.

It occurs only with the dissolving of all sense of individuality, not as a "personal" awakening but ending of the seeming "person" in the Oneness, the All-ness of Being. It is not an expansive spiritual awakening occurring to some "one" who then remains in time as an "individual," or with a simultaneous awakening for the masses. More correctly stated, it is the radical dissolving of all sense of ego, or "I," "me," "my," and "mine," or being a separate-self, or separate person, or individual entity. The result is the Radiant Heart of God, now and forever known *in* the Heart *as* the Heart – being directly, infinitely *here*, and eternally *now*, without doubt or question or even anyone knowing this. It is just what is.

This Oneness permanently remains in the very face of all apparent adversity, challenge or conflict, as the timeless, present moment of all time, which is eternally NOW (for Now *is* eternal). It is the *realized* Truth: that "I AM that I AM!"

AGREEMENT – THE BASIS FOR MAKING
YOUR LIFE WORK

AGREEMENT is the "warp and woof," the very *founda-tion* or *basis* of the world of so-called "objective real-ity." Without agreement, there would be no concrete, external "reality" for anyone to experience. That is, without *agreement*, what is believed to be "real," what is named, called and routinely consider to be "all these solid objects" and/or particular *types* of events, which express or manifest as what is called "ordinary life" – whether pleasant or unpleasant – do not of themselves actually exist. These are all only concepts, the products of thought. It is all only a very long dream.

Just as the past does not exist apart from the thought of it, nor does the future (it being merely a vision), so the present world of so-called objective "reality" is also only a product of thought, just like a dream. It is based on our mutual agree-ment as to its existence, the labeled name and/or nature that *is given to each thing and to all events!*

This is super-simple, but it is generally not seen, understood, or even believed. However, you cannot avoid or get around it – agreement is the very mortar that holds the building blocks of objective "reality" together, or makes it appear solid, con-crete, sensory perceptible, "out there," or what we call "real."

For example, without agreement you cannot prove that ei-ther yesterday or tomorrow exist. No one has ever *seen* "to-morrow" nor can you actually *see* "yesterday." You may have a memory, and share "your" memory with someone else who also experienced the same event that occurred "yesterday" or in the past, but neither can actually see "yesterday" itself. For "yesterday" in itself does not exist. Only NOW exists; and yet even *its* present objective appearance requires our agreement in order to be in mutual accord with it or about it, and when we are communicating about it.

If the entire world apart from you suffered a form of amne-sia, or forgetfulness of memory, and no one remembered beyond the point of the present, you being the only human who recalled the past or could conceive of the future, you would be unable to prove that either of them existed; for neither of them exists in themselves. They only exist as a memory (past) and as a vision (future) *in the mind.* Consciousness, the Self, or pure Awareness – being the foundation supporting the mind, which is the sustainer of the concepts of past and future – only exists *now,* and is the only reality. NOW is the One Reality.

Existence *itself* must exist for there to be the notion or idea of existence, or even of non-existence. But, the existence of objects is "real" only by our agreement that they are. They do not exist independently, or on their own, meaning apart from our consciousness of them.

Without agreement, life would not "appear." There would only be the "appearance" of formlessness having no boundaries, relative positioning, or difference between various objects and events. Without agreement, life would be total confusion. In general, confusion, disorder, contradiction, disorientation, fear, hatred, hostility, or a state bordering on lack of sanity would exist as the nature of "life."

Life functions smoothly only when you understand the importance of agreement and keep your agreements. Most people are not even aware of the importance of keeping agreements. Very few people have conscious insight into the depth of this principle of agreement, and how it is actually the catalyst for making life in the world work efficiently, effectively, easily, and harmoniously.

You can only experience an event; you cannot experience a concept. Reality is that which one *experiences,* and since experience can only occur *now,* then reality can only be or exist NOW, not in the past or the future. It (Reality) exists at the level of experience, not in the mind, or "at the level of" concepts. Therefore, things have only the *appearance* of independent existence. They in fact appear only in the mind, being concepts held together entirely by agreement.

This principle and process is true regardless of what we apply or refer it to in the world, *including the very world itself.* The solid, objective world exists by our agreement that it does and in the size, shape, relative positioning, nature, quality, and quantity that we agree that it does. Only by such agreement does the world itself "exist." Otherwise, the objective world does not exist in itself, or by itself, independent of the observing consciousness that sees and says it exists. Neither do "you" exist as an individual entity living in the world. In truth, the "self" you think you are and the world in which it appears are only a dream.

You may think this is a very radical, irrational, even foolish concept or belief, made by someone whose sanity is in question. Yet, so-called sanity is based on the agreement of society, or those we trust to define "sanity" and determine just what sanity in fact *is*. Society has established and we have more or less settled for a quality of "agreed sanity." This standard of so-called sanity, the level of which is acceptable or agreeable to most of society, is to be seriously questioned. For, actually, ordinary society is quite insane. Yet, in order for life to function, to rationally or logically occur at all, this agreed level of so-called sanity is maintained as the status quo. To go outside this is considered insanity.

But what in fact is sane about the never-ending hostility, war, killing, escalating crime, violence, selfishness, greed, and the gross inhumanity to man that prevails in almost every culture and society? What is sane about all that?

A TIME LINE FROM THE PAST: At the time of writing this manual's first edited edition (before it became a bound book), there is in the news the threat of possible war in order to release American hostages being held in the American embassy in Iran by a group of angry Iranian students. The students are protesting the brutality, greed, and inhumane activities of the ousted Shah of Iran who was put into power and maintained in his position by the Central Intelligence Agency (CIA) of the United States government, for "his favors" to this country. The question of the Shah's methods of ruling his people (with America's approval and aid) will not even be allowed on the table for discussion. Nor are Americans willing to even consider the topic in negotiating the release of our people being held in the seized embassy. Yet, the facts reveal that the Shah's actions or methods in dealing with the Iranian people *were* inhumane and even quite brutal.

What is sane about all of this? Sanity is only our agreement about its "acceptable" degree, or what "we" think is "right." I may think "they" (the Iranians) are very wrong or insane, while "we" are right or sane, but it is all a matter of agreement. "Their" side holds the idea that Americans are beasts and tyrants. How can there ever be any "sane" negotiations between opposing sides when each is holding (and stuck in) such different, conflicting concepts?

So, "we" agree that "they" are barbarians or animals and "they" agree that "we" are tyrants. Therefore, we may all agree to go to war about it and kill each other. This is considered sanity by both sides, or from each one's perspective. Everybody agrees, and out of our agreement to disagree there is war. All of this is termed rational and reasonable behavior by the participants on both sides. And yet, it is sheer insanity.

[NOTE: At the time of preparing the first hardbound edition of this book for printing (1998), there is the aftermath of attempted genocide in Bosnia, and also in Central Africa. A war crimes tribunal has issued warrants for the arrest of the president of the Bosnian Serbs and the commanding general of his forces for crimes against humanity; yet not even the American soldiers keeping peace in the area can or will arrest either of them. Is this sanity?

Then, there is the case of a famous American sports figure arrested and tried for slitting the throats of his estranged wife and her male friend, with all of the evidence overwhelmingly indicating that he committed the crimes, that he had battered and abused her for years prior to her murder. After he was finally charged with the double murders, thousands stood along the highway and cheered this famous person as he drove by them for several miles with the police following in only modest pursuit. And because of his fame and wealth he was able to hire a staff of the best, most well-known defense attorneys in the country and was acquitted while the prosecution appeared incompetent and effete in their presentation of the physical evidence. Is this sanity?

SECOND NOTE: At the time of further preparing this hardbound edition for printing (about 3 years later), the Serbian army meanwhile was finally forced to the negotiating table under pressure primarily from America with the sanction of the United Nations. The war with the Bosnians was halted; but now the Serbians have started it again, this time against the people of Kosovo with the repeating of atrocities and reported attempted genocide of these unfortunate people.

And the president of the Bosnian Serbs as well as his commanding general are still both free men, living apparently in luxury in comparison to the many thousands of people whose homes they were responsible for destroying, not to mention others whose lives they were responsible for taking. And now all the powerful governments of Europe, and America are again standing back, allowing these current atrocities to continue against Kosovo, while its people are begging for help or intervention from the United Nations all to no avail. Is this sanity?]

[A FURTHER NOTE to the first revision of the bound edition: We are all now familiar with "9/11," or the destruction of the twin towers of the World Trade Center in New York City on September 11, 2001, that killed approximately 3000 people in all. And, we are also aware of the American invasion of both Afghanistan and Iraq, resulting in wars that are still today (2005) in progress. These wars are respectively for the purpose of putting down the Taliban and hunting the "wanted-terrorist" Osama bin Laden, and also overthrowing the tyrannical rule of Saddam Hussein, dictator of Iraq, because he was "supposedly developing weapons of mass destruction" later proven to not be true. Both of these instances are resulting in the killing of even more tens of thousands of innocent people. Is this sanity"

To further add to the confusion, disorder and contradiction (or insanity), previously both of these infamous tyrants were openly, strongly supported by America, given vast financial assistance, and even sanctioned by our Central Intelligence Agency (CIA) to do "our dirty work." Of mutual benefit, in the case of Osama bin Laden, it was for his "help" in the name of "overcoming communism" and, in the latter instance (Saddam Hussein), it was in part for "getting even" with Iran for its earlier actions of taking our people hostage in our embassy in Tehran, as mentioned above.

Again, does any of this indicate *sane* behavior? Is it not really an example of so-called sanity, which in fact is actually a prime or candid demonstration of "agreed insanity?"]

None of this insanity would occur without our agreement that it should, regardless of our point of view. *Agreement* is what makes *everything* in the phenomenal world occur in the form and manner that it does. Understanding and acceptance of this simple truth is itself very basic, and is paramount to efficient and effective living in the world. It is also a major key to *phenomenal happiness in the world!* Understand, I am saying "phenomenal" or "material" happiness or "worldly success."

Your world will not work if you fail, refuse, or are irresponsible in keeping your agreements. Since agreement is the very cement holding the *form* of objective life together, when you fail to keep your agreements you cannot hope to have life con-*form* to your wishes or desires.

Choose now, as an idea or notion, what you want from life. Then make an agreement with yourself to abide with your chosen ideal and work to remove all blocks or barriers using the principles of creativity herein later revealed to you. Then get agreement from those in your world who can aid you. And always keep your agreements (which is your *word*) with those to whom you give it. If you give your agreement to someone and then discover that you have made a bad deal for yourself or for someone else by this agreement, go directly to the person or group and openly communicate your present feelings, insights and intention, and wish to change or withdraw your agreement. This clears the way to then make a new agreement, which *can* be kept. Only in this manner (of always honoring your agreements once given) can you ever expect to have your life work properly and happily without constant losses and setbacks. Or, another important point of fact, if you fail to keep your agreements, you can never know for sure what *actually* is not working in your life when your life is out of order. All agreements with others are *really* only with yourself and are reflected back to you in the form of the other person who witnesses or reflects your agreement to yourself.

Remember the principle of keeping your agreements: In making an agreement *always* keep your word; a commitment you make to anyone, you are making with *the Self!* It means to *be aware* when you say you will or will not do a thing AND to *mean it* when you say it – you *mean* what you say, and you *say* what you mean! You don't say you will (or will not) do a thing just to conveniently change the subject or to momentarily "get off the hook," or just to "get someone off your back." You must keep *all* your agreements, such as your agreement to live by or apply all the principles and processes contained in this book, *when you tell yourself that you intend to.* If, for your personal success, you commit yourself to a regular study of this material, along with the methods and processes it contains, but don't keep your agreement to yourself to follow through and apply them, *they will not work for you!*

Remember: If you make an agreement involving others and later irresponsibly either "change your mind" or "decide to do something else" – i.e., not follow through and not fulfill your commitment, which causes others loss or distress – then you are drawing into your life negative or dire circumstances that will undoubtedly befall you in the future, in either this lifetime or a next!

Right now, look at the pattern of your life and see how consistent you are or have been about keeping your agreements. Are you *really alert* when saying you will do a thing? Do you *always* follow though with what you say you will do, or not do? Keeping your agreement with others shows the quality of your character. It is a mark of your integrity. If you always keep all your agreements, with yourself and others, you are already assured of happiness and success in the world by the conscious or intentional application of these principles.

It is suggested that you obtain a copy of my book, *The Handbook To Perpetual Happiness,* published by AHAM Publications, which contains all of the principles and processes one needs to literally "do what you want to do, have what you want to have, and be what you want to be" *in this world.* It also goes more deeply into the part Agreements play in your success in life, which is a subject this book only touches on indirectly.

Again, to further reiterate, the primary message of this book deals with the fact that in truth there is no separate individual to either be successful or not, for no such character actually exists. "He" or "she" is only an apparent person in this dream of mortality, expressing in a seeming historical and present role in this apparent play of life, being played out by the One-Self-We-All-Are.

BEING FOREWARNED IS BEING FOREARMED

N EARLY EVERYONE wants his or her life to improve in some way. And very often you know deeply within yourself that for real improvement to occur, you are yourself going to have to make either some radical or drastic changes in your present lifestyle, or in some of the patterns of your life. So, when it comes time to *really* look at yourself, you must be willing to "tell the truth" about whether you are willing to go through with, *to completion*, the necessary changes *in you* that will be required to produce the changes you desire in your world. And, as mentioned in the last chapter, keeping your agreements with yourself plays a major part in this.

When you work with methods, techniques or programs of radical transformation, or realization, which *actually do work* to produce *real transformation* in the quality of your life, then you can expect to come into a period of radical and intense adjustment, or re-adjustment. That is, especially as long as you are still identified with your body-mind as being yourself and with your conditioned patterns of thought, which continue to rise up out of the past.

You may even begin to question yourself about going on with the work that's required of you, by questioning either the program material, the teaching itself, or the teacher, and perhaps even everyone that's involved in the teaching. This may include questioning even the validity, veracity, integrity, or benefit of what you have *already gained*, or realized about yourself, even though it has *already benefited* you!

As you get near to achieving one or more of your long cherished goals, you (meaning actually, your mind) may either go through a process of intense resistance, frustration, doubt, uncertainty and even fear, or it might present itself as a sense of indifference or perhaps loss of interest in it all. The mind may flippantly pass it off as "no longer being of any importance" or saying, "I think that I am finished with this and am ready to do something else." Or, "I have recently discovered something else that's now more interesting to me."

But even more insidious, if you are one who is diligently pursuing total enlightenment – and you have perhaps already gone a good way into the teaching being discussed – is the mind fooling you into thinking, "I am already complete." You may have read where another teacher or teaching has said this, and you "buy into, or believe it," when in fact you may still have a very subtle ego, that is actually very strong but not seen by you, and is very much alive and "doing well."

When challenged about this by your teacher or current program trainer, or AHAM Sponsor, or questioned by friends and fellow participants in the current program, those sincerely concerned about your hasty decision, you may likely become defensive of your "new position" or "state." Your mind may strongly rationalize and justify your decision to quit by exaggerating your reasons in order to reinforce your position. It will seem and sound very logical, or feel very definite to you. What's happening is you are holding the sense of "I" as being the one who is now complete; and, "I know I am not wrong."

When engaged in consciousness transforming programs that work, as you start changing the basic foundation and structure of daily life patterns, the memories and experiences of the past that depend on old structured beliefs, habits and self-image will rise up to challenge and fill the mind with all sorts of confusion, doubt, and concern. The mind will begin offering logical arguments and resistance against the certain success that is on its way, often bringing up thoughts of doubt and fear, or even suspicions regarding the new or current teaching.

Often the people around you, particularly those closest to you, will begin to resist your changes, especially if they are also addicted to the same old patterns of thought and doubt in their lives. They see your "old self" that you are working to change, as the "good old you" which they are familiar with. Some will resent your changing. This can often occur with your relatives or some of your closest friends and can be quite disturbing and difficult to deal with.

If you have not yet made a solid covenant or agreement with yourself to allow your life to *really* change for the better, these reactions within yourself (and in your friends toward you) could actually become fatal obstacles to your ongoing success. In fact, it is the primary cause of failure with methods that do work when applied, for it causes you to stop short of your goals and not complete the process. After you realize only a few minor accomplishments, or maybe even some major ones, your mind may rationalize a very logical reason for quitting.

It is important to understand that the person you think you are, or that others think you are, is *not* the person you *really* are. When you come to discover or realize who you *really* are, it is more than enough to blow your mind! For you are even nicer and more real, more dependable, more loving, more humorous, more capable, more satisfied and satisfying, more complete and more wholesome than you could ever have imagined or thought. And, usually none of the negative or fearful, ugly, unthinkable and unspeakably horrible things that you believed about yourself (or that others thought or said about you) have any real or actual basis in truth.

Your true Self, in retrospect, is quite different from the outlook of your former self-image, or your *imagined* self-image, and the difference is positive, not negative. So don't let your successful attainments in any way be limited, hindered, delayed or set aside by the strategy of your mind and its conditioned fear. Or, by your well-meaning friends' misconceptions of you, and their lack of understanding about these working principles that pertain to true spiritual life.

This strategy against one's own good *by one's own mind* is what the Bible calls the work of Satan, or the devil. The true meaning of the term, "Satan or devil," translated from the original Hebrew and Greek in the Bible is "the spoiler, the liar, the adversary, the thief who enters your thoughts and feelings and creates doubt, fear, confusion, suspicion, frustration and delay." This often leads to further dissatisfaction and another defeat. Then you blame the method, the material, the message, or the members of the movement working to help you to achieve completion, or freedom, or to improve yourself. You rarely see or observe the real fact of the matter – that your old self or ego is the limited and unreal self, and that your desired Higher Self that is positive and capable, is the real Self.

It is normal for you to have these feelings of doubt, confusion and fear. The reason is that the old psycho-physical structure, your identification with the body-mind and the conditioned past, is now falling apart or dissolving. The whole psychology of your conditioned being *as a separate-self* is crumbling. In the past, it was what maintained, related with, and expressed these old patterns and seemed to provide you with whatever degree of sanity and peace of mind you had and enjoyed. Consequently, your present rationality or reasoning, and even your seeming sanity may itself appear to be in jeopardy. There is the current misconception (being a temporary thought-feeling of "more stress" in your mind and emotions) that causes you to resist it as an enemy to your well-being. However, this "seeming stress" is not really stress but is in fact *the release of stress!* Although it seems like "more" stress or "real" stress, your mind is actually readjusting to your true or more positive nature and releasing your old negative patterns and thoughts that have been so familiar to you.

Understand and accept in advance: *you will most likely have what appears to be negative reactions from positive processes* – processes that are *really working* to produce *beneficial* change or transformation in your life. Therefore, with this prior understanding, you should not be surprised or caught off guard when it occurs. The depth and degree of your experience will depend on how radically different and beneficial are the results you are now capable of achieving, with the ratio being how negative or limited you were, to how positive and free you now begin to recognize your potential to be.

You may have been an "asshole" all your life and now, for the first time, you are actually seeing to just what degree you really were one. So now, you feel unworthy of success and happiness. *But, it is OK!* The past is dead and gone. You can't relive yesterday. Nor can you make a mistake yesterday.

So, love yourself *now*, even in your memories, and let it be OK that in your past ignorance or foolishness you "goofed" or f--ked up. NOW is all that's real, and *God does not punish!* God is love. Only your fearful, guilty mind punishes you by plaguing you with thoughts of the past; and, if you continue to cling to these negative thoughts and feelings, it causes you to repeat them or their effect on you in the seeming future. So, let *all* of that go! Re-cognize (know again) that you can only live in this instant, only today; and by living life moment-to-moment while using AHAM's principles and processes, allow yourself to have a natural, secure, safe, abundant, and joyous tomorrow.

No, that is not even it, or the correct way of saying the Truth. Always have a joyous *today*, and tomorrow, on becoming today, will *always* be joyous. For *now* is all there is!

If you are ready to receive it, there is one simple, yet major truth: It is, there is no individual to be made happy or miserable, there is only the One-Awareness-You-Are, the One Reality that is playing all the roles of life including this "self" you think you are. Remain *in* and *as* IT, and be happy.

Consider this: if you didn't think about it, what would be wrong with your life? Just stop thinking, and *be* your-Self.

[TAKE NOTE: Any time you feel discouragement or any outer or inner resistance, or slip back into negative thoughts and feelings, or have doubts about going on with it and moving forward, or if questions arise regarding your ability to continue with the transformation of your life, return to this chapter and read it again. In fact, read it over and over again until you are no longer affected by your mind and all your negative conditioning of the past, or any negative influence from relatives and friends. Remember when you take a stand to transform your life, all the old habit patterns and conditioned tendencies of the past, based on body-mind identification, will rise up and oppose you. It is like an inner war going on. *You want to accept that this is almost certain to occur!*

This is what has been written in scriptural writings as the symbolical fight between God and Satan. In the Bible, it is called the battle of Armageddon or "good versus evil." In the East, it is represented by the battle of the *Mahabharata* in the Bhagavad Gita. It is also in the great epic, "The Ramayana," in which the *asuras* (demons) represent our bad thoughts and the *devas* (gods) are our elevated thoughts. *Everyone* on the spiritual path of "returning" the mind back to its Source must pass through this time of trial and tribulation. So keep on going, don't give in to the "enemy" (your negative thoughts) and you *will* succeed! You are destined to win eventually, so why not now, and be forever HAPPY!]

PART I

REMOVING THE COBWEBS

or

CLEARING THE SPACE FOR WHAT'S SO

WHAT'S REAL IS ALWAYS REAL

W HAT IS NOW SO is what's so. Nothing else is so. This very moment, just as it is, is *what is*. Nothing else is.

I can never know what anything *is*. If I think "I" know what a thing is, and the knowing is about that "thing" as being something separate or "other" than "I" the knower, then what is known is only a concept appearing in the mind; it is not real or have actual existence. Therefore, I don't really know what any "thing" *is*.

If I think "I" know who "I" am and that knowing is about an "I," a separate "me" that is "other" (meaning separate from "you"), then I don't know who I am.

Am I really conscious that I am Conscious? Consciousness is infinite.

Consciousness (or Pure Awareness) is infinite. It has no beginning, middle, or ending. It is not and cannot be divided into parts. It has no high or above, low or below, middle or midpoint.

Mathematically, the infinite is one. There cannot be two infinities. Even for one thought to exist outside the Infinite would mean the Infinite is not infinite.

The All is either all, or it is not All.

There cannot be an "I" apart from (outside) the Infinite nor an Infinite exclusive of or apart from me.

The "I" that I *think* I am is only a concept. The Self I *really* am is prior to, or beyond even the concept "I." The very Self is Infinite.

Self is pure Awareness, prior to the pure, thoughtless Thought "I AM," the original, primal movement giving rise to pure Consciousness out of which the "I" thought as ego-mind appears and sustains all apparent creation.

Self is the "inexperienceable" experience, the Heart and Core of pure Being, prior to all states, ideas, thoughts or concepts.

Self is That Which Observes or Sees all that the "I" thinks it sees and knows.

The concept or sense of "I" is felt as identification with the body... it is the sensation or feeling in the body that "I-am-this-body."

Again said: Self is pure Awareness (or pure I AM), prior to the thought-concept "I," or the notion "I-am-this-body." Uncaused and unqualified pure Awareness, unknowable by anyone or anything, is the real and true nature of That Which I AM. The Self ever abides as the Heart, which may be felt with respect to the body in the *right* chest of the body, the same spot or location "automatically" or naturally indicated when motioning, gesturing or pointing to the body while referring to oneself.

*   *   *   *   *

Everyone, without exception, indicates this same location or point in the body when referring to themselves, giving unerring universal verification (or proof) that the Heart (in Sanskrit: *Hridayam*) is the primal location of the Self.

The body actually abides in the Self, or Heart-Awareness. The Self does not abide in the body; it only appears to. It is only when identification with the body occurs that the Self is felt as if in the body, or as if located in the right chest of the body.

The body with reference to the Self is like a sponge in the ocean. The sponge (body) is in the ocean (Self) and the ocean (Self) is in the sponge (body).

The Self – being uncaused, unqualified pure Awareness, the Heart – abides as eternalness and infiniteness, and is the Presence, or "now," which is Now, and Always NOW. It is the "here" which is Here, and Always HERE.

Now is one; now is present. Now is Presence. Now – being

Conscious Presence – never moves. Now is eternal. Now is eternity. Eternity never moves.

Time appears to move on the surface of "now" (eternity) as waves appear to move on the surface of the non-moving ocean. The ocean in essence does not move. The ocean is already from shore to shore. Waves on the surface of the ocean or currents in the ocean move, giving the illusion of apparent movement to the ocean, or within the ocean, but the ocean in essence always, already includes the total space of its occupation. Being like the ocean "now" just is, it never moves, it only appears to move. Time – being like the waves on the ocean – is that in which "now" appears to move, just as the ocean appears to move.

Now is eternal. Like the Rock of Gibraltar, "now" remains unmoving as the waves of time splash against it, across it, and recede. But "now" itself never moves.

Now is infinite and eternal and non-moving. It is like an infinite mirror that supports all the reflections of moving objects on its surface, but which itself does not move.

Every event, at the moment of its occurrence, is only happening "now". When every event of the past was occurring in its own time and moment, that time and moment was "now" while it was occurring. Every event destined to occur in the apparent future, as it occurs in its own time and moment, that time and moment will be "now" while the event is occurring.

Just as the mathematical equation of $2 \times 2 = 4$ is not changeable to $2 \times 2 = 5$ (or any other number) and the principle of mathematics survive, "now" does not change. It abides as the non-changing, non-moving basis and principle on which time moves (or appears to move), and on which time absolutely depends.

Likewise, just as 2×2 is always 4, and not just in the moment when you think about it, or chose to use it as a mathematical equation, "now" is always now, and NOT *just in this moment* when you chose to think about it, or consider it.

If I were to ask you, "When did 'now' become 'now'?" The only correct answer would be, "Now has *always* been now."

The past is dead and gone. The future does not exist either, or has not yet come alive. Only "now" lives or is. Thought is only the memory of the past or the vision (desire or fear) of the future. Neither the past nor the future in themselves is now present. Only the thought of these two concepts (or of what either contains) is possible, and that and all thought is possible only "now," or in the present.

Thought is a movement in the non-moving "now," which is uncaused and unqualified Conscious Awareness (being the Heart of the very Self).

The body does not exist apart from the thought or consciousness of it. In deep, dreamless sleep there is no thought; therefore, there is no consciousness or perception of the body. In this state (realm or dimension) there is no body and no mind with an identifying thought of the body. Therefore, there is peace and rest in pure Being, or pure Awareness, the nature of which is true Happiness.

Pure Awareness, Itself, does not cease in deep dreamless sleep, but the "body-as-I" consciousness, notion or concept and identification with it ceases. The activity of identifying Self with the not-Self ceases.

The activity of meditating a separate-self identity and identifying with the concept "I-am-this-body" is the root cause of ignorance and suffering. This identifying the Self with not-Self causes the sense of separation, conflict, discord and dilemma, and the corresponding mental states of fear, anger, hostility, frustration, confusion, conflict, and contradiction. It is the basis of all unhappiness – all felt lack, limitation, bondage and pain.

All the opposite *positive* emotions and qualities, all pleasure, and the love of objects – i.e., persons, places and things – are experienced as well. This gives rise to the false notion, the *illusion*, that pleasure derived from the physical senses is itself the source of one's happiness.

The ego is the activity of meditating a separate-self identity; it is the movement of mind in which thought is identified with the body-mind as being the self. From this perspective, the mind (thought) holds and projects the notion of separateness from God, the conceived Source of being, and everything and everyone in the world seen as "other."

The mind also rises in the dream state, giving rise to identification with a dream body, also identified with as being oneself. This results in experiences of pleasure and/or displeasure from the dream events. The mechanism of conception and perception, and the resultant experience of events in the dream state, are not different in principle and nature from these occurring in the waking state. The waking state is only a long dream.

Logic would say that if the body were actually the Self, it would be always present or known. That is, it would be consistently present and felt in consciousness – i.e., seen and felt *as "my" very being, existence, or self* – even in the state of dreamless sleep, and the states of coma, swoon or fainting, but it is not. Body-consciousness ceases in awareness in those states, yet my actual being or existence does not cease in those states.

That which is Real is *always real*. Reality is not real this moment and unreal the next. I AM present in deep, dreamless sleep, even though the body is not. Therefore, I AM Real – as eternal existence – but the body is not.

> "Without Reality existing, could there be a notion of existence? Prior to all thought, and thus free of all thought, Reality abides in the Heart, the source of all thought (and even the thinking "I"). This Heart (which is unqualified and uncaused conscious awareness) cannot be contemplated. (For It is the very realm out of which the instrument of contemplation – the mind or thinking "I" – arises.) How then is one to know or understand this Reality? By simply being – as It is – in the Heart, *is* Its contemplation." [Introductory verse to *Reality in Forty Verses*, by Bhagavan Sri Ramana Maharshi. (Parenthetical comments added).]

The heart-felt radiance of I AM, felt as if shining on the right of center in one's chest, is this Being-Reality. It is timeless, formless, faceless, thoughtless, changeless, uncaused, unqualified awareness. It is simply I AM. I AM THAT I AM. Just float in this ever-present, joyous feeling of simple being... or I AMness.

As long as there is identification with the not-real as being

Real and the not-self as being the Self, there is dilemma. Dilemma is experienced as fear and desire. This is conflict. This consequential conflict is the motivation for more, better and different experiences of security, and pleasure from the world, in order to overcome, cover up, get past, beyond, through or around this primary misery and discomfort, and into feeling completion, fulfillment, happiness and satisfaction – into non-separate, non-suffering togetherness, and inner peace. But it cannot happen in or from the world or life in the world.

Pleasure and its quest, in all its agreeable and desirable forms, is merely a consolation. It's an attempt at momentary freedom from this always, already present misery caused by being identified with the body-mind, or from being identified with the non-real as Real and/or the non-self as the Self.

Bhagavan Sri Ramana Maharshi said, "If the self has form, the world will have form; but does the Self have a form?" The world is apparently real – as solid objectivity – only to a believed and sensed individual entity or separate-self identity – one that is identified with the "I-am-the-body" notion. The sense of "I" is the ego, the body-mind, the subjective-self that perceives all it beholds by means of the mind, processing input through the five senses. This "I" sees and requires a "not-I" for its continued existence, just as an object is not perceptible apart from the subject that perceives it. An object requires a subject for there to register an objective perception of existence, and the subject requires an object in order for it to remain as a subjective witnessing and experiencing perceiver.

The concepts of "I" and "not-I" rise simultaneously, mutually dependent, out of the unqualified, uncaused consciousness of pure Awareness, the Heart. Consciousness rises as mind into the head, where it abides as the apparent seat of thought, or as a reflection of the uncaused, unqualified Light of the Heart.

The mind itself *is* the ego, the sense of "I" and "not-I." The mind is the repository of all one's conditioning from the past. Events and experiences recorded from the past rise up as memories in the present, veiling or concealing the eternalness of *now*-Awareness on which they arise (which is Reality as Eternity), giving rise to the appearance (or illusion) of time.

This repository of the past is also the conglomerate of tendencies that motivate and/or compel certain apparent individual actions or behavior in response to or in support of current events and experiences. Past events, which were identified with as causing pleasure, are recalled from the repository of the past, bringing up the desire to repeat or experience them again. This creates in the present moment an illusory belief in the future, since a future is needed in order to repeat the desired experience. This likewise and even simultaneously creates fear and disappointment, for there is the possibility the experience cannot or might not occur again, or may not be like it was before. Past events that caused pain, loss or unhappiness are remembered or recalled from the repository of the past, giving rise to the desire and need for their avoidance. This also produces fear – fear of not being able to avoid them now or in the future.

Therefore, from future anticipation, both unpleasant and pleasant, there always abides the possibility of pain, loss or unhappiness. This is often experienced as dilemma, and felt as fear, doubt, and conflict, or as suspicion or uncertainty even when current situations themselves are not unpleasant.

Since I have forgotten most of my past desires, I may not recall now how I once desired what I am now receiving or experiencing, but not presently wanting. Or, I may have forgotten how I once desired an unpleasant or hurtful experience for someone else that I am presently experiencing in or for myself and not wanting.

In consciousness, "I" and "not-I" co-exist as opposite poles of the same Self and in truth are not different. Therefore, whatever I desire for another, I am also unconsciously desiring or inviting to be one day experienced by me. Also, that which I eliminate or improve in myself, I am improving or relieving for others in my world, and even in the larger world.

TIME AND SPACE ARE CONCEPTS

D UE TO THOUGHTS and identification with the body-mind as being "myself" now living in the past and the future, "I" create the illusion of space and time. But these are only false notions, or *conceptualized* "realities" appearing in the ever-present Now, which is the only Reality. The concept of space and time is itself appearing in the mind, while mind only appears to exist in and as the realms of space and time, in all worlds and dimensions. It is entirely body-mind identification.

However, Now is *always* now – in all dimensions, in all planes, in all worlds... even NOW. At this moment it is Now where I am, where you are, where everyone on earth is, as well as on the sun, and on Pluto, the outermost planet in our solar system. It is also Now on the suns and planets in the most distant galaxies in the universe, and in all other universes.

Time is an illusion, a concept in the mind. Absolute Awareness, which in its pure essence is Pure Existence, is timeless. Thought rising on the surface of timeless Awareness (Now) gives rise to the concepts and appearance of space and time.

The body requires space, which is a concept, in order to have room to live and move, *and* the concept of time to give duration to its life. Both of these are *required* in order for the body to occur. Since these are *both* concepts, and are *requirements* for a body to appear or occur, what does this reveal and say about the body? The logical and final conclusion is, the body *itself* is only a concept, it is not real.

In contrast, the Self is spaceless and timeless Awareness, living in Eternity, which is Now in apparent time, and Here in apparent space.

Although it appears as if the Self abides in the body, in Truth the body (being an object, which is a concept in the mind) abides in the Self, which is infinite and eternal pure Awareness – the Heart.

Just as it was believed in the Middle Ages that the earth was the center of the solar system, or then believed universe, and that the sun circled the earth, to most people today it appears that the world is itself permanent or real abiding in believed real time; and, that I (or Self) abides in the world, housed in and totally limited to and dependent on this body.

But in Truth, the Self is pure, uncaused, unqualified Awareness and the world of time and space only appears or occurs as concepts in the mind. The body and the world are only a temporary appearance on this Awareness I AM, while I AM (Self is) permanent and eternal. The space-like Awareness I AM is also infinite, or everywhere present. This means, wherever the body appears to go or travel, there I *already* AM.

Death

That which is born dies, that which is not born is not subject to death. The body was born and the body dies. But with the death of the body, the Self does not die. For the Self, being uncaused, unqualified consciousness (or pure Awareness and Existence Itself) is without origin. It was not born and thus is never subject to death.

Thought is born and thought dies. One's self-image is born and this self-image dies. The mind is born and the mind dies. However, none of this affects the Self I AM, the Heart, being the Cause and Source of all and everything. For "I AM" is the Self and its nature is Eternal Existence as unqualified, uncaused Consciousness, the One Spirit, or pure Awareness.

The space in a cup is why the cup is created. Without the space in the cup, it would be nonfunctional or useless for fulfilling its purpose. The cup's design may be sturdy or delicate; it may be expensive china or cheap pottery or styrofoam. But, without the space in the bowl of the cup it would be useless as a cup. The space in all cups is the same space, and that one and same space also exists outside and all around all the cups as well as within them. When you break or destroy a cup, you do not break or destroy the space inside or outside the cup. And when you move a cup from the pantry to the table or the table to the dishwasher, you do not move the space inside the cup, for the space is already, always all-pervasive.

Similarly, the pure Consciousness or Awareness that I am (Self is) abides apparently in the body as space abides in the cup. When I clearly understand this, then I understand that like the space is not broken with the breaking of the cup, I do not die with the death of this body. For I AM unqualified, uncaused Consciousness and am always all-pervasive like space.

The Truth Realized is that the body moves, but not the Self. For I am (Self is) omnipresent Consciousness or Awareness; the body is but an object in the consciousness that I am.

Progression or Movement

When I say that "I" am going somewhere, I am referring to my body as my "self," or "me." But in Truth, since I am consciousness itself and not the body, all places or locations are in ME and I merely witness the body moving. When I ride in an automobile or other vehicle, I (my body) am merely sitting there resting or unmoving in the conveyance. The vehicle is what's moving. When I give attention to the non-moving relationship of my body sitting inside the vehicle to the non-moving interior of the vehicle, I observe no movement occurring. Looking ahead through the vehicle's windshield, I observe the scenery coming toward me as "I" sit *unmoving* in the seat. Moreover, looking out the side windows and the rear window of the automobile, I watch the scenery moving past and away into the distance as "I" sit *unmoving* in the seat. Just as moving the cup does not move the space in the cup, the movement of the vehicle is not ME (the true Self) moving. For, as pure Awareness (which is like space) I am always, already where I am going, as well as where I have been. In pure Awareness there is no going or coming; there is only BEing.

Sitting on a train while stopped in a station, I look out the window next to me and watch people walking on the platform. I then glance across the train's interior and out the opposite window of my train and see another train also standing alongside my train at its platform. Casually continuing to watch the other train, I notice a movement begin and I conceive that my train is now moving as I watch the passing windows of the other train and sense the acceleration as the view of the moving windows appears to rapidly increase. Feeling that we are well on our way and moving steadily along, I glance back in the direction of the window next to me that was overlooking the platform expecting to see the changing scenery where the platform formerly was... *but lo and behold, to my surprise! ... there is the stationary platform ... and a jolting experience of a sudden stop!* We had not been moving at all; rather, *it was the other train moving in the opposite direction!* The other train's movement superimposed on my vision and consciousness (or my attention), gave rise to the false notion and perception (the illusion) of my own train and "we in it" moving.

In this experience, I get it! Movement is only a concept in the non-moving Consciousness or Awareness that I AM. The consciousness of movement is not itself moving. There is no movement in pure Awareness or in the consciousness itself that is conscious of movement occurring.

Similarly with change, where there is apparent progression or a sequential succession of movements or changes, no change occurs in the pure Awareness, the consciousness that witnesses (oversees) change occurring, whether it appears to occur in the environment, the body, or in one's affairs. The Self, I AM, is the same Self now, and that has always been, even though many changes appear to have occurred to "me" – i.e., in me or around me, the apparent "self." I, the Real Self, have not changed even though the images and concepts of "myself" have changed thousands of times, and continue to change. I am ever the One Self, the one and only Being.

Looking at myself through the filter of mind gives the illusion of change. This illusion is apparently factual, as it pertains to the apparent "self," but ultimately unreal, for it only pertains to the body and self-image, not the Real Me.

Consciousness of time has no time in it. Consciousness of space has no space in it. Consciousness that is conscious of solid objects has no hardness in it. Consciousness of water is itself not wet or damp, nor is consciousness of fire itself hot. Pure Consciousness is not affected by that which it is conscious of, but it may appear to be. This appearance, when identified with, allows for and sustains the concept and experience of duality, of separation and division, which is in fact the basis of suffering – conflict, contradiction, confusion and unhappiness. But, Consciousness itself, the Awareness that is conscious *of* separation, division, conflict, confusion and unhappiness has none of these qualities or characteristics in it.

Separation and Separativeness

The sense of "I" centered in the head or brain in the body is a reflection of the prior pure Awareness, or I AM, that shines infinitely and eternally in the Heart, the Self, the One Reality.

This "I" sense gives rise to the false concept of "other," or "not-I," reflected in the subtle realms "above" and the physical realm "below," but is itself a concept. It is occurring in the Light of Consciousness reflecting off the body-mind, which is "sensorially" felt and identified with as the notion "I-am-this-body" or "I-am-an-individual-being."

The Light-energy of pure Awareness originally shines from the Heart of Being as a reflection, or "I" sense, into the center of the head, the seat of the mind. From there, it reflects instantly down the *sushumna*, the yogic nerve through which the *kundalini* (primal causal energy) travels through in the spine of the body to the solar plexus. There it is for some felt as identification with the body as "I" and the world (with its content of persons, places and things) as "not-I." The stored memory of all past experiences is recorded in the brain and central nervous system and actively triggered by the senses as they register the events appearing or occurring in the mind or the environment.

As light-energy of the sun supports all life on earth, the light-energy of the Heart supports the life and activity of the body-mind or apparent individual being. Just as the light of the moon is the reflected light of the sun that gives light to the earth when the sun has set and not seen, so the Light of the Heart, also not seen, reflects off the brain and its activity centered in the head and shines down the *sushumna* into the solar plexus registering in some as "I-am-this-body." This is the process of body-mind identification in which there appears to be division, duality or multiplicity that produces fear and suffering. This is felt as a contraction and ensuing recoil from the chronic pain of separateness and the resulting desire for return to the Source, and experience of reunification and oneness with the One Reality, or I AM, which is Real God or Self.

The sense of "I" pulsating (contracting and expanding) throughout the body, particularly in the solar plexus, is the activity engaging the mind, recording events as memory, motivating the ego's desire for and thoughts of survival, pleasurable experiences, and personal ambition. That is, the recorded programming of past experiences pertaining to survival, ambition, pleasure or personal control, stimulates the desire for more experiences of this type and is the basis of all seeking. One's craving for sex, money, power or control is generated from or by this solar plexus region of the body.

On the "vibrational" scale of being, this is the gross level of life in the physical body. It is where the energy of consciousness pulsates in manifesting itself in form, or duality, as all apparent physical creations and experiences. The primary formation of this process is the body-mind itself, the apparent (though non-existing) individual being living in this seeming physical world, and supporting the false concept of the world having solid, objective reality, or seemingly existing entirely on its own in time and space.

The apparent "physicalness" of reality is generated and sustained by this activity of consciousness that's being conducted through these channels or outlets and gives expression to and indulgence in the basic desires for food, sex, money, and personal power to control these elements or components of one's life. It is apparently primarily focused in the psychic center located in the region of the solar plexus and all the connecting centers above and below.

This for some results in a strong, tenacious attachment to the body, with the felt sense that the body is the "self," while the world and all its content are "not-self," accompanied by a mild to strong wish to perhaps avoid, or the felt need or desire to control the people, places and things in the world. Basically, this need to control is due to a conscious or unconscious sense of insecurity, arising from the perpetual sense of separateness from the Source, or God, the one Allness of Being.

This body-mind identification and attachment is usually experienced as a chronic knot, contraction, or pinch often felt in the lower region of the body. It may be either subtle or intense. However, with some it may be occurring elsewhere in the body, i.e. in the whole body or spine. Or it may be in other regions up or down the spine in the trunk of the body. These could include a chronic tightness of the neck and shoulders, middle or lower back, or even in areas in or around the head.

Wherever it is located in the body, it is felt as a knot, pinch, or a contraction and often as pain or a sense of discomfort.

An effective physical analogy of this subtle or even strongly felt contraction can be seen and felt by intentionally making a fist. *Do it now!* Hold your hand in a very tightly closed fist for a minute or two; compare the sensation with the tightness or pinch usually felt in the body as the contraction of body-mind identification.

As ordinarily lived the sense of "I," identified with the body, is "unconscious," meaning it's not significantly considered as such. Body-mind identification for most is considered or felt to be normal, natural and what is *always* so; it is usually never questioned or inquired into as to whether it is actually true. So, in ordinary moments of daily life the sense of "self" is usually totally "unconscious," and not at all aware that one's *true* essence and source *is the Heart*, or pure Awareness. Thus, one's whole body is conceived and felt as "I" or "self." As a result those so identified ordinarily live in the constant sense of dilemma, separation, and compulsive seeking as the ordinary basis, principle, and experience of life. This gives rise to seeking: i.e., to the desire and motivation for more, better and different things and experiences in the world that creates and sustains the false notion of "future," and the lived sense of "not enough" – i.e., anticipation, craving, preferences, etc., for more. This also sustains the illusion of individual choice and free will. In addition, it causes the desire for liberation, or freedom from this contraction of limitation and separateness.

This contraction, wherever it is located, felt and identified with in the body, generates the strongest sense and vibration of individuality and separateness. At birth, for many, it produced in consciousness the trauma or shock experienced as a strong, vital resistance to birth, and to the body itself, and the deep and frightening experience of bondage and limitation.

* * * * *

Bondage is the deep dissatisfaction that is always present as long as it is believed and felt that "I am my body."

This birth itself is what is being resisted. And now, paradoxically, "I am" experiencing this resistance as "my" fear and resistance to dying. This will continue the sensed fear of death for as long as there is continued thinking and feeling "I-am-this-body."

In deep, dreamless sleep, "my" existence does not cease even though body awareness as "I" then ceases. In the dream state, the "I" shines in identification with the dream body living in the dream realm during the duration of the dream. In the waking state, which is the more common or universal dream (and what is seen as and called the world), the "I" shines in identification with the physical body. The duration or length of ordinary life is the duration of the waking dream. However, these three states (sleep, dream and waking) are in truth only apparently real. They appear to "come and go" in continual, cyclic interchange on what, in fact, is the prior Context or Higher State of Consciousness, or pure Awareness, or the Fourth State, which is the *real* and *true* State of the Self.

Therefore, the One Reality or true Self, I AM, is ever abiding *prior to* and *beyond* these apparent three states. "I" will die unconsciously unless, during the term or duration of this life, I awaken in true Self-Realization, or pure Awareness, to the Very Self, the Truth, or one and only Reality or Existence.

While in ordinary sleep, when the "I" is appearing in a dream body during the dream state, the dream body and dream world, with all its ordinary dream objects – such as people, places, things and various dreamed events or happenings – all appear to be solidly, objectively real and ordinary at the time. This is how it seems to both "me" in the dream and to all the "others" appearing in the dream.

If it should be said to the character I am in my dream while "I" am dreaming that the dream is really a dream, and not a solid, objective, concrete reality, I would not believe it. For the dream, *while it is occurring*, does not appear to be a dream but appears to be solid, objective reality. I may have gone to sleep shortly after eating a big meal. But if I am hungry in the dream, the fact that my physical body's stomach is full does not satisfy my dream hunger. It requires dream food to do so. This graphically indicates that each realm is complete and whole in itself, and its "reality" is actually *subjective*, not objective; i.e., it is subject to the "I" living in identification with the body in that respective realm.

When consciousness is identified with a body as "I," in any realm, that world and realm are considered real and solid. But the truth is, all activity in that realm is actually grounded in, and is at the effect of, this assumed "I-am-the-body" identification and depends *entirely* on *it* for its existence.

When "I" awaken from the dream while sleeping, the "I" drops its identification with the dream body and instantly identifies with the physical body in the waking state (this world). Then "I" immediately realize that "I" was dreaming and that the dream that *seemed* so real was *not*, and in fact *is not* real. It was all occurring in the mind. The people, places, things and all the actions and events were actually occurring in the dreamer. "I" or "they" were also not separate entities occurring in that apparently real (but actually dreamed) world.

In exactly the same manner, as "I" actually awaken to this dream in true Self-Realization and Conscious Understanding and see that my body is not "me," the waking world is then seen in the Light of Reality. It is seen to be also only a dream and no more solidly real than an ordinary dream.

Likewise, in Reality, all persons, places, things and events are occurring in the real Me, or in the Consciousness I AM, not "I" as a separate entity occurring along with "them" in an apparently solid, objective world.

Just as one may appear as a character in his/her dream forgetting that the waking self is in fact the dreamer and that he/she is not actually the dreamed character presently identified with in the dream, so the One Reality, the true Self, is momentarily forgetting Itself. It is thus identified with the ego or body-mind as being the apparent individual self "It thinks It is." It is, therefore, apparently stuck or caught up in the dream of mortality, or birth and death, which is apparently occurring in what appears to be real time and space.

However, in Truth, only this instant moment that is always only NOW, being infinite and eternal, is what's so, and I AM, Self is, this One Reality; there is no other.

PART II

THE PRINCIPLE AND PROCESS OF CONSCIOUS CREATION, OR CREATING A WORLD OF HAPPINESS

Some may question why a section on "Creating a World of Happiness" and "fulfilling or completing desires" is included in a work devoted to non-duality – the Highest Truth, the One Reality, or pure Enlightenment. This is a legitimate question.

It is a way for anyone caught in the dream – due to addiction to body-mind identification and being compulsively stuck in desire – to have his/her reasonable and just needs fulfilled, to eventually calm the mind's disturbance caused by desire. Such a one is then more capable of dispassion, and surrender of the separate sense of "I." Worldly objects and achievements are then no longer a concern or motivating force in life.

Of course, in Truth there are no such persons, there is only the One Reality, the Self. But, just as Jesus had compassion for the masses of suffering humanity, so this section is for those still thinking they are "separate entities" caught in the search.

If you have not yet attained the state of dispassion (or desirelessness), you have not gotten it about the level of spiritual clarity or maturity the sages say is necessary for Enlightenment. You are still looking to fulfill desires and/or maintain a steady level of unripe satisfactions. As long as you are motivated by the desire for "more," "better" and "different" *things* or *experiences from life* (or this world) in order to "be happy," this urge will distract you from an all-out, unified Self-Inquiry, or from the *single quest* for the Self, or Enlightenment. Sri Ramana Maharshi, among other sages, considered focused attention on the quest necessary for "attainment," or Self-abidance.

Therefore, this section is only for those that need it, *not* for those having *true* dispassion, and/or no further interest in worldly pleasures and pursuits, but are focused *only* on Enlightenment – it being the highest, purest, purpose of life.

When the mind *is quiet* and *serene*, not filled with worldly desires, completion may "come about" naturally and easily.

MAKING YOUR LIFE WORK

I HAVE READ where science has discovered that all solid objects are actually only patterns and forms of energy. Objects are phenomenal manifestations produced by the energy of atoms in intense vibration or circular motion. Electrons and protons revolve with intense velocity, producing a force-field which is perceived by the senses of the body and experienced and interpreted by the mind as shape and form, etc., giving rise to an apparently real, objective world composed of solids, liquids, gases, etc.

Now, as I awaken from this dream of mortal "reality" to my true nature as the Self (the Heart), which is uncaused, unqualified Conscious Awareness, I experience for myself what science is indicating. My body itself is a massive flow of complex energy patterns floating in a universal ocean of conscious energy (bliss, joy and supreme pleasure). But when I identify with the body as being "me," the body is contracted, apparently separate from the people, places, things, or objects in the world; it is limited, disturbed, unhappy, and I am perpetually engaged in the compulsive search for security, peace, freedom and happiness.

The apparent world and everything in it is composed of light-energy in varying patterns, forms, densities, shapes and sizes and varying degrees and velocities of pulsation, gyration, rotation, or movement. The reference point in consciousness, which is "I," is comparable to the speed of light and is the perceiver of all apparent creation that appears as macrocosm or microcosm, increases or decreases, rises and falls, is pulsating in various forms, and dissolving back into formless light that is no-thing-ness, but which is not a void.

The fullness of unqualified Consciousness, pure Being, the One Reality, is the absolute Light out of which all things are formed. I AM (Self is) that Light. All things are given rise out of this consciousness (by my perception of them), and refold or subside back into Consciousness (pure formless Existence) as I release them, and am no longer conscious of them.

No objective thing in the world (including my body, all the objects in the world, and the entire world itself) exists outside of the Consciousness I AM, or pure Awareness.

If this seems unbelievable or difficult to accept, it is only necessary to see that I can "bring anything" into my consciousness by simply thinking of it, or about it, or *becoming conscious of it*. Anything that I say I "do," or am going to do, I "do" in consciousness *first* – by holding an idea about it – prior to its actual occurrence as an event. When I go (in body) anywhere, I have already "gone" there in mind before my body arrives. When I create or build something, anything, I create or build it in thought (mind) prior to its appearance in physical form. The Truth is, when I am going somewhere, the Self is *already there*, for it (Self) is *everywhere*. It takes time and movement in space for a body (including my body) to go from place to place, or arrive anywhere, but the Self is always, already existing everywhere.

Anything I build or create, I build or create in my mind by means of thoughts or ideas, prior to the physical fact. The physical event gives evidence of the subjective ideas that I am now holding in mind. Anything I am now experiencing in my life that is undesirable, is present in my life because *I* have created (perceived) it that way. No one outside of me is doing it *to* me.

Therefore, in order to re-create my life or change the events to the way I desire them to be, I must first accept *what's so* (the way things presently are) and then clear the space for the new creation. I cannot create, form or build something in the same space now filled with something else. I must first clear away what is already there, and I can only clear away what I "own."

For example, I cannot build a new building for myself on someone else's property or where another building is already standing. I must first purchase and take legal ownership of the present property and building where my new building is to be constructed, then remove the old building and clear the space before new construction can begin. Likewise, that which is now appearing in my life that I wish to change can only be changed when I take responsibility for it by "owning" it. I must either "buy it," so to speak, or accept that I am re-

sponsible for it *just as it is*. I may try to argue or reason that
what is wrong in my life is not "my" responsibility, that
someone or something outside myself is causing my upset,
disturbance, difficulty or unhappiness. But holding to this position is only ignoring the facts and reinforcing my ignorance,
unconsciousness, and separateness. It is my "wanting to be
right," which is only avoidance of the truth or relationship
with what's so. This only strengthens and prolongs my suffering and limitation. If it is happening to me, or is seen in my
own consciousness, then I am the creator of it, or the cause of
it, regardless of the appearance of what *it* is – good or bad,
happy or sad.

I can clear the space by simply accepting that it is my own
creation and stop reacting, resisting and resenting what is now
present that I want to change and stop insisting that "I" am
right and "they" are wrong. When I accept that I am the cause
of the situation and not the effect, then I own it. I can only
change what I own. Insisting on "being right" is not owning
what needs to be changed; it is only owning "being right"
which changes nothing. But by taking responsibility for the
situation, just as it is, I am able to choose what I prefer, then
get agreement and create my preference, or change the present
situation to one that I prefer.

First, accept what is now appearing and take responsibility
for being "cause" in the matter. Thus, I must cease resisting
the experience and just *be with* the experience. I must fully *ex-
perience* the experience, rather than continuing to non-
experience the experience. To non-experience the experience
is to resist it. Non-experiencing it is to "think about it," to reason it out, trying to avoid being responsible for it, or blaming
someone or something else for being the cause of the matter.
It's hoping it will change by itself, or just "go away," and end
soon on its own.

For example, it is not pain itself that causes someone unhappiness, but rather it is one's resistance to pain, one's belief that
pain is bad or wrong. One's avoidance of pain by *not experiencing it directly*, not moving into it consciously, is what prolongs it and causes unhappiness.

This means that when I resist pain and refuse to experience
it directly, my suffering increases. But when I accept the pain,

move into it and *experience it directly* (rather than thinking about it, and resisting it), my suffering subsides and the pain is even transformed into a kind of pleasure.

Similarly, with anything I choose to change in my life, the process is to first *accept it.* I own it, I take responsibility for it. I experience it *directly* in a state of "accepting acknowledgment" of it *as it is,* accepting it as being *my own expression* of the past, even though that is perhaps now forgotten. Then, by being in harmony with it, by re-creating this same past creation in place – just as it is, and as my own – I thereby clear the space for its transformation to occur, into its new form.

In this clear space, I am now able to choose how I *prefer* it to be – i.e., its new form. I can now mentally hold a vision of it in this chosen new form, and by staying with the feeling that it is *already done,* watch it change into this more agreeable and enjoyable manifestation.

Now, being at cause in the matter, when I change my concept or idea about a thing or person, that physical thing (or person) ultimately bears witness to my changed notion about it. And its form (or the form of its transformed relationship with me) eventually changes in the world of outer "reality." The outer is now one with the inner. "As within, so without." No other method is adequate or certain. To attempt to change the outer while continuing to retain the same inner concept (or holding the same thought, idea or feeling about it) is fruitless and only results in conflict or continued frustration.

My consciousness is one with (and the cause of) that which I am conscious of, but my consciousness is *greater* than that which I am conscious of. *(Poor English, but true statement).* To change that which I am conscious *of* into that which I *prefer it to be,* I simply withdraw my consciousness from it (from seeing and feeling it in its present form) and see and feel it in me *already being* the way I *want* it to be. Even in the face of its present unchanged form, I continue to mentally see and feel it in the pattern and the form I *desire* it to be, until the fullness of that feeling rises from the Heart into the head and reflects down into my solar plexus where it is registered throughout my whole body-being as *presently complete* in its new form or transformed appearance. Having totally saturated my entire body-being with the feeling of the *desired end result*, I simply wait patiently until this "new creation" presents itself completely in my world for all to see.

This process, which is the principle of creation, is very simple and quite effortless when I am conscious in Truth of who or what I am (the truth of the underlying and permeating Self). The only effort required to produce desired changes in my world, and in the events of my life, is to accept responsibility for what is now present in my space and then choose what new form and direction I prefer it (or them) to take. By choosing and holding the feeling that the change is *already complete*, the sustained feeling *that it is done* will (and must) ultimately manifest itself in my physical world.

When I assume the mood, the now-feeling, of my desire as being *already* fulfilled, the energy from that sustained mood is eventually fashioned or molded into the manifested form of my desire fulfilled. My mind, being a focused aspect of the full scope of universal mind or infinite intelligence, works through the medium of Universal Substance (the building material of all creation) to produce an alignment of events and happenings which ultimately produce the desired result as a physical fact. How does it manifest? Not necessarily miraculously, but more likely quite normally. For example, a new acquaintance comes into my life with just what I need, or the phone rings with good news, or some hidden, forgotten, or lost item is uncovered or turns up. In some simple and otherwise unforeseen or expected or anticipated manner, life rearranges itself in alignment with my purpose without any other efforting on my part, other than continuing to hold the mood that corresponds to my desire being *already* fulfilled.

It may appear to some people to be "miraculous," especially if you have already attempted all other ordinary ways and means without success, and now it just easily happens with no other apparent effort. The true *miracle* is in the *natural law* of creation itself. Very few people are aware of or willing to accept its working hypothesis.

This *is* the law of creation. I am (Self is) that law. For all things rise out of consciousness, are sustained by consciousness and refold, reform or dissolve back into formlessness when I am no longer conscious of them.

* * * * *

If you are interested in going more deeply into these laws of creation, and the simple yet very effective processes for manifesting your reasonable and just desires, it is recommended you read this writer's book, *The Handbook To Perpetual Happiness*. Especially read in Chapter Six, "Eliminating Obstructions to Present Freedom, Happiness and Success," and "The Block-Buster." The latter is a powerful process for consciously removing all the blocks, barriers and obstacles in your life or consciousness, whatever they may be, that are now limiting or hindering your present success or desired achievements.

This Must be Said

Again to remind you: The *one cause* of all suffering is the false assumption of and continuous meditation of a separate-self-identity. It is: 1) identifying with the body-mind as being oneself living in this seemingly "real" world of duality – and, 2) the belief that the world has solid, objective reality or existence entirely on its own – i.e., independent of the mind, or one's consciousness of it.

This gives rise to the felt and believed "individual-self," or "I" (the ego) that has desires and fears, and is subject to cause and effect, or karma. Living from this believed perspective means constantly having to deal with one's attitudes and unwise actions of the past, and produces the trials and tribulations of life going on with all the people, places, things, events or situations in the world, or around oneself.

So, these instructions for "making your life work" and intentionally using the mind or consciousness correctly, or to fulfill desires, or to bring about major changes in your world, is *only about what's occurring in the dream itself*, this "dream of reality." These instructions are *NOT* for living the Highest Truth or fulfilling the Highest Purpose of life, which is to Awaken to the dream and *abide in* the Self apparently caught in the dream.

So, this chapter, "Making Your Life Work," as well as the next chapter on using "The Law of Reversibility" for achieving your desires, may expose you to the *danger* of prolonging your dream state. Or to be precise, to actually prolonging your suffering. Why? Fulfilled desires make the events occurring in the dream more palatable, or pleasurable, so you are less motivated to *fully awaken*. But rather may wish to more deeply indulge in the illusion (*maya*) of phenomenal existence, i.e., the "ongoing sleep" or "unconsciousness" of the dream.

One living from or aspiring to a Higher Level Consciousness or Insight, that is, from the perspective and wisdom of the Self, is more into completing what arises or occurs *just as it is* in this lifetime.

It is not about desires and their fulfillment that is important, that is just more karma to be dealt with in the non-existing future – since all life actually occurs only in this instant, in the infinite and eternal NOW! What matters most is abiding in this present moment *as it is*, accepting what occurs *as* it occurs.

THE LAW OF REVERSIBILITY

T HOMAS EDISON was, in a manner if speaking, working with the Law of Reversibility when he invented the phonograph. This law is based on the principle that any transformation of energy or force is reversible. Electricity will run a motor to generate mechanical energy, and, conversely or inversely, mechanical force will generate electricity. Heat produces friction; friction generates heat. Edison knew this law or principle of basic physics. He also knew from his boyhood that you could hum on a piece of paper wrapped around a pocket comb and produce a somewhat musical sound. And that by talking or singing with your lips near or slightly touching a single sheet of paper held in front of them, that sound currents produce mechanical vibrations on the surface of the paper. He knew, based on the law of reversibility, that if sound, or the human voice, could produce mechanical motion then mechanical motion must reproduce sound, or the human voice. One day he got the idea, and set out in his laboratory to discover *how to make it happen.* He already knew that it *would;* it was just a matter of figuring out *how* to make it work.

This inversion and/or transformation of energy is a principle that applies in all dimensions and all realms – physical and metaphysical. It is always at work with all of us, bringing into manifestation our thoughts and feelings as living experiences.

Thus, the Law of Reversibility is, in a way, the very principle of creation itself that we *always* use to form or manifest what happens to us in our lives, whether we are consciously aware of it, intentional about it, or even whether we believe it or not.

*   *   *   *   *

Every experience that occurs to "me" activates a particular response in the mind as an attitude, mood or feeling. This very mood, attitude or feeling in turn generates force that reverts back, reinforces itself, and continues to reproduce its physical equivalent as an actual manifestation. That is, it produces the very quality or type of experience, event, object, or situation that corresponds with the thoughts I am thinking, and the predominant feelings I am holding. This is *always* occurring. It has *always* occurred this way *and always will!*

People ordinarily observe, believe and align with *only* that *half* of the principle that says, "That which occurs *to me* is what 'causes' me to feel, think, and act the way I do." They usually do not consider the *other half* of the *whole equation or cycle*. This is the principle and process of creation: All thoughts charged and magnetized *with my predominant mood or feeling* actually set in motion an invisible yet sustaining force-field that aligns events, calling them into expression or manifestation in the actual form that they take or occur in, in my life and affairs.

Jesus was speaking about this law and principle when he taught his disciples and followers, as is recorded in Mark 11:23-24: *"Truly, I say to you, whoever says to this mountain, 'Be taken up and cast into the sea,' and* does not doubt in his heart, *but believes that what he says will come to pass, it* will *be done for him. Therefore, I tell you, whatever you ask in prayer,* believe *that you* have *received it, and you* will *receive it."* (Emphases added.)

A Word of Caution

The power released into expression in the use of this principle, or Law of Reversibility, is an absolute power. It can be used in any situation to accomplish *any* goal, aim, or purpose – good or bad. Therefore, a word of caution is in order:

It is *very* unwise, and *not* recommended, to use this principle to affect another person's life without his or her foreknowledge, agreement, and consent. Nor should you use it in your own life to produce specific results without forethought and clear insight as to how these results will ultimately affect *all* areas of your life. As an example, one may desire a loving one-to-one relationship with another person and may have in mind a *specific* person who is felt to be the *very* person. If that person is not now in agreement with being "the one," it would be *very* unwise to use this principle and process to bring it about. For even though you now think he or she may actually be the "perfect one," later there will be revealed all the presently unknown and unseen qualities and characteristics the person has that you *will also have to live with,* and these could be *very* unpleasant or even the cause of pain and upset.

The proper way of using the process in such an instance would be to *not* fill in the face of a desired mate. Don't try to conjure, charm or invoke a *known* person, but rather choose such a person's qualities, like the personality, character, mutual interests, general physical features, and mental and emotional disposition that you are looking for in a person. Although these may be the characteristics of a person you know, *do not attempt to influence* that *person*. It is only the *qualities* that the person has, or represents to you, that you really want anyway, and not the *actual* person. *Any person* with those same qualities and characteristics, who loves and appreciates you, will be found to be far more acceptable and satisfying.

Also, with regard to some specific goal or object you desire that is also being desired competitively by someone else or others as well – only use this principle where you awaken the feeling of attainment for yourself while *also* awakening the definite and good feeling that your competitor is receiving an *equal* or *comparable* degree of success, joy and benefit as well.

Resistance to Feeling Fulfillment or Completion

If you are unable to awaken or maintain the mood or feeling of completion corresponding to your desire being *now* successfully fulfilled, then you need to look deeply inside yourself for any or all feelings of jealousy, envy, resentment or unforgiving attitudes held toward yourself and/or others. You can release these by awakening the feeling of forgiveness, love and joy for an imagined good fortune going to your perceived adversaries and by imagining them as being your friend and ally. Neutralize any negative feelings and awaken the sense of self-forgiveness for your own past deeds and mistakes. The revelation of Edward Carpenter, in his prose poem entitled, "I Accept You," is very healing. It is from his book *Towards Democracy*, written from the viewpoint of God or the Higher Self speaking to you as an apparent separate self or seeker.

I ACCEPT YOU

I accept you, altogether, as the ocean accepts the fish that swim in it.
It is no good apologizing for anything that you have done,
For you have been nowhere yet, nor done anything,
But what I have supported you.

* * * * *

Having uncovered and looked at all inner negativity about myself and others, and being totally willing to release them, if I still find it difficult to maintain the mood of my desire as *already* being fulfilled, it is because I am still more affected by past programming (which is now unreal) and by its effect on the mind, than I am by the Truth of the one Being that is always, already uncaused, unqualified Conscious Awareness.

I now consciously realize that my personal connection with the Heart, as the Heart, the very Source of Being, is strong enough *in itself* to yield all my conscious desires. "That which is in me is greater than that which is in the world." My consciousness of *Being* – or *as Being* – is greater than that which I am conscious *of* being. I am able to change that which I am conscious *of* being by withdrawing my attention into the Heart – into my consciousness *as* Being. In the Heart, I am not conscious of being anything, I am just *conscious...* i.e., conscious *as* pure Being. I AM THAT I AM. I am peace. I am love. I AM.

Now, how does it feel being the person I desire to be? I let that feeling rise. It feels good. Feeling good feels *Good!!*

* * * * *

A simple analogy from life will help explain and sum up how to apply the creative principle and process of the Law of Reversibility, so as to be, do and have that which you *desire* to be, do and have. Say, you go to a movie, arrive only minutes from its end, and see the happy, successful ending of the story. You see the hero or heroine honored, recognized, and celebrating his or her success or wish fulfilled. They "ride off into the sunset, and live happily ever after." Then, already knowing and being assured of the successful conclusion, you wait for the movie to be shown again from the beginning. As you watch the story unfold, you now witness how in the plot the hero or heroine goes through a series of the most trying and problematic experiences, i.e., unloved, falsely accused, condemned, ostracized, bankrupted, homeless, hungry, imprisoned, and near death. Every imaginable bad thing happens to them, each bringing tears, moans, doubt and despair in the minds and hearts of the audience. But, even though you too feel, identify with and project yourself into the drama, and for a time live vicariously through some of the challenges the hero is undergoing, deep down you still rest in the assurance that the happy, successful conclusion is *already certain.* For, you already *know* what is true! You have *seen* the happy conclusion.

In the same manner, you now awaken what you would feel if what your desire was now *already* assured *as your experience.* You "see" the end of "your movie" and live the already-happy conclusion *as your present feeling.* You do this by first resting in the uncaused, unqualified conscious awareness of the Heart, where "then" is NOW, and "there" is HERE. You draw forth or bring into mind a vivid scene that depicts *the action* of the successful conclusion or completion of your desire. You "live through" that scene, like a vivid dream, where you are *already* thinking, feeling and *acting exactly* as the person you want to be, *doing* what you want to do, and *having* what you want to have, *experiencing* what you want to experience as your *present here and now accomplishment!* You "see," "hear," and "feel" *mentally* the experience of your friends congratulating you on your good fortune. You *vividly live* in the experience. Then, if time and circumstance allow, you drift off into sleep (a short nap will do), fully saturated in the joy of success!

Close your eyes and feel: *I already am the person I desire to be. When I open my eyes and move through what is at hand to be done, deep inside I will continue to retain the feeling of the successful end of "my movie."*

Now, as the events of your life daily unfold in consciousness, bring into being the magnetized pattern or picture of *the end of your movie.* The outer appearance of the events and their nature may seem absolutely alien and contrary to your happy conclusion. They may bring tears and moans from anyone looking on as an observer, but so did the events in the movie analogy. No matter what happens or comes up, *you don't get drawn into it,* but instead rest in the *assurance* that these events are necessary and are compatible to the successful end of your movie, even though they may not now appear to be. The same was so with the hero in the movie. In time, the circumstances *will* change, until they are fully expressing what your deep inner mood is and has been all along, that is, if you have remained *firm* in your conviction of *a happy conclusion.* Just don't give in to any of the negative thoughts and feelings.

*   *   *   *   *

When I react to each negative experience with forgetfulness of the Law of Reversibility and allow my feelings to change into alignment with the negative and I become negative, then I am creating or forming the substance of consciousness to create or give me more negative experiences. But, as I inquire, and rest in the Self, even in the face of all negative events, and draw my attention back into the Heart of being, I can allow *any* event to occur without it bringing any upset up in me.

In the absolute center of a spinning wheel, there is no movement, yet the non-moving center supports the entire wheel. The fast moving changes occurring on the rim of the wheel do not affect the perfectly still center. Rather than identifying with the changing highs and lows, ups and downs occurring like a glob of mud stuck on the rim of the wheel, I draw my attention back into the quiet, still center, the Heart, and merely observe – with understanding, humor, compassion and peace – the rising and falling events appearing around me.

Like an actor who is playing a role that calls for distress in a play, I cry when it is called for and laugh when it is appropriate. But I rest in the *prior* pure Awareness, the Heart, *as* the Heart, knowing it is not happening to ME. I am only acting out my role in the drama, the end of which is *already assured*.

That which is ME, the true Self, is not affected by events. I am one with that which is prior to it all. My Consciousness *as Being* is greater than that which I am conscious *of* being, even in this present moment. All moments are *as* this moment. Now, I am conscious that I AM. My true nature is peace, freedom, love and happiness, and I rest comfortably in this direct, pure understanding. I AM that I AM. I am the Heart. I AM *is* the Heart.

There is neither I, nor other than I, there is only....

*   *   *   *   *

PART III

THE SACRED WRITINGS

A REMINDER: All references made to yourself in First Person singular, are an affirmation to yourself *about yourself*. Remember, this is *your* book written to *yourself* about *you*, meaning, the Real You.

As you read, consider this as being a message from the Higher or true Self writing or speaking to the body-mind, which may be the apparent individual or separate "self" you have previously thought or considered yourself to be, but which in Truth is not. There is no separate one.

Simply remember, there is no separate, individual self; there is only the One Reality, the One Absolute Being manifesting *as* the mind and its creation of this apparent world of multiplicity – i.e., these apparently multiple objects and seeming body-forms or illusory separate selves, which is not unlike the traditional Vedanta analogy of the rope appearing as a snake in the dim light.

THE MESSAGE OF THE SACRED WRITINGS

DOWN THROUGH HISTORY, in various times and localities of the world, certain Sages or Enlightened Beings have revealed or shared their realization of Truth or Reality, their awakened or illumined Awareness. The record of their experience and their teaching, as well as the freeing effect all this had on those around them, was written down and spoken about by their followers. These records were cherished and kept by their disciples and other loyal followers. Many of these stories at first were only verbally passed on to devotees or followers whose lives were benefited and transformed by them. In many cases, it was much later that the stories were actually written down, as there were very few who could read and write.

Initially their stories were told by witnesses living during or shortly after the time of the events. After their passing, the accounts were directly passed down by word of mouth by their enlightened disciples who also kept their enlightening quality alive and in tact by the influence of their own awakened realization. Later, however, they were written down as legends to preserve them and the teaching and to make them available for study by all later generations. However, in the written records and commentaries that followed, the *transforming* consciousness was lost due to the lack of *actual enlightenment* of later believers; only intellectual and/or doctrinal beliefs were the result. In some instances, these recorded accounts have become the very bibles and sacred scriptures of the cultures in which they originated or occurred. The growth and later dissemination of these basic teachings eventually contributed to the formation of the world's major religions.

We hear present day theologians or bible scholars and their students declare that the Bible is "inspired by God" or that the Bible is "the word of God." This is certainly true. But, it does not mean that God has "spoken" through only one "bible" or "holy scripture," nor does it mean that God has totally ceased "speaking" His word of Truth today.

God's so-called "spoken word" is today as *real* and *true* as it was in biblical times. Since God is the Source and Essence of Being itself, and even of time itself – i.e., living in the eternal *now* prior to time, beyond all time, yet within all time – then all time is "God's time."

God is the very Self of all selves, the very Being of all beings, and is not, in absolute Truth, an individual "Entity" or Divine "Person" that man often conceives and projects God to be. God is the One subjective essence in which the world and all it contains, including man, is only apparently occurring. God, as pure Awareness, is not masculine or feminine as some theologians maintain. The Supreme Essence, which is the Source of all, is not limited to any form or gender, but is the Seeing Awareness in which all appears and is seen.

"God" is the name we give to That which is nameless, which is the Source and Support of *all that is.* That Source was called "Spirit" or "Father" by Jesus. Jesus' Conscious Awareness was steadily, continuously, and consciously "one-with," or not different from that Source. Jesus described this experience, and this insight of *everyone's* relationship to God, the Source, in first person terms, such as *"I AM the way, the truth and the life; no one comes to the Father* (the Source) *except by me."* (John 14:6) This means simply, that one's own Self, or pure Being, is the one and *ONLY direct* and *immediate* way to *realize* or "know" God. This also gave humankind – i.e., his immediate disciples and later followers – an understanding of the *devotional* sense of *love* and *union* Jesus had with the one Source. Also, Jesus must have had great love for Joseph, his earthly father, for he expressed his spiritual relationship in human terms, the love of a son for his father, and by referring to God as "Father."

Later on, and even to this day, most theologians and other so-called Bible scholars and students have greatly misunderstood and misinterpreted this *first person* account of his realization of oneness with God. They take it to mean that he was (or is) *himself* the *only* Son of God. *This is absolutely ridiculous!* And, it is directly *contrary* to his own words and teaching. When questioned by the Jewish leaders of his day about this very point, Jesus answered, *"Is it not written in your law I said, 'you are gods'?"* Here, he was quoting Psalms 82:6 that says: *"I say, you are gods, children of the Most High, all of you."*

Other Self-realized Teachers have expressed this Awakening in other terms. Some, such as Sri Ramakrishna, have referred to the Source as "Mother," or "Divine Mother." The name is actually immaterial, for it is an attempt to describe or explain this *grand experience* that cannot be fully described. It can be indicated or pointed to, so that we can also turn attention in that direction and perhaps have this same insight-experience.

To someone who had never tasted sugar, how could you describe the taste of sugar? You could say, "It is sweet." But what if he had never knowingly tasted anything that was sweet? You would have a difficult time. In fact, he may never know what you actually mean.

Or, imagine a person being born color-blind to the extent that he sees everything around him as it would appear on a black and white television set. You are walking with him through a beautiful flower garden. How could you describe or discuss the beauty of the colorful scene, with all the varying combinations, shades, hues and tints of colors appearing around him? He is looking directly at what you are describing to him but will never see the full beauty of the flowers as you see them.

Now, imagine the same person to be also devoid of the sense of smell. Here are these glorious blending fragrances and aromas in the air, and the beauty of the varying colors, but the person is totally ignorant or unconscious of the extent and the depth of it all and sees or experiences only partially.

This is the problem Jesus and all Sages or Awakened beings have in describing to the un-awakened, or spiritually ignorant, what God or Reality or Truth *actually is*. To attempt to do so, they must use examples, stories, parables, analogies and allegories. Unfortunately their much later followers, such as in the case of Jesus and today's Christians, only have the "doctored" or misunderstood scriptures to go by, or read, without the benefit of His enlightened experience or the clarity of His direct disciples. They are now, in many instances, interpreting the analogies and parables literally, missing the meaning of what Jesus and the Great Prophets were attempting to convey.

In some instances, even the disciples or the early scribes who recorded the handed down words of their masters did not have the direct, pure insight or enlightened experience of their mentors. In their misunderstanding as to what was *actually* being conveyed, they "jumped to wrong conclusions" or made erroneous assumptions. Errors in the descriptions or meaning of the words used were very likely incorporated into what is believed and even defended as today's Bible, or "word of God."

This includes the interpolations or personal notes made as entries in the margins of the original diaries. These were often written solely for the personal convenience, clarity or under-standing of the scribe that was recording the event. These notes were later innocently or perhaps even intentionally in-cluded in subsequent drafts by successors, assistants or nov-ices "working their way through school" so to speak. So, what do we end up with? Today, what we have as the "official" or "finished" Bible may be very different, even "poles apart," from how the original testaments or manuscripts started out.

Combine that with the religious bigotry of many overzeal-ous theologians or fundamentalist "religionists" (the present day equivalent of the Pharisees during Jesus' time) who have widely varying views of what they consider to be the "true doctrine" contained in the Bible, and we can see why today there is so much controversy between different religious sects, and even the widely varying views within the same sects or denominations. This is *all* due to lack of enlightenment – that is, to the faulty *intellectual* interpretations made by those who are infected with superstition, fear and over zealousness re-garding the Bible's meaning. The Bible and all the pure sacred writings of the world are really about spiritual Enlightenment. In this sense, they are not actually different, even though in their present form they may appear to be.

The question may then arise, "Of what official or true benefit are the Bible, or the other Sacred Writings, if they are filled with so many errors and interpolations of others?" The an-swer is, there is no enlightenment, as such, in the Bible itself or the sacred writings, nor was there to begin with. Enlighten-ment is only in one's consciousness and is directly available to each of us. It is "attained" by meditation, not by reading the

Bible or other religious books. The Bible and other sacred writings are only "pointers" to the Truth. Or, they are helpful for generating or sustaining one's faith since they are the record or testimonies of those who have *already* attained Enlightenment. They are more like road maps or codes of ethics for all of us to follow. Again, they "point" to the state that must be "awakened to" in and by everyone.

So, the Bible and other sacred writings are the record of Enlightened Beings trying to describe the indescribable. For God, the Source, First Cause, Spirit, Real Truth, Divine Being, the Supreme Self, Divine Mind, Infinite Intelligence, the All in All – or whatever name you choose to call That which is prior to the mind itself – cannot be described. It is *prior* to the mind. The mind is the instrument we all must use in attempting to explain anything being explained. But God is not an object that can be perceived or adequately explained, even in or with the mind. *God is Truth*. Truth cannot be adequately explained or defined. Every definition is a limitation that restricts or confines God to the apparent "size" or "shape" of the definition. God is beyond all forms, definitions, or explanations. The mind is the instrument we use to attempt to describe God; yet, God is that which gives light or awareness to the mind.

This is like a movie projector in which the light from the bulb inside shines through the film, casting an image of the pictures contained in the film onto the screen. The film is like the mind. God is like the light bulb. The light bulb is behind the film and lights and projects the images into "manifested expression" on the screen. But the film's images cannot express, contain or manifest the light bulb itself, for the light of the bulb is what projects or gives expression to the film. Being *behind* the film, *prior* to the film, beyond the film, it shines in and through the film as the manifesting light to the film.

Likewise, direct perception of the pure Light of Consciousness itself cannot be done with the mind. But, if the film in the projector comes to a span of frames that are clear, with no images or impressions imprinted on them, then the pure light shines through the clear space and the quality of the light is seen. But, that is still not the bulb itself; it is only its light.

When we empty the mind of all concepts, opinions, beliefs,

theories, images, thoughts and ideas, and let it rest quietly without a single ripple of movement, and without going unconscious or to sleep, then the light of its source is capable of being experienced.

But for absolute realization, the clear mind must ultimately merge or be absorbed in the Source and become as the very nature of the Source – the Light. This means the total loss of ego or the sense of being a separate individual "self." At first, to the mind, this becomes very frightening, for it is thought to be loss of identity, or like "losing one's mind," or dying. Yet, it is the true birth or re-birth or resurrection of the Self. It is Awakening to the Higher Self, the very Self of all selves.

The Bible and sacred writings are describing an experience that each of us must have for oneself. That experience is the ultimate Realization that God is the Source of all, including our conscious Awareness. God is the very Self. It is not that we as separate entities are God, but that "our" consciousness is not different from God's Absolute Consciousness. Moses, Buddha, Jesus, Bhagavan Sri Ramana Maharshi and other Enlightened Beings have all realized this as the very Truth.

Jesus' testimony throughout the New Testament is the revelation that the "I AM" is Lord, Source, Father or Self of all. Jesus did not mean that his *"personal 'I'"* was the *exclusive* Lord. When Jesus said, "I am," he knew that the very I AM which was *his* Source or Self was the one Source, Self or Cause of *all* beings.

Jesus stated this Truth *continuously*, as I AM (is) the truth; I AM (is) the way; I AM (is) the door; I AM (is) the resurrection; I AM (is) the life; I AM (is) the beginning and the end (the alpha and omega). Jesus' I AM is the one I AM that I AM. There is only *one* I AM, *one* Self, or God. God is I AM. Man's unconditioned, unqualified Awareness is this "I AM." This uncaused, unqualified, unconditioned Awareness is *eternal* – being without beginning or ending. It is the One Truth. It is the One Cause and Seer of all we as apparently separate, conscious beings *are*. I AM is the doorway through which everything enters and leaves our lives.

Withdrawal of attention, once and for all, into this pure Awareness, abiding in and as the Heart of Being, is the *only* "way" to Liberation or Salvation. It is the *true* Resurrection. Jesus' crucifixion and resurrection represents the crucifixion (crossing out) of ego, or body-mind identification, and resurrection into or *as* the Transcendent Being, the One Reality of the Supreme Self, or pure Christ Consciousness, which is the natural state prior to body-mind, time and space.

When we say, "I am," we are *unknowingly* speaking of the one Self, the Source and Cause of *all that is*, but we must *realize it*. Like the color-blind man in the flower garden saying he sees the full beauty of the flowers, we ordinarily do not realize what we are saying when we say, "I am." Jesus fully realized what "I am" meant. Jesus is like one with full color vision trying to describe the beauty of the flowers to a "color blind" humanity. Jesus says, "I am" and sees. We look and say, "yes, I am" but do not see. But we *can* see. Remove the veils from your spiritual eyes and the one I AM is *your* I am; it is the consciousness of God *in* us, *as* us.

Jesus was not the only being in history to *realize* and *know* the Truth regarding "I AM." We all say, "I am." But do we see the significance of what we are saying? Do we have clear vision and insight into the True and Real meaning of the statement? Do we really know *who we are, what we are?* Jesus knew. Others have also known. Their Awakened Knowledge is also recorded as the sacred writings in other cultures.

All sacred writings of all cultures and all societies are the same thing. In India, their sacred writings are the Vedas, the Upanishads, the Bhagavad Gita (the Song of God) and others. In Arabic countries, among the Muslims it is the Koran. In Israel, it is the Torah, the Talmud, the Qabbalah and others. The Mormons have "The Book of Mormon," etc. All "bibles" or sacred scriptures are commentaries, discourses, descriptions of God, the Supreme Being, revealing Himself as the Source of manifestation (man), or man's Higher Self. All are "the word of God." Although it appears to some as though the overall meaning in different scriptures is different, they are only different ways of describing or explaining the same Truth, the One Reality.

Since God is really unexplainable, the attempted explanations often create apparent division in man's religions. All religion is one; it only appears as many. When God is realized in the Heart as the very Source of being, as Being itself, division and separation ends. Division and separation are what Jesus called "sin." He said that the purpose of his life and work was to overcome sin – which is schism or separation. Yet, unfortunately, many of his professed followers still divide and separate themselves from the rest of humanity, from other religions and even from other Christian sects and teachings. Even Hindus are divided from other Hindus. Separation is not exclusive to Christianity or any single world religion. Mankind is dividing itself and the result is conflict, confusion, contradiction, hatred and war. Such division itself is sin.

Love is unconditional acceptance; it is not separating, dividing, or alienating anyone from anyone. It is remaining one with the pure Being of *all,* in the Heart. Jesus unconditionally accepted *everyone,* just as they were. He made no judgments but was pure Love in expression. Ordinary Christians will say, "Yes, but that was Jesus. He was the Son of God, and was capable of that quality of unconditional love; we are not." Such a statement is itself separative, for it maintains the sense of separation from Jesus and God, the Source, being the very sin Jesus gave his life to overcome. *Everyone is capable* of that quality of unconditional love. Jesus instructed all his *true* followers in this very fact, saying, *"Love everyone as I have loved you."* (John 13:34) In fact, this was Jesus' commandment to his followers – not just his suggestion – when he said, *"If you love me you will keep my commandments."* (John 14:15)

Love is not seeing "others" but seeing all as expressions of the one Universal Awareness. It is not judging, finding fault, condemning, competing, or being envious or jealous of others. It is allowing "others" to be themselves, freely, without judgment. It is giving everyone the space to be as they are, to make mistakes, to even do "wrong," to fall or fail – even to "sin."

When we are not allowing another being the space to experience life in the way he or she seems compelled to live, we do not love. Yes, his or her actions may leave much to be desired, and may even be creating pain for himself and "others" around him. But if there is any judgment or aversion, it is to be toward *the ignorance* and *the behavior*, not toward the being expressing *as* the actions. The *ignorance* should be despised, not the being. For one is *not* one's ignorance, but is only momentarily stuck, or caught up in it, or is presently misguided because of it. We should love and have great compassion for those caught in the snare of ignorance, for their folly is causing them much distress, confusion and pain, whether they see and admit it or not; or, it will *eventually* do so if it is continued in.

Love heals; hate irritates. So withdraw your criticism and your attention from the apparent division, the seeming separateness you may see in the world. Meditate on the Self and thereby awaken to the true Self, which *is* Love, and let your natural Being express openly to all mankind. You will then be a living example of the message of Jesus and all the Sages or Enlightened Beings of *all* traditions and cultures. This is the underlying message of all the sacred writings of the world.

THE CHRISTIAN BIBLE

L ET'S NOW PURSUE FURTHER CONFIRMATION in the Christian Bible and its teaching for the simple Truth we have been discussing. Jesus said, *"If you continue in my word* (live by my teaching and my example) *you are truly my disciples* (dedicated to the highest purpose of life), *and you will know the Truth, and the Truth will make you free."* (John 8:31-32)

We are always, *already* happy and free of conflict and suffering when we abide in the true Self, as did Jesus, and when we re-cognize (again know) that the body, mind and ego are not the Self. Jesus said, *"Truly, truly I say to you, before Abraham was, I am."* (John 8:58) The Self exists *prior* to time and space. It is uncaused, unqualified consciousness, *prior* to being conscious of *anything*.

By changing our concept of a thing – i.e., no longer identifying with it, or its present effect on us but rather embracing the mood and holding the feeling *that would be ours if the thing was already happening the way we want it to be* – it will eventually change and no longer affect us. It will cease to cause us pain or upset. This is a simple conscious process for being free of all conflict. Where *is* the problem, if you don't think about it?

* * * * *

The Real Cause of Suffering

Pain or upset are not caused by any event or experience in itself, but by the system of beliefs, the emotional demands or requirements which I impose on or expect *from* life, and the effect these expectations have on my thoughts and feelings. If I held no preference or requirement about a thing, no demand as to how I think and feel it *should be*, then I will not be in the least affected, either by the way it is, or is not. Simply see that it's *the thought about the thing* that's upsetting, not the thing.

So, the thing itself is not where the upset is located, or where the feeling of disapproval or disappointment or pain is being experienced. Rather, it is in my thoughts about it, at the point where my preferences or beliefs are being held, maintained and insisted upon. It is *in me,* in my thoughts about it.

When I understand and accept this simple truth, that the cause of upset in my life *is due to my thoughts,* to my own set of beliefs and requirements, then my willingness to unconditionally accept life and any situation, *just as it is,* will free me from upset – now and forevermore!

*   *   *   *   *

Consider this simple yet significant question shared by the conscious Australian teacher, "Sailor" Bob Adamson: "What would be wrong with my life, or my world, if I didn't *think* about it?" In truth, there would be nothing whatsoever!

In its simplest terms, the cause of suffering is thinking! It starts with identification with the body-mind as being the Self. While abiding in the Self, or pure Awareness, prior to body-mind identification, there are no upsetting thoughts and there is no upset. In dreamless sleep, there is no body or mind and no thoughts, and there is no upset. You, the Self, are there in the presence of uninterrupted Bliss. Upset enters only when the "I"-thought arises, or when the body, mind and world are seen *and thinking is resumed and identified with!*

*   *   *   *   *

My primary suffering and sense of bondage is the contraction in the form of the idea "I-am-this-body." When I realize the Truth known by Jesus – that *"I and my Father* (the Heart, the Source) *are one"* (John 10:30) – then I too will understand that my concept of myself as being the body is maintained by my identification with the body, held in my mind. I will then cease identifying the Self with the not-self (the ego or body-mind) and experience the prior bliss and peace of my true nature, which is always, already happy, full and complete, and which now abides infinitely and eternally *prior to* all bodies, worlds and realms, and all experiences in all domains.

Only the body is born, and only the body dies. The Self was never born and so will never die. As with Jesus, the truth is: "Before Abraham was, I am." (John 8:58)

* * * * *

Jesus did not consider it blasphemous to know, understand and declare that his very nature was one and identical with God, the Source, which he called Father. *"This was why the Jews* (the fundamentalist religionists of his time) *sought all the more to kill him, because he not only broke the Sabbath but also called God his Father, making himself equal with God."* (John 5:18)

Again and again, he demonstrated that he was the true Self, the realization of which is the living prophecy (or real purpose) of the sacred scriptures. He referred to this Truth as direct and immediate relationship with God, the Source of being.

> *Philip said to him, "Lord, show us the Father, and we shall be satisfied." Jesus said to him, "Have I been with you so long, and yet you do not know me, Phillip? He who has seen me has seen the Father; how can you say, 'Show us the Father?' Do you not believe that I am in the Father and the Father in me? The words that I say to you I do not speak on my own authority; but the Father who dwells in me does his works. Believe me that I am in the Father and the Father in me, or else believe me for the sake of the works themselves.* (John 14:8-14)

Jesus was in truth a Spiritual Master, a Sage, a Guru (conscious teacher) of the highest stature. But, unknown and unaccepted by most Christians there were, before and after Jesus, many Enlightened Beings or Gurus of an equal degree of God-Realization. Most of them were born and have lived in India.

One well-known enlightened being was Sri Ramakrishna, who lived in India during the mid-1800s. He had at least 25 direct disciples who also became enlightened by his spiritual influence and guidance. Swami Vivekananda, one of his chief disciples, also became widely known throughout the world. He came to America in the early 1900s as the official delegate from India to the first meeting of the Congress of World Religions. He and some of his brother disciples who came later were responsible for establishing Ramakrishna Missions in various cities in America, as well as forming the Vedanta Society in America.

In more recent times, Bhagavan Sri Ramana Maharshi was such an enlightened being, whose spiritual influence and grace also guided many of his followers into this Highest State. Also, during his time and living after him, was Sri Nisargadatta Maharaj, a very ordinary householder and ciga- rette merchant who lived in Mumbai (Bombay) India until his death in 1981 at the age of 83. There have been thousands more similar Enlightened Beings throughout India's history.

Jesus was evidently visited by such beings when he was born. The story of "the wise men from the East" who "sought him out" at the time of his birth indicates this probability. Even to this day, Tibetan Buddhist Lamas search for the birth- places of their sages who have been reborn in physical bodies and attempt to return them to their monasteries to carry on their spiritual mission as conscious teachers. This happened as recently as 1995, when Buddhist priests from Bhutan and Tibet came to Seattle, Washington, located a small boy living there and took him to Bhutan. They considered him to possi- bly be one of their recent senior Lamas who had reincarnated there. There was even a documentary movie made about it, ti- tled *"The Little Buddha."*

Jesus was evidently recognized by the wise men in this same traditional fashion. But rather than returning him to India or Tibet where he had probably lived his last life, they possibly chose to allow him to fulfill his destiny in Judea, or perhaps convinced his parents to take him to the Buddhist monastery which existed at that time near Alexandria, Egypt.

Jesus certainly *was* the Son of God; there is little doubt about that. But this is *not* what made Jesus unique or special, for we are *all* sons and daughters of God. Jesus was unique because *he was Consciously Aware and Awake to the fact* – that he was one with or not different from God. His uniqueness was that he lived most or all of his life *from* and *as* this Awakened Con- sciousness and was able to awaken so-called "others" into it.

Non-Acceptance of Enlightenment by Organized Relig- ion

Even though Christians by and large believe that Jesus was *"the only Son of God"* (John 3:16), based primarily on their misinterpretation of this particular verse in the Bible, they don't understand or accept that *everyone* who has spiritually Awakened to the same quality of Self-awareness or consciousness as Jesus (which is Christ Consciousness) is also a *true* son or daughter of God, *no less than Jesus*. Jesus, himself, said exactly the same thing. *"In Truth I say to you, he who believes in me* (awakens to this state of consciousness I AM) *will also do the works that I do, and greater works than these will he do, because I go* (merge with or ascend) *to the Father* (the Source)." (John 14:12)

However, fundamentalist or orthodox Christians have historically refused to accept the Awakening or Enlightenment of anyone other than Jesus, who have realized the Self, even when it occurs within the Christian Church or tradition. They accuse anyone saying that he or she has "realized God" of heresy and blasphemy, as did the Pharisees during the time of Jesus. Two dreadful examples are the infamous 300 years of the Spanish Inquisition and the Salem "witch trials" in the 1700s where people were branded as witches, tortured and burned at the stake for heresy, or making similar assertions.

To organized religion, it has always been acceptable to *seek* God, to set goals for being more God-like, and to always be involved in *the great quest for God*. But it is not ordinarily acceptable to *find* God, to realize your own true God-Self or Christ-nature and live consciously one with God *daily*, as your *actual present-moment experience* – in bliss, humor, compassion, and joy. This is just not acceptable! If this *does* occur and is found out, or is confessed and openly stated, there are those among the ignorant masses, including most professed Christians, who will cry out in unison: "Blasphemy!" "Heresy!" And brand their followers as being "Cultists!"

Throughout much of history, those great Beings – sages and saints – who *did* realize their own God-nature have had to conceal it in order to avoid persecution or even death. A distinctive feature of Jesus' life is that he disclosed his Realization openly where and when it was not popular. *"Greater love has no man than he lay down his life for friends."* (John 15:13)

Persecution of those who have realized God is not confined to Jesus' experience with the early Pharisees. It occurs in the current Moslem and Christian world as well. Just as the early Jews had Jesus executed for "blasphemy," others have since persecuted and even executed many of their saints (e.g., burning Joan of Arc at the stake). Mainstream Moslems persecuted the founder and early leaders of the Sufi sect, as well as the founder of the Baha'i faith. Only Hindus and Buddhists have revered their sages and saints, their sadhus and lamas.

This persecution of saints and sages still occurs today, despite the fact that the message and meaning of all *true* saintly beings is love. Jesus taught only love. Mohammed demonstrated love. Old Testament prophets extolled love.

When Jesus was accused of blasphemy for saying he was the Son of God, he said to his accusers who were about to stone him for saying this, *"I have shown you many good works from the Father; for which of these do you stone me?" The Jews* (the fundamentalist religionists of that time) *answered him: "We stone you for no good work but for blasphemy; because you, being a man, make yourself God." Jesus answered them, "Is it not written in your law, 'I said, you are gods'? If he called them gods to whom the word of God came (and scripture cannot be broken), do you say of him whom the Father consecrated and sent into the world, 'You are blaspheming' because I said, 'I am the Son of God?' If I am not doing the works of my Father, then do not believe me, but if I do them, even though you do not believe me, believe the works, that you may know and understand that the Father is in me and I am in the Father. Again, they tried to arrest him but he escaped from their hands."* (John 10:32-39)

Thanks to the Bill of Rights that guarantees Americans freedom of religious expression, no violent acts can be *legally* perpetrated against someone for realizing and expressing his/her *oneness with God.* But many still try, and it is quite probable you will be either ridiculed, or harassed, or ostracized if the word or "your" realization "gets out." At least you will be doubted and treated with suspicion and possibly even with contempt. So be very sensitive and discreet with whom you share your deeper spiritual insights and understanding so that you do not bring about unpleasant reactions from society.

We are all Sons and Daughters of God

Remain firm *within yourself*, however, about the truth of your divine nature. Although others generally will not accept you and your awakened spiritual understanding when it does occur, the Truth still remains that you *are* a son or daughter or *living expression* of God. God *does* dwell *in you, as you.*

St. Paul wrote in Romans 8:16-17:
"It is the Spirit himself bearing witness with our spirit that we are children of God; and if children, then heirs, heirs of God and fellow heirs with Christ, provided we suffer with him in order that we may also be glorified with him."

We are *all* equal to Jesus *in Truth,* being children of God. But it requires our spiritual discipline ("suffering with him") to release all the un-Godly, unloving, ignorant, fearful, separate and "separative" or doubtful thoughts and conditioning that presently conceal the Truth from direct realization. All concepts about who we *think* we are – as limited beings – must be released, so that the pure Awareness of the true Self, covered up by these false concepts, may be revealed.

When we try to remain alert to the Truth of our Being but continually fail, Jesus points out that *"the spirit is willing but the flesh* (body-mind) *is weak."* (Matthew 26:41) Our identification with the body as "I," and the addictive habits of thought that pull us into unconsciousness are very strong. The conditioned patterns that compel us to pursue "more, better and different pleasurable experiences" in the world for the sake of sensual gratification must eventually subside, or come to an end.

At the time of death, if we have not yet realized our transcendent nature as eternal Being prior to body-mind identification, we may suffer greatly. That is, have great fear and strongly resist death by trying to avoid this inevitable event, which otherwise would be a most beautiful experience of bliss as we are released from the limitations of the body-mind.

Jesus said, *"Be of good cheer, I have overcome the world."* (John 16:33) He realized and demonstrated, prior to his physical death, that by our Awakening and "getting beyond" identification with the body as "I" (and our connection with the world), we are *already* the Truth beyond the world, and fear of death is gone forever.

Jesus knew and taught that our own consciousness is what creates or gives light to our world, when he said, *"You are the light of the world."* (Matthew 5:14) The I AM, man's own con-

sciousness, contains all that is – and *is* all that is. Before we
are aware of anything, we are aware that we *are*. Awareness
itself, or that *we exist*, is prior to (and the Father or Source of)
all that we are aware *of*. It – Awareness itself – is what we *are*.

The Pure Teaching of Jesus

Much of the Gospel of John contains the direct and pure
Teaching of Jesus; that is, with reference to his knowledge of
himself being one with and not different from God's Awareness. He stated emphatically that this is the truth of *all of us*.
He also said that even after he was "gone" from this earth, "a
Counselor, the Holy Spirit" would "come," acknowledging
that other Enlightened Beings would enter our lives to teach
those who are open and ready to receive the Truth. Indeed
there have been many; many have already come.

Here is a supporting biblical reference containing a Conscious Commentary, taken from the Gospel of John in the
New Testament:

> *Truly, truly, I say to you, he who believes in me....*
> (i.e., aligns himself in consciousness with the pure
> Awareness of being, the One Reality or Source)

> *will also do the works that I do; and greater works than these*
> *will he do, because I go to the Father.*
> (i.e., finally and totally merge with the Absolute
> Source of Being.)

> *Whatever you ask in my name....*
> (i.e., align yourself with in consciousness, by your-
> self Awakening the inner feeling that *it is already*
> *done*)

> *I will do it, that the Father may be glorified to the Son;*
> (i.e., The I AM will bring it about. The glory being,
> that what you ask for while feeling that it is *already*
> accomplished, will *be* accomplished.

> *if you ask anything in my name, I will do it.*
> (Everything needed is naturally provided, if you
> simply abide as the prior pure Awareness, the true
> Self, or Christ-consciousness, with all sense of

"need" totally dissolved. If there is unwavering faith (a *certain* feeling) that what you ask or pray for is *already accomplished*, it will be accomplished.)

If you love me, you will keep my commandments.
(i.e., maintain the same quality of Conscious Presence as did Jesus, or as your present Enlightened Teacher, Guru, or comparable spiritual guide.)

And I will pray the Father, and he will give you another Counselor, to be with you forever, even the Spirit of Truth, whom the world cannot receive, because it neither sees him nor knows him; you know him, for he dwells with you, and will be in you.
(There are always Conscious or Enlightened Beings on earth. The Presence and Grace of such Ones are able to intercede and/or open the spiritual Heart of true devotees to the inner Source and Stillness – *"pray to the Father"* – and bring about a quickening to their own enlightenment. However, only those who surrender the ego, who are *truly receptive* and *in harmony* with such a Conscious One when known or "found," will receive, realize or truly benefit from this pure quality of grace.)

I will not leave you desolate; I will come to you.
(The true Self is always available. It is only concealed or hidden by the mind and world while the ego or body-mind is apparently manifesting.)

Yet a little while, and the world will see me no more, but you will see me; because I live, you will live also.
(When identified with the ego or body-mind we do not "see" or realize the true Self. But we will eventually, for the Self is who or *what* we *really are* – "*I live so you live also.*" But a Conscious Teacher – "*the Counselor*" – is *required* to assist us in removing the obstructions to this pure Awareness or true Self.)

In that day you will know that I am in my Father, and you in me, and I in you.
(On Spiritually Awakening, when the body-mind obstructions are removed and the Self realized, it is seen that one is not different from the Source, "*the*

Father," and Christ Consciousness is our nature.)

He who has my commandments and keeps them, he it is who loves me; and he who loves me will be loved by my Father, and I will love him and manifest to him.
    (One abiding in the Self, attending *only* to the Self, or meditating steadily on the One Reality, is *"keeping my commandments,"* or following the guru's instructions, and thus the Self will soon be realized.)

Judas (not Iscariot) said to him, "Lord, how is it that you will manifest yourself to us, and not to the world?" Jesus answered him, "If a man loves me, he will keep my word, and my Father will love him, and we will come to him and make our home with him.
    (One who Inquires, or meditates only on the inner Self, realizes within himself the same quality of consciousness as God *or* the Guru; he realizes that God *is* the Guru manifesting in human form. But one not attuned is unable to understand even intellectually the Truth of the Source of his own being.)

He who does not love me does not keep my words; and (that) the word which you hear is not mine but the Father's who sent me.
    (One who does not surrender to the Truth or turn his/her attention to the Self [or Christ] *"does not love"* Christ, the Source, or these words of truth. He is therefore incapable of realizing the Truth they contain.)

These things I have spoken to you while I am still with you. But the Counselor, the Holy Spirit, whom the Father....
    (the Source, pure Awareness, the Higher State of Consciousness or true Self...)

will send in my name....
    (i.e., send One of the same nature, or degree of realization, to function as your guide or guru)

he will teach you all things, and bring to your remembrance all that I have said to you. Peace I leave with you; my peace I give to you; not as the world gives do I give to you.
    (The peace of the Heart, the true Self, is beyond

anything known or even attainable in the world.)

Let not your hearts be troubled, neither let them be afraid. You heard me say to you, 'I go away, and I will come to you.' If you loved me, you would have rejoiced, because I go to the Father; for the Father is greater than I.
   (The true Self, the Source, pure Awareness is Itself greater than that which we are conscious *of*, including the world and all that manifests in or to the body-mind, or ego, or the "I"-thought.)

And now I have told you before it takes place, so that when it does take place, you may believe. I will no longer talk much with you....
   (It is better to simply remain quiet, in the Silence and Stillness of pure Awareness, than to analyze the Truth or engage in intellectual discussions or processes *about* it with the mind. The mind can never "know" the Truth)

for the ruler of this world is coming.
   (The ego, or body-mind, or the separate-self, may *appear* to "know," or "to be in charge," or "to be in control," when the Self is forgotten or not realized, but it is not.)

He has no power over me....
   (The ego actually has no power over the *true* Self)

but I do as the Father has commanded me, so that the world may know that I love the Father.
   (This is being surrendered, and totally merged in the Source, itself shining as pure Peace, Freedom and Joy. This is *pure* Love.)

(From John 14: 12 - 31, the Revised Standard Bible.)

Most Christian theologians, being intellectually oriented but *not* spiritually Awakened or enlightened, have interpreted the Bible and the teachings of Jesus entirely in the mind – i.e., mentally and emotionally, physically and historically (meaning literally) – and not spiritually or metaphysically. They may *think* their knowledge is experiential, but it in fact is only the experience of their own minds, not the Higher or Transcendental Realization of pure Being, *prior to* time and space.

Generally, their conditioned beliefs follow the thinking of traditional, doctrinal fundamentalism, much like the strongly prejudicial beliefs of the early Pharisees that denied Christ. Their limited beliefs are not only emotionally embraced, but are passed on to their adherents. They are basically doctrinaire, "fear-of-hell" oriented, and judgmental of all who *in their view* are "sinners," meaning who embrace different, "unorthodox" beliefs or concepts other than their own.

They also often join forces and embrace the conservative political views of the "far right," and attempt to gain legislative control to have laws passed that *require* everyone to follow their own "brand" of Christian doctrine or beliefs, such as being *against* birth control, but *for* capital punishment, and practicing their own "form of prayer" in schools – contrary to the American Bill of Rights which separates church and state.

Their limited and false beliefs, concepts and far-drawn conclusions that divide and separate themselves from the rest of society have been "spoon fed" or handed down to their gullible fear-oriented adherents and very strongly proselytized to new converts throughout Christian history. The narrow bias that is contained in the interpretation of scripture by these so-called "orthodox" theologians, is unfortunately what is usually the most widely known, taught, embraced and disseminated (or at least tolerated) in the world of Christianity.

It seems they never really knew or understood, or they just lost sight of the true meaning, purpose and intent of Jesus' message of spiritual Enlightenment for all humanity. This is because they have been more interested in preserving their own fundamentalist ideas and concepts, and their own social standing in their church, or Christian community, or the world, than in spiritual enlightenment. The result is that they and their members (past and present) actually know little or nothing at all about spiritual Enlightenment, and are very far from realizing it now, since it is not lived or taught in their churches or by any so-called orthodox denomination or sect.

To summarize, the real mission or purpose of Jesus' life has been grossly misunderstood. Mankind in general, and Christianity in particular, has suffered a great deal as the result of these unconscious doctrinaire views. What's more, these unconscious views have now become the accepted "authority" for most so-called Christian doctrine and belief.

The fact is, the Bible – when studied from the context or con-sciousness of spiritual enlightenment – is realized to be *with-out* doctrine; there is not one iota of doctrine contained in the entire New Testament! *It is just not there!* Or, *paradoxically*, it is *all* doctrine, based on the misconceptions of *unenlightened* men.

All Bible "Doctrine" is Man-made

All so-called doctrine, which is believed to be contained in the Bible, is *entirely* created in the minds of men – i.e., it is only the notions of the church leaders and "believers" of funda-mentalism. They have created it *entirely* in, and projected it out of, *their own minds*, based on their own limited concepts. They have successfully influenced their followers to *believe it* along with themselves. Thus, these theologians and church leaders have themselves historically given (and continue to give) this pseudo-doctrine its assumed authority by calling it "the indisputable *word of God,*" and getting ongoing agree-ment from all those in the Christian world who are equally ig-norant of, or to, the Transcendental Awareness of pure Being.

This also has "sealed" its existence and longevity in time, while elevating these ecclesiastics into high positions as "relig-ious authorities." This has elevated their prestige, not to men-tion their egos, by giving them an important and remembered place in so-called history, at least among their sympathetic fol-lowers in the clergy who also embrace their conceptual views. The clergy "share the spotlight" by handing the same doctri-naire down to *their* gullible congregations who were and are often filled with fear and superstition, and so are willing to ac-cept just about *anything* given to them as "being from God," or "on high." For it comes with the promise of "saving them" from their phobias: the loss of individuality, and their fear of "eternal damnation." Since there were very few with either the true knowledge, ability, power, or the inclination to "go against the tide" and challenge the early theologians or so-called "church fathers," the result is that the long-held concep-tual theories of professed doctrine in the Bible has continued. Its false beliefs have survived, and the doctrine is still em-braced today by the majority of fundamentalist Christians.

The same tendency to hegemony (supreme domination and control by a particular group) is true among the fundamentalists of the other major world religions. Just look at the result: it had engendered persecution within each of the separate religious groups, and horrible wars or bloodshed between the differing religions, and all this "in the name of God," or "Christ," or "Allah," etc. The recent rise of the Taliban in Afghanistan and its doctrine of fundamentalist Islam is just as limiting and inflexible as are most fundamentalist Christians.

To some people (obviously those who hold many of the doctrinal views being described here, regardless of their chosen personal religion) these statements may sound pejorative, and thought to be *intentionally* provocative, if not inflammatory. It may even be thought they are an *intentional* outburst against *all* fundamentalist believers or orthodoxy in particular, and thus against *all* orthodox churches, temples and mosques, or against religion itself. Thus it may *seem* like the intention here is only to be divisive. But this is *not* the intention! This is being said *only to bring light to the facts,* and without judgment! It is a fact that the strong-minded adherents of most of these fundamentalist, religionist views have caused much pain and suffering to otherwise innocent people throughout history.

The unfortunate fact is, *anyone* – who candidly and uncompromisingly looks into it for oneself – can see that throughout history, as much if not more blood has been spilled by religious fundamentalists – all "in the name of God" or "on behalf of Christ" or for "Allah" – as has been caused by political conflicts. Jesus, who taught "Love thy neighbor as thy self," and "Love one another as I have loved you," had nothing to do with any of this. Nor does "Jehovah," or "Allah the merciful."

So, this is being brought up *only* for us to realize that God (which is Love itself, according to Jesus) and Jesus himself *never taught or even suggested* conflict between differing people. Nor did he advocate condemnation of those who hold different spiritual or religious views. However, he did condemn the Pharisees, who were the fundamentalists, or the "conservative religious right" of his own time, for their bigoted and divisive attitudes and behavior. The result of Jesus' criticism of religious fundamentalists is that they were responsible for his crucifixion. And, unfortunately, these very same narrow and divisive views still prevail among many so-called "Christians" to this day.

Competition Between Early Religious Sects

Various accounts of historians indicate that the religious competition during early biblical times was quite strong. This was particularly so in countries bordered by the Mediterranean Sea, all along its southern, eastern, and northern coastlines from Egypt throughout the Holy Lands, and from Greece to Rome and later even to early Spain. In Christianity's incipiency, its early missionaries strongly competed for a position in the social community among the people living along the various Mediterranean trade routes. The "rank and file" were competitively solicited by all the religious sects of the time, including those of the Greeks, Romans, Persians, Hebrews and even Buddhists from India, China and Tibet.

So early Christians, then competing with all the different religions during that period, and out of their lack of understanding of the *real meaning* of Jesus' message – that spiritual Enlightenment (or reunion with God, the Source) is the *real* and *highest* purpose of life (this misunderstanding is still not much different to this day) – exaggerated their arguments, trying to prove their "new religion" as "better than" all the rest. Their big claim, of course, was *"our leader is the very Son of God!"*

And, it is quite plausible, in order to cut the competition off from making the same or a similar claim, they rushed forth to exclaim...*for a quick clincher*: "In fact, he is the *only* Son of God!" This is not unlike two small boys arguing about whose daddy is the biggest and the strongest, each saying that his daddy is. Then one quickly responds: "My daddy is the biggest and strongest daddy in the *whole world!*" Now how does the other boy overcome, outdo, or overshadow such an all-encompassing claim? Perhaps with only a louder but still weak (because it was not stated *first*), "No, he is not!"

Buddhist Influence on Jesus' Early Training and Teaching

Buddhism was already a strong and influential religion in the Far East, having spread from its much earlier beginning in India, to Tibet, China and Japan. It was rapidly growing in all directions with organizational aptitude and purpose, its purpose and message being the Dharma, spiritual Enlightenment. It, being a growing proselytizing religion, already had an active monastery at Alexandria, near the mouth of the Nile River, when on the recommendation of the "wise men from the East," Jesus after his birth was taken by Joseph and Mary to Egypt.

Also, it *has* been confirmed by a few historians and early researchers that Jesus did in fact also travel to India and Tibet and even studied and meditated with Buddhist Lamas and priests in at least one Tibetan monastery. I myself knew an elderly couple, both have since died, who together spent a few years in Tibet. He was a Unity minister (clergyman). I met them when I was a student minister training at Unity School of Christianity in Lee's Summit, Missouri. They told me about a fascinating incident that had occurred to them when they were much younger, while visiting an ancient monastery in Tibet. One of the Buddhist monks took them down through dark and narrow subterranean passageways lighted only by oil lamps and torches, into a room containing scores of very old cylinder-shaped scrolls. They said the scrolls were approximately 30 inches (75 centimeters) long and were inserted in round niches recessed in the walls approximately 12 inches (30 centimeters) in diameter.

They explained how the monk, after making a short search of the index of either the contents or locations of the various scrolls, very carefully removed one and, with even more care, partially unrolled it. The monk said the scroll was hundreds of years old and explained that the index entry carved in the wooden spool stated it was perhaps the third or fourth ensuing and exact copy made of the data it contained, reproduced from the previous, older scrolls of similar antiquity. Each of them had been exactly copied in their time due to their age, going back to the original. My friends said the monk explained that the work of some of the other monks there – and their only or primary job, day in and day out – was to reproduce by hand the ancient scrolls that were beginning to crack and crumble or fall apart from age. It took a few years to reproduce each scroll. And, with a few hundred such scrolls to be reproduced, it was a never-ending job that consumed the entire adult lifetime of some scribes.

The monk translated what he read from the scroll explaining, "Your Jesus visited this very monastery and stayed here for a few years meditating, working and studying with our monks of that era; he returned to where he had come from in an evidently illumined or elevated state of consciousness."

It was believed by the monk translating the scroll to my friends that other monks had said records showed that, "Your Jesus also spent time in India either before arriving in or after departing from Tibet." My friends recalled with interest that the dates of the period seemed to indicate in the monastery scrolls that Jesus would have been there studying with the Tibetan Buddhist monks very near the time period that the Bible has no record or account of his activities, other than *"he increased in wisdom and stature (or years) and in favor with God and men."* (Luke 2:52) Biblically, this was during the time before he appeared in Judea at about the age of 30 to be baptized by John the Baptist and begin his ministry. (Luke 3:23)

There is something else in this regard that is interesting to note. It is surmised by some historians, who are not influenced by traditional religious doctrine, that Jesus' earliest spiritual training may have actually started at the Buddhist monastery in Alexandria, Egypt, or before the age of 12 when, as is recorded, he questioned and debated the teachers and priests in the temple in Jerusalem. (Luke 2:42-48) This would have been during his early and later childhood, which the New Testament confirms was spent in Egypt before his return to Judea with his parents after the death of King Herod.

King Herod plotted to kill the baby Jesus when *"the wise men from the East"* (Matthew 2:1-12) went to the king asking his aid in locating the young infant who was *"born king of the Jews."* (Matthew 2:2) It is biblically recorded that the plot was revealed to Joseph in a dream in which an angel of the Lord prompted him to flee with Mary and Jesus to Egypt (Matthew 2:13) following the visit by the wise men. The wise men were prompted by their own vision (or dream) not to return to Herod's palace and disclose the babe's location, as Herod had requested them to do.

The possibility (and even the probability) is very strong that Jesus did have early Buddhist training, which either *began* his spiritual process or ultimately cleared his consciousness for spiritual enlightenment to occur. As briefly mentioned earlier, this might possibly have been his rebirth, or continuation of a previous life in Tibet, where he was an enlightened Lama. Or, it could have been the completion of doing *sadhana* (Sanskrit: "spiritual practice") in a former life.

It is fairly obvious that Jesus had some very intense *karma* (destiny) to complete or fulfill from a former life by his painful ordeal on the cross. The law of karma, by his own words, is irrefutable. He said, *"He that takes the sword will perish by the sword,"* (Matthew 26:52) and *"truly I say to you, till heaven and earth pass away, not an iota, not a dot, will pass from the law* (karma) *until all is fulfilled."* (Matthew 5:18)

Christianity's Claim to Exclusive Connection with God

Perhaps ignorant of or refusing to accept then available stories of Jesus' early training in other religions, Christianity's "all-encompassing claim" of his being "the only Son God ever had" was made into doctrinal or ecclesiastical law. It thus became part of the catechism of the early Christian Church.

Today it conforms to the beliefs of most Christians, being written into the spiritual records or accounts, e.g., the New Testament, that Jesus is the *only* Son of God. This leaves little room for interpretation or intelligent reconsideration; such as, he is just one *Avatar* (world Savior) among the many known and worshipped, as he is widely actually recognized, honored and considered by many Hindus throughout the world.

Evidently, it would seem – at least to most Christians – "there is no other child in God's family" or for that matter even a wife for God. It is as though "the world of the divine" is only a "one-child and motherless family." As to who is Jesus' *spiritual* or *divine* mother, no Christian theologian has come forth to reveal who this "grand goddess" might be. Is this possibly because that in the patriarchal-oriented Judeo-Christian world (which is also the case with the Muslims), there seems to be no room for or recognition given to a Divine Mother or comparable Divine Feminine; it is only a system of Divine Men? As a result, look how long it has taken for women to be given their true equal rights with men. In fact, they are still not yet *totally* equal, there is still great disparity. Even a semblance of equality has scarcely begun to occur for the women in most countries outside of the Western world.

When you ask some Christians about God's mate or female partner they answer, "God doesn't need a wife to procreate." Their argument is God's creation of Adam, the first man, without a mother to give him birth, and the creation of Eve from Adam's rib. Or, some contend that God "cohabitated" with Joseph's wife, thus implying she committed adultery making even Jesus' birth an act resulting from "sin." We can see just how ridiculous or outlandish it gets when people are strongly identified with the body-mind as being the Self. Of course, the contention still is that Mary *was* Jesus' mother, although Jesus is not really an ordinary human to most Christians; he is divine even though he was *partially* human, etc. Or, more often, their answer to this type of question is, "You must have faith." Even some Christians who are professional scientists or medical doctors have trouble dealing with these issues.

In truth, Jesus was just as ordinary a man in the human sense as anyone. And yes, he was and is unique; there is no doubt about that. But his experience was *not*, nor is *exclusive*. What *makes* Jesus extraordinary is not that he was (or is) the Son of God, for so are you and I – *we all are!* His extraordinariness was his *Awakened Consciousness* or his *knowledge* of the fact. It was his direct Awareness *of* and *as* being the Son of God, or the One Supreme Self, and his Consciously *living that* in the ever-present moment *with full understanding of the fact!*

Jesus knew as a matter of *direct* insight, understanding and continual steady realization that his Consciousness or Awareness, *and that of all of us,* is rooted in the One Supreme Being, the Energy of pure Intelligence, which is the very Self of God. He knew, not as a belief, opinion, or concept, but by *direct experience!* His life is the perfect model that he taught by, and urged all of us to use or follow as an example in order to realize and directly experience this Truth for ourselves.

He said, *"The works I do, do you also, and even greater works than these will you do."* (John 14:12 paraphrased) Similarly, in this regard, the apostle Paul wrote, *"Have in you the same mind (awareness of Self) as Christ Jesus."* (Phil. 2:5)

FINALLY, do these above assertions mean that all or most

religion, particularly Christianity, is not good or beneficial for true spiritual seekers? Or, that it is to be entirely discounted? No, it is not all limiting or detrimental, religion does have its place and its benefits. Even though all major religions are limited, or dualistic in their nature and view of life, religion is still beneficial to aspirants at its level who are seeking God, for learning morality, good behavior, kindness, by sincerely "taking up" religion at its level of their spiritual quest. It at least benefits the aspirant by helping to *purify the mind* and making sincere seekers more *devotional* to God, and respecting of one's fellow man, or more loving if only among others in his religion. Ultimately, this contributes to some extent to us all, for *any degree of love genuinely expressed* in this apparent world of conflict, confusion, and contradiction *is better than no love at all!*

The Truth is, there is only one Self, One Reality now manifesting *as* all the apparent persons, places and things comprising this and all worlds. This One Absolute Intelligence emanates as the single Universal Awareness *always, already appearing as* these apparently different levels, forms, and expressions of manifest existence, including all the major religions. IT is even NOW, at a subtle level, fulfilling the various needs of *everyone*, to the degree that we are capable of receiving IT.

It also means if you truly "hear" and "understand" this argument of the Highest Truth – regarding the Self, which is Real God or the One Absolute Intelligence – you do not need *any* religion. If you truly "get this," then, from the spiritual point of view, you are *already beyond religion*. Or, you are ready to not just *believe*, but to *realize* the Truth and remain ever happy, free and at peace *in and as the Self!*

The way and the means of "achieving" this is to simply *do nothing* – i.e., just abide in the *true* Self, you *always, already are!*

If this still seems to be "not yet possible," due to interference from the mind, then an effective aid to *completion* is practicing or consciously living the principles and processes found in this book. They are based primarily on the pure, direct Teaching of Bhagavan Sri Ramana Maharshi, as well as *all* the Enlightened Teachers in the world, in particular the *pure* Teaching of Jesus Christ, free of the doctrine of fundamentalist orthodox Christianity. They also have been proven *true* and *dependable* in the life and experience of this writer.

MOSES' REALIZATION OF SELF

BHAGAVAN SRI RAMANA MAHARSHI often said that the entire Vedanta (i.e., *the sum and substance of true knowledge*), as well as the meaning and purpose realized in *all* the scriptures of *all* religious cultures or *all* the sages and saints *who have ever lived*, is contained in the one verse of the Old Testament: "I AM THAT I AM." (Exodus 3:14) The way to realize this Supreme Truth, he said, is: "Be still and know that I AM (is) God." (Psalms 46:10 paraphrased)

Exodus 3:14 is the *only* passage in either the Old or New Testaments of the Bible written in all capital letters. This indicates that it is *the most significant statement contained in the entire Jewish and Christian scriptures!* It not only sums up the total teaching to be realized from the Bible, but also is the culmination of many lifetimes of meditation or spiritual practice.

Moses received this revelation directly from God. This was his direct, intimate realization of God dwelling in him, *as him,* or being his very own Self. It was his Awakened Realization that Universal Awareness is itself the individual consciousness in us all. But mere *intellectual* understanding about this, as being what Moses realized and understood for himself, is not enough. It must also be *directly awakened and realized* by *each of us for ourselves.* That is, we must not just know *about it* and *believe* it, but spiritually Awaken to it as did Moses.

Moses was an Israelite, a Jew. At the time, his people were slaves in Egypt. As well as being historically factual, this has a psychological or metaphysical meaning, which is the higher meaning that has any real spiritual significance today, even for the Jews.

According to Charles Fillmore's "Metaphysical Bible Dictionary," (published by Unity School of Christianity, Lee's Summit, Missouri), the word Israelite means a "chosen one of God," while "being in Egypt" metaphysically means, "being in darkness or ignorance."

We are all, in this sense, Israelites, for we are *all* sons of God,

and thus "chosen of God." Also, all people who do not know
and realize the Truth of their being, that is, their oneness with
God, are slaves to spiritual darkness or ignorance. They must
"slave and work hard" to survive or really succeed in this
world, and they have very little if any real or lasting happiness – happiness not mixed with pain, suffering and/or upset.

Metaphysically, "Moses" means "drawn from the water,"
which represents the aspiration in man to withdraw, or "be
drawn from" the spiritual ignorance of ordinary life in the
world. This is departing from the state of separation, seeking,
and suffering, and Awakening to the Truth, the One Reality,
or the Self ever-abiding in the Heart of being *as one's natural
state.* "Moses" is spiritually orienting man's aspiration to lift
himself into a higher understanding or higher consciousness.

As an infant, Moses was saved from being slaughtered when
Pharaoh's soldiers had been commanded to kill all the new-
born males of the Israelites. This means that when we aspire
to Higher Truth, even the world and its armies cannot stop
God's grace or His influence from protecting us.

Moses was the son of Amram and Jochebed. They represent
holding a high conception of oneness with God. When we are
caught up and living in the illusion of separateness (darkness)
but are having a high degree of love for God, which grows
into a closer awareness of oneness with God, then our desire
to bring forth this higher consciousness will find a protector.

Moses was placed in a basket and floated down the river
toward where the daughter of Pharaoh had her daily bath,
where he was seen by her and taken and raised by her. We
must care for our infant-thoughts of Truth and surround them
with the woven combination (basket) of faith, love, and trust.

Pharaoh represents our own ignorance, our gross material
consciousness, and worldly or body passions that would en-
slave and even kill our new-born attempt to realize the Truth
and live it consciously. Pharaoh also represents our beliefs, or
false or limited concepts about Self, the concept "I-am-this-
body."

Moses was actually raised as the adopted grandson of Pharaoh, symbolizing that the intellect with its power and ability,

identified with the body-mind, can actually be used intentionally to express and perhaps realize our higher spiritual nature by consciously putting it to use for this higher purpose. Moses was educated in the highest "schools or temples of learning" of that time in Egypt; this represents the illumined intellect being used to turn awareness inward toward the Self, or God. Even with all his "formal schooling," higher knowledge or intellectual understanding of physical laws and scientific principles of the time, Moses was still dissatisfied. He was deeply interested in knowing the Truth of Being, for it to be directly revealed, understood and experienced – not just learned concepts and theories that are usually considered to be "higher education," or as intellectual or "book knowledge."

Mere *intellectual* understanding or knowledge *about* the Self, *is not enough* – the truth must be fully *awakened*, or *realized directly!* It must be *assimilated* and *integrated* into one's being as the *very basis* from which one expresses – *sees, moves* and *acts*.

Real knowledge is *not* contained in books. Books give only the record or repetition of other people's knowledge or beliefs, their *recorded* experience and knowledge, which is often with little actual, direct experience on the part of the one who is learning. What is usually considered "knowledge" by the average student is what has been read, heard and collected in one's mind or been mechanically stored in memory and repeated by rote. That is only the record of someone else's experience. Real knowledge is actually the *present, direct knowing*. It is the *very intelligence itself*, pure consciousness *itself*, and this is not in books; it is "in" the Self. This quality of Direct Knowing cannot be found or obtained in books, including this book. It is *direct expression!* This true knowledge can only be realized *directly* by personal *insight* and *experience*, which is *true* understanding. Books, especially sacred scriptures, can *point to it*, but you must *realize it for yourself!*

The word "education" comes from the Latin word *"educare"* (lit. *e* = out of, *ducare* = to lead) which means to release or uncover that which is *already* innately *there*. Knowledge is no more contained in books than food is contained in a cookbook. If you are hungry, reading a cookbook will not satisfy your need for food; if anything, it will only increase your appetite or craving for real food. This was what happened to Moses.

He deeply desired to have real *understanding* about *who* and *what* he really was, as pure Being, not just mere concepts.

Moses was not told that he was adopted; therefore he always thought he was an Egyptian, a born member of the royal family. On growing into manhood, he learned that he was an Israelite. This was a real shock and gave him great concern over the plight of his newly found "people," his true kinsmen. He desired to help them get free from their bondage and suffering, their state of physical-mental suppression. Moses had a clearer, higher understanding than most of those around him and felt compassion and responsibility to do something about their plight. Probably, at first, he had ego motivation mixed in with his high ideals – like personal ambition or the "recognition" to be gained from "doing good" for others. This can also kindle doubt in one's ability or capability.

Having volunteered, thus allowing his destiny as a leader of his people to be fulfilled, to help set them free from their bondage to suffering and limitation, he must have felt the great burden of responsibility and questioned, "Why me? Why has this great responsibility fallen on me; why is it occurring to me?" There possibly arose doubt and uncertainty. "Can this really be done? Who am I, to be doing this?" Haven't we all at one time or another experienced this question when something worthwhile we attempted or started seemed beyond our capacity, even though at the start we were ignited with the passion or zeal of its high purpose and benefit?

Moses, like all who have a deep interest in life with a desire to help others, also may have had a desire to trace his own roots. He was, perhaps, at first not satisfied just being an Egyptian (living an ordinary, worldly life) but wanted a higher understanding of himself, or true Self, and so was in search for his Source. Then he learned that he was really an Israelite (a chosen one of God). This was at first only intellectual knowing. But his desire and quest for the direct experience of true Self-knowledge and understanding pierced to a deeper level of Inquiry. It is possible that Moses was long asking, wondering and inquiring into the Source of his being, his true Self. He was perhaps asking, "Who am I?" "Where did I come from?" "Why am I here?" and "Where is the promised land that I am going to?" What is true, *before* birth and *after* death, and what is the real purpose of life beyond all this suffering?" What is this apparent "self," that has all these questions – that "knows" and yet "does not know"?

The biblical record says that one day while Moses was on Mt. Sinai (being on a mountain metaphysically means to be in a high state of consciousness) his thoughts or meditation had reached a high point, a pinnacle. As Moses was thus elevated in consciousness by this penetrating inquiry to know and understand himself, not just his physical roots, ancestry or lineage, but rather his true *purpose* in life and the *meaning* of life, God's voice came to him "speaking from a burning bush."

This has many possible meanings, each according to the nature of one's personal concept of God or Self.

For example, we may not be able to guarantee the existence of the world or what it contains or even the existence of God its assumed creator, but at no time can we deny our own existence. Without doubt, *we do exist*; and, our existence is not dependent on thought; that is, we do not have to "think" to know that we exist. Our existence is self-evident.

So, prior to the body-mind – or birth certificate, driver's license or any other form or identification – and even personality, there first exists the Self *that we are* that is *pure I AMness*. Although usually *misconceived* as being the "I"-thought, it is not a thought, it is the pure Awareness prior to all thought.

Concurrently, the fact is, consciousness *must be* before anything else can be! That is, before we can be conscious of any thing, *we* must be – meaning, we must first be *as existence* and *consciousness*. So again, consciousness *must be*, and *must be the One Presence* before recognizing anything else as "other," or *anything* having objective existence, including the body-mind.

Thus, very simply: Consciousness, or pure I AMness, *is itself* the Self. This is the highest meaning of this biblical message.

But there are interim meanings that are also significant and helpful to anyone unable to fully grasp or realize this highest meaning. Another possible meaning of "the burning bush experience" is that it is possible Moses was at the time gazing at a bush while deeply contemplating or meditating. When his mind slowed down, being focused outwardly on the form of the bush, and at the same time attending inwardly on the Source of Consciousness, the mind could have stopped. The experience of the mind stopping, with the eyes open and focused on an object often gives the effect of the observed object being engulfed in a sea of light, or like it is on fire. Light is the nature of all things, and in this state, prior to the mind, all things appear in an effulgent radiance of light as though on fire but not being consumed.

Also, another possible meaning is, in the Yoga system of meditation the spine has seven "centers" (*chakras*) ranging from the "root" *chakra* at the base of the spine (named, *muladhara*) to a center in the crown of the head. The crown center or *chakra* (the seventh) is named the *sahasrara*, or thousand-petal lotus. When the life force, or energy of consciousness called the *kundalini* (or serpent power) is stirred, in advanced yogis it rises up the spine to the crown *chakra* and is sustained there. For some of these advanced yogis, there occurs an inner vision of bright light in the head which radiates throughout the thousand petal lotus. This experience, which itself could be likened to the vision of a burning bush, results in the yogi being immersed in a state of bliss, an actual transcendental experience reported by many practicing yogis.

However, as already stated, the highest meaning *for all of us* is, that consciousness must be before anything else can be, and the name of that pure Consciousness is I AM. It is the cause and source of *all that is*, shining in oneself *as* the Self, the I AM. Thus, "I AM THAT I AM," recorded in *all capital letters* in the Old Testament (Exodus 3:14) is, as Bhagavan Sri Ramana Maharshi said, the summation of *all* the scriptures of *all* religious cultures. He said this is the final or Supreme Truth, and to "Be still and know that I AM *is* God." He said this entirely sums up *the very best method of spiritual practice!* Stop thinking and just abide in the Self. He later summed up and reduced the method of Self-Inquiry (explained fully later, see page 232) to "simple Self-abidance" and that to just two words: "Be still."

"Being still" is to not think; it is remaining quiet in the Self, in pure Awareness – prior to the mind, prior to the "I"-thought.

THE TEN COMMANDMENTS

MOSES' REALIZATION OF SUPREME TRUTH is that Pure Awareness is the One Reality, and the True Self. With this important realization also came a code of ethics or laws for appropriate living, whereby all of us – being equal – could live together in harmony, peace, love, happiness and prosperity. However, it is also written in scripture (recorded in the King James New Testament by St. Paul), "The letter of the law killeth, but the spirit giveth life." (II Cor. 3:6) We must understand the *spiritual* meaning of these precepts. When understood in the Light of Consciousness, these ten practical "laws" are actually principles for *effective living*.

The FIRST commandment (Exodus 20:2) is the statement of Supreme Truth: *"I AM the Lord, your God... You shall have no other gods before Me."* Self, or I AM, *is* God. I AM *is* the Lord. The word "Lord" in Hebrew, when spelled with capital letters, is the divine name YHWH, which here is connected with the verb *hayah*, "to be." It means the simple principle of *Being*. The commandment states, "You shall have no other gods besides *me*," which is your very Being, or I AM, the very Self.

*   *   *   *   *

The Self (I AM, First Person singular, Consciousness Itself) is the Lord and creator of all that I AM conscious of being. This is the Truth. To give creative power or authority to any other force or power outside this pure Consciousness is to live a lie, and is "not permitted." Doing so causes one to continue in separation (sin), seeking, suffering and death.

*   *   *   *   *

The SECOND commandment (Exodus 20:4) speaks of the suffering that is experienced when we are ignorant of our true Self and its nature, and when we refuse to heed this highest precept and instead believe in a separate third-person *entity* as the "Lord God" and worship this *imaged* "God." It says, *"You shall not make for yourself a graven image, or any likeness of anything that is in heaven above, or the earth beneath, or the waters be-*

neath the earth, nor shall you bow down to them or serve them. For I am a jealous God visiting the iniquity of the fathers upon the children of the third and fourth generations of those who hate me, but showing steadfast love to those who love me and keep my commandments."

It means that we are not to hold *any* second- or third-person image, belief, or concept of God and worship that. God is not and cannot be a second or third-person object; God is eternally prior to both subject and object, being the very Self, the Supreme Context for *all* subjects and objects, thoughts or beliefs.

When we place our faith and trust in *anything* outside the One Self (God), and separate ourself from the Source or God, we are *"those who hate me."* The result is living at the effect of life, or of such apparent "things" or "situations," and thus undergoing countless cycles of bondage, limitation, loss and suffering as *"the children of the third and fourth generations."*

The THIRD commandment (Exodus 20:7) tells us, *"You shall not take the name of the Lord your God in vain."* The name of God is I AM. Contrary to one's beliefs, we are not offending God by using profanity such as "god damn," etc. Actually, no such second or third-person "God-entity" even exists that could be offended. "He" simply does not exist. The notion that such an anthropomorphic God *exists* as a living separate Entity is *itself* the problem with many religionists. For it is "creating" and living in the false notion of being separate from the Source, which is itself "sin" the very cause of all suffering.

God, in the purest sense, is really not (nor ever could be) offended by anything; for God is All and all is God. Since *everything* is the Self of God, how could any part of the Self be offensive to itself? Can one's hand be offended by one's foot? It is man's separated sense of pride and ego that feels offense or offended, and takes offense – not God, which is the Self.

The third commandment is about using the unconditioned "name" and "nature" of God, the Self, to *condition* or *identify* It with the sense of lack, limitation, untruth, separation and seeking. The "name" of God, the very Self, is I AM. *"I AM has sent you... this is my name forever, and thus I am to be remembered throughout all generations."* (Exodus 3:14-15) Take note that the capital (upper case) letters used here *are actually contained in the scriptures,* indicating that God *is* I AM, or *is the very Self.*

*   *   *   *   *

When using such self-derogatory statements as "I am sick," "I am incapable," "I am unhappy," "I am unworthy," "I am a miserable sinner," or "I am no good," this is actually violating this law, or the Self's integrity, by improperly using the Self's name and contaminating its pure nature with false limitation.

The name "I" give myself (which is the one Self), or the state of consciousness "I" identify with as being "myself," is what determines the nature of each and every experience.

*   *   *   *   *

The FOURTH commandment (Exodus 20:8) deals with what the Bible calls the Sabbath Day, the "day" or period of rest from all further acting, creating or "doing." The commandment says, *"Remember the Sabbath day and keep it holy. Six days you shall labor, but the seventh day is a Sabbath to the Lord your God; in it you shall rest and not do any work."*

The creative significance of this simple yet all-powerful principle, or law, is: once you have determined the specific form and final feeling of a desire, feeling it fulfilled (see p. 62), and are "seeing" it *already* done in the mind, then resting or remaining still in the natural "feeling of completion," with no further effort, allows it to naturally manifest in the world.

Without further effort, you simply allow the *awakened feeling of completion* (with regard to the situation) to occur, or come about in your world. You do not hold on or return to former thoughts of uncertainty, or allow any feelings of doubt or lack, or any sense of separation between you and your wish fulfilled.

As already explained in the Law of Reversibility, when you assume the natural feeling *that would be yours* if what you want was *already* so, or was *an accomplished fact,* and just rest in this feeling as your "ongoing and predominant mood" – i.e., as *already having, doing* or *being* whatever it is that you want – this steady feeling of completion will bring it about as a physical fact in your world. This is simply the creative process and how it works to bring about the manifestation of a thing, *anything desired*, in your world.

The FIFTH commandment (Exodus 20:12) is *"Honor your father and mother, that your days in the land may be long which the Lord your God gives you."* One meaning of this pertains to the Universal Law of balance between the masculine and feminine creative energies. Both male and female energy are required and utilized for the occurring of all creation, as well as for having a happy, well-balanced life. The idea, or male aspect (assertive, father, seed-thought) of a thing must be planted or impressed in the passive or receptive female feeling nature; that is, impregnated in the open feminine quality (mother, or earth quality). Once this occurs, the idea is conceived and in due season is born as a physical expression or manifestation.

This commandment also means that man is both male and female, and woman is both female and male. We are all both, male and female. The proper balance of male and female energy in one's nature, with the combined qualities and characteristics of both, will produce a balanced life and result in long life and happiness in the body. This also means to love and respect *both sexes* as equal.

This commandment is also about the simplicity of the principle of life manifesting in duality, or physical form: that for any *thing* to exist, its opposite must *also* exist. *Both* are needed in a total creation – up *requires* down; right *requires* left; east *requires* west; heat *requires* cold. These opposites are interdependent. Very simply, this is the principle of opposite polarities co-existing in all manifesting objects. The appropriate balance of opposites occurring in the context of *any* idea lends to the successful outcome or completion of that idea and *brings it into being*. When the opposite position to a new idea is first accepted, considered and utilized *within the context of the new idea*, it lends itself creatively to the successful completion of the idea, and to the success of the project. This makes for a successful outcome and for long-lasting results.

Also, this commandment is about the importance of accepting and fully loving both your father and your mother, which is psychologically important to your emotional well being. Any lack of love in the world-dream, causes distress, conflict and unhappiness to the one who is unloving. This is *especially* the case when you fall out of love with your parents. The basis for loving *all* people in your life begins and ends with your basic love for your parents. So, if you are out of love with either of them, you are out of love with all of life. (See page 185 for a process for forgiving your parents).

The SIXTH commandment (Exodus 20:13) is *"You shall not kill."* To kill is to take away the life, spirit, joy or creative expression of another being. It is not allowing or giving another being the space necessary for the free expression and creativity of life, which they naturally feel and want to express and experience. This is a direct violation of love. Love is true, unconditional acceptance of another, or of life itself, in the form or manner it is presently occurring or expressing. You are "killing" another being by not allowing him or her the free space to be him/herself in the world, that is, by not approving of "his or her right to be," or accepting him/her as he/she is. This *does not mean* that you have to tolerate or put up with "rip-offs" or allow someone to do harm or inflict injury to you or someone you love (which should be everyone). It does mean, however, that with love and compassion you should restrain other beings that would do harm to you or others, for they are ignorantly doing harm to themselves. So you, by restraining them, are aiding or helping *both them and society.*

As the commandment states, it is wrong to kill or to intentionally inflict injury or pain on another. We don't have the power to *give* life, so we should not *take* life. To kill or take anyone's life is to cut a part of *yourself* off from the Source.

The law of manifested life in the world is that "for every action there is an equal and opposite reaction." In the East, this is called *"karma."* The law of karma, with regard to killing, will eventually cause you to experience pain and even death in return, if not in this life then in the next (if there is one). Or, perhaps someone or something close to you, that you hold near and dear to you, will be killed or taken from you.

Karma pertains only to the body. It continues in life as the Law of Gain and Loss (Balance), also as accountability or retribution. It occurs for as long as you retain a sense of individual being, or as long as you think you are a separate-self, the "doer." However, when the sense of individuality – the sense of "I-me-my-mine" as the body, or "doer" – is finally dissolved, there is no longer anyone remaining to receive the results of these actions, since all karma is ended. However, this does not occur with your ordinary physical death. It occurs only with ego-death or by Awakening to the true Self *as* pure Awareness, or abiding in the Heart *as* the very Heart of being.

The SEVENTH commandment (Exodus 20:14) is *"You shall not commit adultery."* The word "adultery" in the original Hebrew is from the same root meaning as the word "idolatry." It means, "making an idol of." Its deepest meaning is that we are not to expect or seek happiness in the outer, physical world but rather understand that the Source, or God, is the only *real* bliss or happiness. When you attribute or give more importance to the world – i.e., its principle and seeming power, and its contents or objects – than to God, the Source of all, this is idolatry or adultery. Jesus meant that the man *"Who looked at a woman with lust in his heart,"* (Matthew 5:27-28) or desire for pleasure in the world, was already caught in the pull of the world and thus was cut off from *real* Happiness, which is only in the Source, or pure Awareness itself. This means that you believe and feel the physical expression of life, i.e., the world and all its glamour, vanity and ego attraction for persons, places and things is greater or more important than the Source, the very Essence of being, or the Truth itself.

Another meaning of this commandment is just the opposite of how it is usually believed and interpreted. It is telling us to keep and hold or see *everything* as a gift from God – including sexual pleasure – and know it to be always, already clean. To adulterate sex is to make it mentally and emotionally unclean or physically unsafe. It is to think or see sexual expression as immoral. Sexual expression is perfectly normal and natural to bodily life, and may be expressed in any way that one desires, heterosexual or homosexual, as long as each participant truly enjoys it and *willingly* consents to participate without coercion or manipulation. Simply stated, appropriate sex is whatever form of sexual expression one enjoys between mutually consenting or agreeing adults. The key words are "mutually consenting adults." This means not being coerced or forced *against one's will*; and, sexual partners *must* have reached full maturity, or be both legally and emotionally mature adults.

As far as marriage being a prerequisite for appropriate sexual expression, or that partners be already married to each other, it may be best but it is not necessary. This is only society's notion of morality or ethics, not God or nature's law. However, if you *are* married, then you *do* keep your marriage vows or agreements. Extramarital sex (or sex outside of marriage, or even outside of a *committed* relationship) requires the *prior* agreement or consent of the spouses or mates of *both* partners concerned, i.e., both your own *and* the other person's partner. What is commonly known as the "Golden Rule" also applies in this regard: *Whatever you wish that another person would do to you, do so to them; for this is the law...* (Matthew 7:12)

Also, if you are consciously engaged in living the life of *sadhana,* or spiritual practice, and you still have sexual urges or feelings, then it is *not* wise to engage in sexual play or expression with someone not also on a comparable level of spiritual commitment and dedication. This is because you actually "take on" the consciousness of those with whom you are intimate. So, if you want to maintain a high level or state of spiritual consciousness, you should not have sex with anyone living at a lower state of consciousness. This doesn't mean they are necessarily bad, though you should be alert to this possibility. What matters is that their level of consciousness, if lower than your own, *will* tend to "pull you down" when you want to *always* be working on *uplifting* or raising your level or quality of consciousness. Eventually, the desire for sex (for those intentionally involved in spiritual practice), will probably naturally drop away, like ripe fruit falling from the tree.

In Truth, no "thing" *in itself* is unclean. Some things are appropriate at one time and are inappropriate at another. Or they are healthy and OK for one but not for another. This law is telling us to *accept* life and everyone and everything in it as perfect *in its own way* or as being good, true and beautiful *in its proper time and place,* and to have compassion when something or someone is out of place, or out of time, or not in order.

This is clearly stated by St. Paul in the New Testament Bible. (Romans 14:14) *"I know and am persuaded in the Lord Jesus Christ that nothing in itself is unclean; but to anyone who sees it as unclean, to him it is unclean."* Most of mankind is caught up in various types or sorts of "right-wrong" beliefs, concepts and perceptions. Many are trying to enforce their "games" or "trips" or *will* on everyone else, such as, "I am right, and you are wrong." However "right and wrong" are merely points of view, which often change with the circumstances, or a new set of events or participants, and/or with the situation at hand.

You may allow one person a liberty with you or in some situation, which you would not allow someone else, or even allow yourself that latitude. So you see, points of view are like beauty or ugliness; they are "in the eyes of the beholder," and not in the person or thing itself, or even the objective world. And this commandment means we should see *everyone* and everything as being beautiful, for in truth *everything* is God.

The EIGHTH commandment (Exodus 20:15) is "*You shall not steal.*" This commandment pertains to integrity, and to prosperity and your physical and emotional well being. The psychological significance of this rule is that attempting to obtain a thing without honestly *earning* it – i.e., without first developing in consciousness the contextual right for owning it – cannot be done successfully, and it be *retained* once it *is* acquired.

For example, to hold negative ideas or feelings about money, that it is evil, or that you are not capable or worthy of having money, and then to try to acquire it, is in fact a form of stealing. You must earn, in consciousness, *everything* you have.

*   *   *   *   *

If I am holding conflicting or contrary thoughts and feelings about something, and yet trying to draw their opposite counterpart into expression in my life, this is in violation of the Law of Reversibility and will not work. It is trying to steal or acquire what I have not *earned* in consciousness.

What I steal is *not truly mine*, according to the attracting law of consciousness. Thus, I cannot happily keep it for long. It will either be stolen from me, lost, dissipated or produce discord and unhappiness in my life somewhere down the line.

*   *   *   *   *

So, another way of considering this commandment is, "You *cannot* steal," because you cannot retain, maintain or fully enjoy that which you have taken from someone else or another, by going against the infallible Law of Consciousness, or rightful ownership.

The NINTH commandment (Exodus 20:16) is *"You shall not bear false witness against your neighbor."* Very basic and obvious, this commandment means that we are not to lie about or misrepresent anyone to someone else, or even to our true Self.

This commandment also has other deeper and subtler meanings. Not understanding this fact, many well-intentioned people often ignorantly violate the subtle or little known aspects of this law. They are inadvertently violating it when they actually want to help their neighbor, believing that they are truly "caring" about their neighbor or friend. When we are holding deep and strong feelings of worry, concern, anxiety and distress for our neighbor's apparent need – i.e., their lack, limitation, trouble, ill health or sickness – and in this state of mind we anxiously fret about and see the circumstances as being "real" for them, we are in fact "bearing false witness against them."

We are in fact activating the Law of Reversibility to produce and project an atmosphere around our neighbor that adds to his problem. Since any polarized thoughts and feelings such as these will manifest themselves in the world, then it is our responsibility, out of love for our neighbor, to hold for him *only* thoughts and feelings that correspond to the happy or successful *end* of his problems.

*   *   *   *   *

I should see and feel the Truth *for* him, that he is a living expression of God and is *fully capable*, that he is *already* clear, whole, happy, healthy, free, peaceful and prosperous!

*   *   *   *   *

This is the highest, beneficial consideration we can have for "another." There is a big misunderstanding about this with most people in the world, who often see others as "victims." The world believes that love is "caring" about a person.

Look up the *primary* meaning of the word "care" or "caring" in your dictionary. Then ask yourself if a person "feeling that way about you" is really doing you any favors or expressing what you truly *want* to feel from him or her. The dictionary's primary definition of "care" is *"concern or anxiety; an object of anxiety; caution; charge or oversight; trouble; grief; to be anxious, concerned; to be affected with solicitude."*

Holding these thoughts and feelings, and arousing them in another in need is more like you're their tormentor than their friend. To be *carefree* (free of care) with regard to another is to *love* them and give them the space to express themselves and live out their troubles without hindrance, thus ending their troubles. This does not mean that we become indifferent or without compassion for someone's current dilemma or pain, but rather we don't lend our energy *to it*. Instead, we lend our energy to the Truth: that in the very Self or spiritual Heart of our neighbor, there is *already* freedom, fulfillment or whole-ness that *will eventually* manifest in his or her life and affairs.

Since in truth there is no "other," our neighbor is *really* an aspect or expression of the One Self, "our" Self. This means that if we want to assist him (while he or she is currently expe-riencing some dilemma or pain), then we deal with and clear that corresponding quality, tendency, or condition *in ourselves* – which our neighbor is presently experiencing and activating or stimulating within us by our association with him.

Thus by either completing or clearing that quality or condi-tion out of our consciousness, we are simultaneously helping our neighbor, the entire world, and ourselves. Jesus knew and used this principle and process when he "healed the sick" and "cast out demons." He was in fact "casting out" of his own consciousness any thoughts or feelings of disease, obsession, lack, limitation or incapability in regard to the "other person."

Jesus, being consciously one-with everyone and *all* creation, did not see people in his space or world as "separate," "other" or "different" from himself. Therefore, when someone pre-sented to him a painful or troubling experience or problem, it compassionately "awakened" in him (his Consciousness) the denial of the presence of that problem *for the person*. Since his consciousness was not different from pure Being, he was able to "remove" this apparent problem from the mind by with-drawing the mind into the Heart, the Source of being, where the problem did not exist, and thus was able to "disappear" it.

Since in truth all are one, as Jesus "healed this quality in himself," it also healed in the moment in the other person. He was able to "do" this by "lifting" the other person – who was a reflected counterpart of himself – into his own level or state of consciousness, or at least temporarily. He often said on those occasions, "Go and sin no more." This meant, do not return to the former lower level or state of consciousness. If they were able to obey, the healing lasted, the condition did not return.

When we are steadily conscious *as* the very Self, the Heart, we too are an instrument for healing all conflict, suffering, disease, lack, limitation and unhappiness in the world.

The TENTH commandment (Exodus 20:17) "*You shall not covet your neighbor's house; you shall not covet your neighbor's wife, or his manservant, or his maidservant, or his ox, or his ass, or anything that is your neighbor's,*" much like number Eight, is about greed and the process of prosperity. It is important for succeeding or acquiring what is beneficial, with integrity. Coveting is the negative quality of consciousness that generates greed, envy, jealousy and resentment toward those who "have," and feeds or contributes to the feeling or sense of lack or limitation with the accompanying thought-feeling "I don't have."

*   *   *   *   *

When I observe someone affluent, successful, and demonstrating good fortune, what is the usual, immediate response it awakens in me, *truthfully?* If it brings up thoughts of lack in that area of my life, or the feeling that "I am less fortunate," then this qualitative thought, feeling or mood reinforces the sense of lack and limitation in me. If it produces thoughts of envy of their good fortune, then it even separates and possibly unconsciously alienates me from similar good fortune, and from many of those people who are happy and prosperous.

Conversely, when I understand the Truth, knowing that "all is one, and one is all," then when I see another person's manifestation of affluence or demonstration of good fortune, it is also potentially coming closer to me. If I maintain the feeling of joy and real happiness *for the good that is happening to someone else,* I am then maintaining that mood in myself, and that mood will eventually contribute to producing for me a similar quality of good fortune, or a state of natural well-being.

An even deeper more significant meaning of this commandment is the fact that desire is *itself* the cause of suffering. Therefore, we should not desire what we see others having, doing, being or expressing in their life, but willingly accept whatever is currently so and true with us, or is now present.

* * * * *

IN SUMMARY, Moses' insight and understanding, revealed and recorded in these Ten Commandments, discloses that these are *first* the product of spiritual Enlightenment. That is, they are a direct result of Moses' conscious realization of the Truth, *which is what's so for everyone.* Jesus' realization of this very Truth came a few centuries later. And, that being: "I AM *is* the Lord." Pure Awareness – "I AM" – is the Lord, GOD, the Source of all that we are consciousness *of.* And Consciousness is the Law of Creative Expression, or creator of all that we are conscious *of* being or experiencing in this world.

* * * * *

Whatever I am now conscious as being, identified with, and hold to as a steady, consistent psychological mood or feeling, will in time become a physical fact or expression in "my" life.

* * * * *

It is best to *not* identify with this "I." But if you do, the rest of the commandments (after the first two) are guidelines for a freer, happier, healthy, prosperous and peaceful life. They are principles of conduct for living in this world, rules for guiding your life for making living easier, simpler, more efficient and without upset, or free from opposition from those around you.

They are practical processes of living, but only when seen and understood in the Light of Consciousness or Enlightenment. Otherwise, some tend to limit and restrict your natural expression of true freedom, peace and joy.

Study them well, as explained here, and *living* will be easy and enjoyable, allowing greater freedom of expression in this world-dream. I AM is *really* the One and only Reality, there is no "other."

THE TRUTH IS ALWAYS THE TRUTH

IF THE ULTIMATE TRUTH was not the *present* Truth it would not be the Ultimate Truth. For the Ultimate Truth to be such, it must be *presently* so, NOW – i.e., in *all* time, in *all* places, in *all* things, in *all* situations and with *all* people simultaneously. There is no "future" Truth to be attained ultimately or some day. There is only the *present* Truth, the One Reality or Truth, and that is *what's so in this instant!* Just *get it,* Truth is not a concept or belief; it is what is real. And, paradoxically, only this instant is real.

All events occurring in so-called "time," while they are in fact *actually occurring,* are only occurring or happening NOW, or *in this instant!* We are only conscious of them now; anything else is our memory or thought about them, and even thought or memory can only occur *now.* You can't think "then" – in the past or the future – you can only think now!

* * * * *

If the Truth is not being presently realized or seen, it is not because the Truth is absent or not present, but because of identification with ignorance. It is due to the commonly held misconception and felt sense of "me," or being a separate, individual entity identified with the body-mind in time and space, and feeling oneself as being apart from the one Pure Awareness or Universal Self. It is taking as real this "dream-world of appearances" – i.e., time and space that are *only* concepts – to be the Truth, the basis of Reality. Therefore, it is due to this inadvertent, unconscious ignoring of the Truth. This ignorance gives rise to myriad false concepts, thoughts, and other mental impressions appearing as the seemingly solid, objective world of persons, places and things in time and space. Rather than abiding in the One Reality, the pure Awareness and substratum underlying all that is appearing, it is living as a seeming entity objectively identified with and at the effect of the world. This is suffering; it is being stuck or caught in the perpetual quest for freedom, peace and joy *believed to be* in the world, which in truth does not actually exist independent of one's consciousness *of* it.

If I look only at the "form" of things (oblivious to their true essence), I am failing to recognize *That* which is essential or real – which is Consciousness itself, *prior* to all these manifested "things" that "I" am consciousness *of*.

A pot's essential or very nature (the truth about it) is the clay of which it is fashioned. To see only its form, or its function, and not its essence, is identifying with its appearance, which is *relatively* true but not *absolutely* true. The pot may break and no longer be useful or considered a pot, but it is *still* the clay out of which even the *broken* pot is formed. Facts – the forms of Truth – change, but the essence of Truth does not change. Ultimate Truth never changes.

*   *   *   *   *

Happiness, freedom, or liberation, peace, understanding, wisdom, prosperity, real love, joy, etc. are all present when we realize *here and now* the ultimate Truth of the Self, of who and what we *really* are, and live *from* and *as* that Realization.

Yes, there *is* a difference between facts and Truth. Facts change; a fact may be "true" today but *not so* tomorrow. Truth is *always* the Truth; or it is not the Truth. For example, it was a *fact*, prior to 1919, that you could not cross the Atlantic Ocean in a single day. Then in June, 1919, two British military aviators, Capt. John Williams Alcock, pilot, and Lt. Arthur Whitton Brown, navigator, together successfully flew the Atlantic in just over 16 hours, proving that you *could* cross the Atlantic Ocean in a day. Charles Lindburg accomplished this *alone* in 1927, receiving the "lions share" of worldwide acclaim for his "solo feat." So, the previous fact (the inability to cross the Atlantic Ocean in a day) was not the Truth. If it *had been* the Truth, then neither of these pioneer aviators then, nor you and I today, could cross the Atlantic Ocean in a single day.

Realizing, understanding and *living* the ultimate Truth of being – as this present-moment *experience* – is the only true freedom from suffering, fear, limitation and death. This is Jesus' meaning as recorded in John 8:32: "*You will know the truth, and the truth will make you free.*" Events may change, but when we live continuously in the Awakened Heart (the very Self), then Truth *is our refuge*. When we abide undisturbed in the bliss of the Self, we witness changing events occurring in the world with humor and compassion, knowing full well that they can never alter our present and eternal state of true Happiness.

Jesus fully understood the Essence and radical Truth disclosed by Moses in the Ten Commandments and correctly reduced all Ten Commandments to only *two;* but even further, he reduced those two to only *one.* Jesus knew that the *one law,* or rule of good conduct and happy life, was Unconditional Love. He said that the First Law (meaning primary or first in importance) is to love the Source, the I AM, the Self; to accept and live *as* the Self *unconditionally, presently;* i.e,. to awaken to the Truth that you *already are* a son or daughter of God – even as you *now* are, or appear not to be. You are an expression (a wave) rising out of the Source (the ocean) that is God, and that is *really you!* Jesus said to be totally and steadily *dedicated* to this understanding and realization, *"With all your heart* (being), *with all your soul* (feeling), *and with all your mind* (thought). (Matthew 22:37)

Jesus also said to *"love your neighbor as yourself."* Since in pure Consciousness there is no "other," then to "love another" indicates the mark of *real* love to oneself. To truly love the Self – pure Being or Consciousness – is to "radiate" the Heart-energy, or "light of perfect unconditional Love," which accepts and uplifts *in the moment* the world and everyone in it. It "awakens" others to the same quality of Self-love now sleeping in the Heart of one and all. This quality of love "heals" the world, and so it truly *is* the Great Law. Since the Self *is* God, to love your neighbor *as yourself* is to love your neighbor *as being an expression of God in your life.* When we abide in and live *from* the Heart, we see God or Self manifesting or making Itself known in everyone and everything; for everyone and everything we see *is* God or Self. The very Self of all selves is the one Supreme Self, or real God. And that Self is not different from "my" self or "your" self, for in Truth there is neither "my" Self nor "your" Self; there is *only* Self.

When we recognize that we always abide in and consciously function *from* this natural state of true Being, life more often presents us with loving, peaceful, happy experiences, and everyone and everything in the world is blessed *by our very presence.* Of course, there may still arise in the mind or come into our experience what normally would be negative or upsetting or undesirable thoughts and events. The difference is that there is not identification with them, and they do not affect us in the former negative or limiting way they once did. Rather, they merely come and go, appearing either humorous or un-important, or we quickly and easily see them as such. Or, we remain undisturbed and accept them in the moment and are capable of effectively and appropriately dealing with them. This is living in present-moment-now-happiness, eternally abiding in the Heart, radiating the Heart, and never needing "anything" or "anyone" outside the Self for our happiness, as joyous, lovely and delightful experiences continue to naturally happen in our world.

Sin, then, is the division of the one unconditional Reality into the seeming world of duality, the appearance of "I" and "other-than-I." Salvation or liberation from sin, by contrast, is awakening to the Heart, and *living* the awakened Heart. It is abiding in the Absolute Supreme Reality, *prior* to or beyond the apparent dichotomy. It is realization that there is no sepa-rate, individual "self," only abidance in the one Universal Awareness, which is always, already our true being.

SECTION TWO

REVELATIONS
IN
SAT SANGA
(CONSCIOUS COMPANY)

Sat Sanga: A Sanskrit phrase meaning "Conscious Company," or "Association with pure Being, the Self, the Wise, or with an Enlightened Being."

PART IV
THE TRUTH OF BEING

A REMINDER: All references made to the first person singular are meant to be an affirmation of Truth applicable to yourself. Remember, this is "Your Book" written *by* you, *to* you, *about* you – i.e., your *true Being*. So, read it fully recognizing it to be the Higher Self writing or speaking to Itself, or the *apparent* "you."

SAT SANGA

THIS COMMUNICATION is a Conscious Process occurring in *Sat Sanga* (Association with true Being or real Truth).

* * * * *

Pure Being is always occurring *as* ME (the Self) and *from* ME (the Self), but is not "me" as a separate, individual "self" – it is always shining as I AM THAT I AM. There is no "entity" that is separate and apart from this I AM, or as an "I" that "knows" this. There is only this Consciousness, and I AM *is* This Consciousness shining in the Heart-cave (with some, perhaps felt in the right center of the chest in the body) as the *eternally present* now-feeling of Pure Being, or simple I AMness.

Sat Sanga is abiding *as* the conscious Heart of God. It is *Conscious Company* with That which *is*, not different from That Which Is. It is abiding with Truth, with what is Real. It is the Supreme Absolute Self of all selves, awake and being the very Self of "myself." It is God living and expressing as Self, or I AM – NOT a separate one believing "he" or "she" is living apart from God and the rest of the world.

Abiding in *Sat Sanga* is abiding in the Presence of Self. Real Presence or Pure Awareness is not a state that a "someone" abides in; it is That which *always, already is*. It is the clear space or environment where pure Consciousness, Understanding, or Awakened Realization of the living Heart (I AM THAT I AM) is occurring in the present moment, *as the eternal now*.

Since IT is *all there is*, it cannot be "reached." It is like space, and the one that wants to "reach" it is like an object trying to "reach space." Only the direct realization that it is impossible to *NOT* be in space will put the objective seeker or seeming self at ease. The realization that there is *nothing but Presence* or *Awareness* will dissolve the confusion of "trying" to *be present* or "trying" *to abide as* pure Awareness.

The ego (the concept "I" or "I-am-this-body") is seen as it

really is – only a concept and not at all real. The separate-self-sense, the very sensation of energy going on in an apparent "me," (or body, emotions and mind), and to which the name "I," "me," or "myself" has been given (and which is tacitly inferred and thus taken for granted), is not real; it's not the real Self. It's merely a conceptual mind pattern that's called "ego."

This energy pattern: i.e., the sensation, knot, contraction, tightness and/or discomfort, or seeming sense of pleasure associated with the body and calling itself "I" and "I-am-this-body," is not the real Self. All this is *only* an appearance, a point of reference in consciousness, and is really the mind.

This "I" that says that thoughts, feelings, actions and things are "mine" and thus are the very sense of "mine" (the very feeling that goes with feeling "this or that is mine," and the very sense of "possession" or "possessiveness itself") is not the real Self; it is all occurring in the mind. Even perception – i.e., "doing" and "experiencing" that depend on "I" (the first person) that sees all actions as "my actions" and all experiences as "my experiences," and which sees all that it perceives as second or third persons – is not the real Self; it is all occurring in the mind.

*   *   *   *   *

This division of conscious awareness into "I" and "other-than-I" ("not-I") is dissolved as consciousness lives the Truth in the present moment in the Awakened Heart, or *Sat Sanga*. Drawing attention consciously into the Awakened Heart, one experiences the ongoing strategy of this mechanism dividing Self into the sense of "self" (small "s") and "other," or separating this "self" from the Source. When the Truth of this process is penetrated by directly observing and seeing it, it allows the machinery of thought to slow down and eventually stop.

Separation is an apparent activity occurring in the unconditioned awareness I AM, apparently conditioning the unconditioned consciousness or Self into its many perceived manifestations, but which do not in fact affect the true Condition of the Self. It is ever one, never changed, or changing).

The ego-self (the "I," "me," "mine" feeling) is an alleged activity occurring in the Self or *appearing* in the Self, the One Reality. However, the ego is not really an entity, or an "I," "me" or "self" apart from the Source or the world of "others." That is only a concept, an appearance that is actually the activity of meditating a separate-self identity. It is a present-moment-activity (if or when it is going on) of identifying with the activity of perception itself, as a reference point in time and space. Prior to this re-cognition, "I" is the believed "me," separate and apart from "others." In this unenlightened state, "I" is only a concept, just as "others" is only a concept.

As we Awaken from this dream to the Conscious Presence of the Living Heart, the Source, the very Self of Real God – the one Self alive in all selves – we re-cognize (or know again) that "I am not this body" with its five senses that perceive a separate world.

Nor am I the mind that perceives and records experiences of the body's senses. Nor am I the functions of action, mobility, digestion, assimilation, circulation, respiration, or the respective organs of each of these functions. Nor am I the memory-record of all past experiences with its residual tendencies and phantom objects. Nor am I the subjective perceiver-of-all-things past, present and future, abiding apart from all things as a subjective-self different from all objective mind-forms or physical forms. But, rather, I am the Supreme Context, the ultimate, transcendent Condition, in which all seeming separate conditions or content abide and are apparently occurring. I AM the Heart. I am the ever-present eternal-now-awareness, this one simple, basic being, itself.....I AM THAT I AM.

As I rest in the prior and eternal radiance of the Heart (the purity of no-seeking, no-dilemma, no-conflict), separateness and "separative-ness" ceases and becomes dismantled. I ever abide in peace, love and eternal-now-happiness – the non-dual, no-dilemma, no-desire, absolute Oneness. This is the eternal and real nature of the very Self – I AM. I am the Heart, the infinite space in which all experience – compatible and even incompatible – is always, already now occurring. All positions and oppositions are within the space of this consciousness I AM. I am the context that allows creative life and its apparent conflicts, confusions, contradictions, differences and sameness to occur.

When "I" is identified with the body-mind and polarized with some specific point of view or position (which I label "right" as compared to "wrong"), "I" experience separation, division and opposition. But this seemingly dualistic process is merely changing conditions in the one unchanging and unchangeable Condition I AM. The trinity of perception – meaning the "seeing I," the object seen (or "other") and the process of seeing (the activity of perceiving) – is only a process of apparent conditioning occurring in the unconditioned Condition I AM, the Heart. This apparent trinity cannot exist apart from the ego, which itself rises out of the pure Awareness, the one Self I AM, and very Self of all. All of this is not occurring *to* the Self however, but *as* the Self, for the Self shines infinitely and eternally prior to and beyond all of this, being untouched or anyway modified by any of these apparent modifications or occurrences, just as the cinema screen is never affected by any of the apparently compatible or conflicting pictures appearing on it.

INDIVIDUAL BEING IS A CONCEPT
CONDITIONED BY THE PAST

EVERYTHING I say "I" know, and believe to be true, is all reducible to "my" point of view. I may have thousands of points of view (even millions) about thousands of different ideas, things, and situations. But all of this is still reducible to one primary reference point or point of view – that there is an "I" or a "seer" who is "me" *having* these many apparent points of view. The very sense of "I" as a separate perceiver is the primary or fundamental "point of view" that alone separates, divides, generates, supports, and contains the content of all these other points of view. It is also the basis and cause of all suffering.

When clearly looking, it is seen and realized that all points of view held and defended as "being right" are grounded in the past. These have their roots in the apparent past and rise here and now as memories brought up in this one ever-present moment being seen as a current expression of the one pure Awareness. Life is *always* new, only occurring *here* and *now*. It is ever fresh. It is *always now!* It is not, in itself, dependent on or subject to the past for its existence. Life – the "ever-new" – always rises and shines or presents itself by its own power in the eternal ever-present-moment of NOW. In any moment of experience, I can never know what a thing, in itself, *is*. It is *always* new, or *as it is*. The mind is what turns the new into the apparently old, comparing the *now* event with the past and wanting to repeat or reject it.

When very alert and observing with steady, unswerving diligence any current event or situation *as it occurs*, the very *first* reaction of the mind or consciousness to that event is *ignorance*, or "I don't know." This is so very quick it requires a very still, thoughtless mind and steady, alert attention to see. No matter what arises or approaches, the mind *at first* does not know; it always goes through this very rapid process of classifying and identifying what is presently occurring with the past. This is to fulfill its primary function and purpose – insuring the survival of the being "we" think we are.

The mind *must* "know" in order to survive. Its survival depends on it *always* knowing; and, its knowing must *always* be "right." Its very existence depends on it *being right!* This compulsive need has much to do with "saving face," which to the mind is tantamount to it and the ego-self's very survival.

This means the mind *instantly* scans the entire record of the past drawing up a relationship from the past with which to identify, classify, and associate the new event. It classifies, then qualifies and reconditions itself by recording the new situation (and/or any modifications) as more new data to be used in its function of "future knowing." It is like a sentry guarding the entrance to a building or "secure" area, always challenging everyone entering, checking credentials and assuring that it knows *everything* and *everyone* before allowing them entry. It checks the impressions of each current event or situation against the *total record of the past* to determine its relationship with the past (its previously programmed data), thus verifying and establishing the identity and/or nature of all that is occuring in the moment.

This entire process is actually the activity of avoiding relationship with what is now arising, or *what is so*. However, what is current or now arising needs no classification, qualification or conditioning. It is whole and complete in itself. It has something "new" to offer *in the present*. But the mind, by always mechanically performing this very efficient "reasoning process" or activity, makes each new experience into the old or familiar, thereby rationally defending its positions and/or points of view each grounded entirely in the past.

The mind's one function and purpose, in this constant process, is *its own* survival and that of the apparent psychophysical entity with which it is identified – that is, the body and the ego-self. Its very being, existence, structure and form are nothing more than the total record of all its past successes, its "hits and misses" in surviving. It is only *apparently* real, much like the "personality" computer programmers or operators "relate or communicate with" in their computers. It is as if the computer itself takes on a state of consciousness and feels that "it" knows what a thing is. But a computer, which only records data and "plays or gives back" its recorded data, does not know what the thing *is* that it records, stores and "delivers" back as data to the operator. A computer's mechanism is much the same as the working of the human mind.

The mind, shining only by means of the reflected light that it borrows or draws from pure Consciousness or Awareness, superimposes this "phantom consciousness" on the brain and central nervous system as a pseudo-self, or sense-of-"I," giving rise to the false notion "I-am-this-body."

This concept of "I," as a separate-self, an individual entity apart from the whole, having different points of view and enforcing and defending these points of view, is what the Bible calls the primal Fall of Man. Communicating the Truth, so as to overcome this false illusion, has been the work of all Enlightened Beings since this "fall" first *appeared* to occur. This was the work and mission of Jesus and is the primary message of all the Holy Scriptures, both in the East and the West.

The New Testament Bible states, *"Awake O Sleeper, and arise from the dead, and Christ will give you light!"* That is, see with the Light of the true Self, *not* the ego. Also it says, *"He who has eyes let him see, and he who has ears let him hear"*; that is, see and hear with the "eyes" and "ears" of Spirit, not with the mind. Jesus and his disciples were not going about preaching to people napping, or in bed asleep. They were as wide-awake as anyone reading this now. Nor were their listeners very likely deaf and dumb, but had ears and eyes capable of hearing and seeing with, just as you the reader.

* * * * *

Jesus was like the man with color-vision (mentioned earlier) taking people who are color-blind on a walk through the multicolored flower garden of life. Some see, as if watching "black and white" TV, what Jesus sees in full color. This is the way it is until one awakens his or her "color vision" and *really* sees what's present, and *always* present. Seeing life through the mind's conditioned content of the past, as being "my" present point of view with what arises, is like seeing in black and white. Seeing in this manner, "I" may believe I am seeing all there is to be seen, or from the one Presence. But little do I know, until Awakening or seeing with "color vision," and see the new, the fresh – free of all contamination from the past, which is now obstructing this present clear vision.

"Color vision" is lost when identified with the false concept of "I" as being a separate entity, different from the Source, which is the *ever new*. "*I see through a glass darkly.*" (I Corinthians 13:12) The ego is a phantom consciousness attached to the body-mind and sustained by its identification with the mind's contents from the past. This false "self" is the Fall of Man or is one's falling out of the grace of the true Self.

Falling out of grace is identification with the seeming individual, the separate-self sense, or personal "I." It results in the apparent division of consciousness into this seemingly objective reality – that is, a world composed of people, places and things apart from and separate from "me," the believed perceiver, and the simultaneous, compulsive craving for more, better and different experiences in the world.

It is also re-enforcing, defending and prolonging tenancy or residency in the world and in the body as a believed separate entity. This entire process is symbolized in the Bible as the Fall of Man, and represented by Lucifer, the *"son of the Dawn"* (Isaiah 14:12), who chose to separate from God (Source) and emulate or compete with God, and is now apparently doing so as the Ego in manifestation, or as one's own sense of separation from God, Truth, Reality, the ever new, the eternal Now.

"How you are fallen from heaven, O Day Star, son of Dawn! How you are cut down to the ground, you who laid the nations low! You said in your heart, 'I will ascend to heaven; above the stars of God I will set my throne on high; I will sit on the mount of assembly in the far north; I will ascend above the heights of the clouds, I will make myself like the Most High'." (Isaiah 14:12-14)

This is the ego-mind, identified with the body as "self," with all its content of experience from the past, living as though it is a separate entity. It is the mind making everything new into the old. The Self is not new, *it just is*. That which is new always becomes old; but the Self (God) *is eternal.*

The mind only *appears* to create; it forms consciousness into apparent objects, giving rise to the apparent world. It forms spiritual substance only conceptually. The power of all apparent creation is from the Self, God, the Source. It is the very Self or pure Being in which there is no actual creation.

We can intentionally use the mind to fashion consciousness into the apparently "living" or "manifesting forms" of our desires; but to do this *efficiently* and *effectively* requires discipline and clarity of mind. It requires definiteness of purpose, and clear understanding of the mind's formative process.

To turn this creative work over to the mind, allowing it to determine or dictate what *it* perceives about life to be the truth, is to live in bondage to the mind. This is suffering and is what most people ordinarily do. To live in separation, cut off from real oneness, happiness and love, as though God's presence is not now present, is living in ignorance and is itself what is "causing" all the evil there is in the world.

Fear (felt from the sense of duality, or separateness from God) with its resulting pain is ignorance, and often results in evil actions in an attempt to get free of this pain and suffering.

*   *   *   *   *

To perpetuate "my own" or "another's" sense of separateness, and use fear as the weapon to manipulate or keep this sense of separateness, division and partition alive, is the *unpardonable* or *unforgivable* sin. However, it is only unpardonable *while it is occurring, or being sustained.* Grace or pardon comes directly and immediately on ceasing this limiting activity, thus ending fear and suffering.

It is a direct and immediate release from sin and suffering, because in Truth there is no separation from the Source, the One Reality, and never has been. This is only an illusion, a false notion.

OUR TRUE BEING OR EXISTENCE
IS DEATHLESS

REALIZATION DISCLOSES – as Bhagavan Sri Ramana Maharshi often stated – our *true* being or *actual* existence is *itself* pure Consciousness. Again, Consciousness *is* our being, our *actual* existence. Apart from the pure Intelligence of Consciousness *itself*, there is nothing – no *thing*. That is, there is no psycho-physical entity or individual person that is in fact "us." Our mind, body, and sensory processes appear or occur *in* consciousness, no different than our appearance in the ordinary dream state. That is, these apparent objects, forms and functions are merely appearances in the One Reality, the pure Awareness or true Self ever shining-abiding prior to and beyond time and space. We routinely, though inadvertently, refer to our body and our mind as "my" body and "my" mind, overlooking or unconsciously ignoring what our verbal communication indicates – the fact that we are *neither* of them but rather are the *possessor* or "owner" of both. They are our "possessions," both being "objects" to all of us, or in the One Self. The possessor is *never* his/her "items or objects of possession," such a notion would be absurd.

We as pure Being always exist infinitely and eternally as pure Awareness *before* the birth of the body and even *prior to* the mind, the latter being only the apparent "seeing subject," a seeming "self-image" or point of reference in consciousness called "I" or "me." The mind can imagine almost anything, but it cannot imagine our death. All it can imagine is the body being apart from us, perhaps "lying in a coffin," or perhaps "lifeless following some accident," but we as Awareness, the Self, are still here existing; we are still presently abiding *as* conscious-existence itself, the One Reality *prior to* the mind and its "imaginings." Even to imagine unconsciousness, such as coma, sleep, fainting, etc., *we still must be present* as the witness awareness of these so-called unconscious states or conditions.

There is *no* death, meaning no death for the Self. That which dies or dissolves *is not us*, not the Self. It is a concept, an apparent *possession* with which we are temporarily identified, which wears out, becomes damaged beyond repair, or eventually runs down and becomes so ineffective it is discarded.

This is much like American society's fad for throw-away items, such as cigarette lighters that run out of fuel, or plastic razors that lose their cutting edge after using only a couple of times, or cameras you use and discard when out of film. Years ago when I smoked cigarettes, I usually owned a personal cigarette lighter that I refilled with lighter fuel when it ran out. I no longer smoke, but I do use lighters for lighting incense sticks. The kind I have now I throw away when it runs out of fuel, and I buy another one even though the working mechanism of the one empty of fuel still works perfectly well. The point is, the apparent reality of this world is constantly changing whenever we agree for it to change, or *"the time has come."*

The same is believed to be so in some religious traditions with regard to re-embodiment, or reincarnation. For them, the body is believed to be much like these various "dispensable items." When it is no longer healthy, capable, or functioning satisfactorily it is like "tossed aside." Some believe the Self "picks up" a new one – perhaps a better or different "model"; after having a "male" model, it is believed the Self may try a "female" one, or vice versa. If the last one was white, it may take one that is black or of another race and color. It is according to the trends, or the apparent (if real) time-period in which the Self apparently "re-embodies." Or, it's believed to be based on the conditioned patterns in consciousness, i.e., particularly strong desires, needs, unfinished projects, karma, or incompletions that may still be active or unfulfilled.

Radical realization of the true Self, the real and true nature of being, is Liberation from this compulsive process or cycle of births and deaths, which includes freedom from the fear of death and dying and the end of all conflict with regard to ordinary life. True Happiness, which is infinite and eternal, abides *within us,* in the Self, *as our actual nature,* and is with us at all times. Unfortunately, most of us have *entirely forgotten this* and are looking *for* happiness from the experiences of life in the world by way of bodily pleasures and comforts.

Existence *as Consciousness* is our real nature. And the duration of Consciousness (*our* "duration" or existence *beyond* the body-mind) is eternal or everlasting. This is the Truth – consciousness is what we *are*.

With regard to the question of re-embodiment or reincarnation, many people are very interested in the subject. Others (i.e., Christians and Muslims) are concerned about "going to Heaven" when they die. Sri Bhagavan Ramana Maharshi often had spiritual seekers asking him about re-embodiment. His usual response was, "See if you are now embodied, or *are the body now*, before being concerned if you will be reincarnated." Heaven as a realm, like this world, is only a concept.

It could be said that reincarnation is an apparent fact, the Self has always been (or lived) and has *apparently* expressed itself occasionally in or through other bodies, but reincarnation *as such* is not the truth, it is a misconception. The Self, which is pure Consciousness, or infinite and eternal Awareness, has not actually "incarnated" as a separate "entity." The fact is, there is no actual "entity" or separate "self" existing in the first place – now, or in the past, nor will there ever be in a so-called "future." This is all an illusion occurring *entirely* in the Self. The truth is, there is no past or future, there is only the One Presence, this infinite and eternal present moment.

That which is born dies, but that which is not born – the Self, pure Awareness – can never be touched by death. It can never be added to or subtracted from.

* * * * *

Prior to all concepts, I AM. When all concepts are not – I AM. I am That *which is*. I am (Self is) Consciousness itself, prior to all that I am conscious *of*, including all that I have done or not done, have been or haven't been. I (Self) don't have to *do* (or *not* do) anything in order to *be* the Self I AM.

The Self (the Absolute Supreme Being, the very Self I AM) has no *individual* sense of "I." It has no "self" concept. It has no concepts at all. It *just is, prior* to all concepts. It simply is I AM – not an "entity," or the "I"-thought that is "am-ing." Neither does the body have a sense of "I." The "I"-sense appears *between* these two (between the all-encompassing Being, or pure Consciousness, and the body) as a mysterious *apparent* "phantom entity" or ego. It attaches itself to the form: the size,

shape, figure, features, and duration of the body, and identifying with the body and its mental-record of experience and
calls all of these "me" and "mine" – i.e., "my" body and all
"my" experiences are "me." This "I-am-the-body" notion is
the ego. It rises *between* pure Consciousness and the body,
partaking of both, but different from either or both.

This sense of "I" seems to be "real," or existing *in our consciousness*, but is actually only an unreal shadow – or a mere
reflection of the true Self, of its Light reflecting off the reflecting media the instrument of the body. The ego has become so
entrenched *as* "our" conceived experience that it appears real,
while the Self appears unreal. As a result, we call the ego our
"self," or "I," or "me." This ego (or body-mind) draws its in-
telligence-light from the Self (just as the moon reflects the light
of the sun), attaches itself to the bodily senses and depends on
them and the Self for its life in order to function and survive.

This entire "identification process" is what is biblically
called or known as "original sin," or "the fall of man," and is
symbolized in religious mythology as Satan, or the devil, the
"fallen angel" that is imitating God by drawing power from
God and using it for selfish, evil, greedy or personal means
and purposes.

This is exactly the story of apparent humankind, of "each of
us" who has forgotten the true Self and instead identifies with
the limited body-mind as being the Self. We fearfully strive to
prolong life in the body, and compulsively effort to achieve
selfish, personal, separate goals in this world, instead of realizing our true Self or true Being, which is always, already contented – i.e., happy, whole, lovable, free and at peace.

This conceived "evil" alliance (the identification of pure
Consciousness with the body-mind as being the Self) is also
the deep dissatisfaction and discomfort in consciousness, the
limited self-image that constitutes all obsessive, compulsive
behavior, all fear and suffering. It is both suffering and the
cause of all suffering.

Without being identified with this "I-am-the-body" notion,
and caught in all this compulsive "thinking" and "doing,"
there is only happiness, peace, and deep satisfaction. All life
then happens simply, *as it is*, without any effort, without hav-

ing to strive and seek or compulsively "do" anything.

In fact, it's one's sense of "doing" – or *believing* one to be the "doer" – that is this "me" contraction felt in the body and/or on the field and ground of consciousness as one's sense of struggle and effort. It is the very sense of *"being an individual."* It is what causes us to seek pleasure in the world, to ease the body-mind; to be free from, or palliate this contraction, this perpetual sense of suffering and the chronic feeling of insecurity, loneliness, alienation, confinement, restriction, or bondage. It is the cause of our continued, compulsive quest for "more," "better," and "different" experiences in and from the world, wanting reprieve from one's chronic dissatisfaction.

It was epitomized in the 1960s and 70s by the Rolling Stones musical group and their hit song: "Satisfaction." The song's lyrics go like this: *"I can't get no satisfaction / I can't get no satisfaction / I can't get no satisfaction… though I try, and I try, and I try, and I try… I just can't get no satisfaction."* (The use of the double negative, or poor English, is in the lyrics). Interestingly enough, the "Stones" (as affectionately called by their fans) are still "going strong" in the year 2005, forty years after their hit song that is also still about as popular, even today!

Only in this chronic sense of innate *dissatisfaction* does one's pattern of compulsive seeking have a *positive* purpose and result since it motivates the *pursuit* of liberation, salvation, and freedom from this entire, habitual configuration of the mind's conditioning, this meditation of a separate-self identity.

But, the Truth is, we are not bound to begin with, *and have never been.* It is all an illusion! The ego is only *mis*identification with the body-mind as being the Self; and, as such, it is totally unnecessary. When we finally "hear" this message of Truth and respond accordingly by dropping body-mind identification and abiding in the Self (that is, remaining quiet and unmoving in the pure Heart of the Self) the entire configuration is dismantled; it is finally seen and dissolved.

This re-cognition (knowing again *what's so*) reveals no "self" or "individual" even existing or being subject to death. We realize and live *in and from* freedom, peace, and happiness, which is always, already our *true nature* – throughout *eternity*.

Like St. Paul, who said in the Bible (1 Cor. 15:55), *O death, where is thy sting? O grave, where is thy victory?*, realization discloses there is *no death* for the Self. Death is only with regard to the body-mind, or the "self-image," which is merely an illusion, a "character" or "role" being "acted out" or played by the Self in this "drama of life," this apparent waking-dream!

Therefore, death is not anything of real importance to be concerned about. It is happening only as an appearance *to all the "other characters"* still living in and identified with their continuing "roles" in this world- illusion, this waking-dream.

LIVING THE LIFE OF HAPPINESS

THE LIFE OF HAPPINESS is experienced when we live appropriately. Living appropriately means living *fully conscious*, in harmony with *what is*. It is being at peace with *what is*. It is being present with *what is*. To be present and at peace is to hold no position *for* or *against* what is, to be free from anxiety about it; to "not care" about what is. This is not the "not caring" of irresponsibility, but rather the absolute *acceptance* of what is, with full responsibility for being at Cause with it, at Source with it. It is absolute *approval*, total *acceptance*, and total *responsibility*. This is not "me right" and "they wrong." It is holding no position whatsoever. It is "being the clear space" for what is so *to be what's so*, without any mental, emotional, or physical interference from a "me." In this moment (any moment) of total acceptance of what's so, transformation can occur in the quality of events appearing or happening; and they will become absolutely humorous compared to their former distress, fear, pain, ugliness, or even panic.

Living *at Cause* is not being at the effect of what's occurring. Living "appropriately" is consciously *choosing* what is occurring in your life. Conscious choice, or "choosing," is creating or forming your life in the size and shape of happy, pleasant, loving experiences. This is "living consciously" in true happiness moment-to-moment, without a gap in its flow, with not even a "mille centimeter" of space for unhappiness to enter or appear. It is creating a "clear space" so that the true order and real happiness that is already innately present, as one's very nature, is allowed to shine and be expressed and reflected in the outer events manifesting in your life.

Appropriate living is now *acknowledging*, or *being fully responsible* for having yourself setup in the past, all that is now presently *arising in the mind* that is appearing to be upsetting in your life. It is not crying or complaining about life appearing as unpleasant. Then, having accepted the present experience and assuming responsibility for your present thoughts now arising out of memory about it, you are capable of being *at cause* in the matter, not at effect.   This makes you capable of seeing all the ongoing events of life consciously, free of upset. This means experiencing these ongoing, momentary experiences joyously, being lived out to completion.   This is thus winning all the "games of life" that you had previously set up.

When you have become proficient at effectively playing and winning your "games of life" by either withdrawing or completing everything without the need to further "play out" any previously anticipated games (i.e., all specific intentions or reasonable and just desires), you are then ready for the Larger *Adventure-less* Adventure, which is *living beyond time and space.*

This is the final, total sacrifice of the "doer" – the "chooser" or "player," the seeming separate "self" – into the Absolute, or eternal Self-Awareness.   This is no longer reacting, modifying, or altering what is appearing or occurring.   It is allowing life to fully present *itself, as it is,* while you steadily abide in Unqualified, Faceless, Formless, Choiceless, Timeless, Uncaused Awareness, the pure Heart of Being.   Regardless of what is happening or appearing in any given moment, just re-cognize (know afresh) that it is only an *apparent* modification in the unchanging, unmodified Condition or Context of Reality.   It neither adds to nor subtracts from the *true* Changeless Condition, which is always, already happy, whole, total and complete.

Order has its own Power, which maintains *itself* when you live appropriately.   You do what is appropriate, and what is appropriate is brought about or "done" as your experience. You arrive in this clear space and understanding by fully *accepting* what is occurring in life, which is Life itself naturally manifesting in alignment with appropriate and orderly living. You simply watch this happen without you "doing" any of it.

A simple, efficient, effective, and functional way of living every day *conscious* and *clear* is to *make a commitment* to acknowledge your *needed actions* for each day, the night before, and always *"plan your work and work your plan."* Predetermine tomorrow's schedule of events and activities tonight before retiring for the evening and then go to sleep resting in the feeling of completion – that tomorrow's activities are *already* occurring in a timely and efficient manner, as "planned."   On awakening, *work your plan* by *staying with your plan.* Observe life itself "working your plan as 'you' have laid it out."

This is *"letting go and letting God."* Life itself simply *lives* "your" commitments and keeps "your" agreements – which "you" have made – and is always responsible for *fully seeing to the completion of each task* before *commencing the next.* As each task is being performed, "live happily in the present-moment feeling" (the now-experience) *of each event,* as life – the totality of being – itself sees it through to completion. In this way or manner, "you" are not the "doer," but rather the One Reality, the Absolute, is now "doing" everything. "You" are merely present and seeing it being done, like an observing Witness.

NORMALLY OR SIMPLY STATED: observe all known or re-vealed purposes, "future" goals, and results; plan the day's ac-tivities the night before; go to sleep in the felt peace, content-ment and happiness of the completion of everything "you" have agreed to *today* as "being done" *tomorrow;* retire into sleep – *loving yourself* and *everyone you dealt with all day.* Then, wake up fresh; and "work" (or observe the working of) your day's plan. "Do" all this while Inquiring, Witnessing and/or Observing it as though watching someone else doing it, or un-til "you" become *the very action itself.*

Living and working in this conscious manner, is living in present non-seeking Being, as the non-doer. Then the very force of life *itself* becomes the Doer of what is being done.

A Vignette

Thinking is slow; Being is immediate, instant, pre-sent, already.

Thinking takes time; Being is timeless.

Thinking is becoming; Being *already* is.

Thinking is (of) the mind; Being is (of) the Self.

Thinking is movement toward or from; Being is always, already present in all times and places.

Being is the very Consciousness that is the Light and Substance of *what is.*

A WORD ON "BEING RIGHT"

IN THE SO-CALLED ORDINARY "THINKING PERSON," the impulse of conscious attention is usually objective. It is focused "outside," on objects in the world, on "others" – i.e., the apparent "persons," "places" and "things" having all these dualistic varieties and activities. Ordinarily, in the perceiving of all that presently occurs (during the very process of perceiving or observing itself), little if any attention is given to the seer or one seeing, or to the source or nature of pure Consciousness itself abiding *in* or *prior to* the "seer" and the "seeing." Instead, attention is given almost entirely to the "seen."

The source or cause of inanimate objects is outside of them, they are not their own cause, but rather are caused by or are the result of something or someone else. However, the source of consciousness, or Conscious Being *itself*, must be inside oneself. Why? Simply because self-consciousness radiates from within itself; it shines independently or entirely on its own. It is its own source and cause.

Inanimate objects are not conscious *of* themselves – i.e., they do not shine or feel "self-existent," or "self-evident," or radiate from within themselves with their own "point of view" – as do conscious beings. Overlooking this very simple fact throws man into the whirl, or maze, or error of attempting to know and understand himself *with the mind*, or from the outside, or objectively, as in the world of objects and events. The inner Source, or Consciousness itself, is "the place" in which to inquire or investigate and have *true* insight and understanding of Self, not by analyzing the "not-self" outside the Self.

Analyzing is thinking. Thinking is always of the past. Thus, ordinary analysis is always grounded in the past.

The mind analyzes, measures, or compares every experience in relation to every present and past experience. Then it determines the course of action in how to relate, respond, or react to the current event in order to remain safe, happy, secure, and in control. Being in control of the situation amounts to "being OK," or more correctly, to "being right."

Since to the mind survival amounts to *always* "being right," as well as *ever appearing* to be "right" – without any question or doubt about it if or when challenged, since that is threatening to being right – and since here, "right" is what has worked in the past to keep one secure, safe, surviving, logical, sane, reasonable, respectable, correct, or justified – all of which is "being right" – then acceptance of what is presently occurring it usually not a primary consideration. In fact, it might not even be of secondary importance or consideration. This means that "acceptance" most often takes a back seat to "being right." Acceptance therefore is first *dependent;* it appears to be dependent on "being" and remaining "right." This means, *any* situation, or idea, is itself unacceptable if it opposes, challenges or threatens one's sense of "being right."

Jesus said, *"If your right eye offends you pluck it out, and if your right hand offends you cut it off, for it is better to loose one of your members than your whole being be cast into oblivion."* (Matthew 5:29-30) This means that our demand to "be right" must be surrendered or sacrificed if we are to find peace. Our *demand* that people see our point of view ("right eye") or that they act in the manner we dictate ("right hand") is the cause of much of life's misery. Yet, to cut off our position of "rightness" is often like amputating our hand or plucking out an eye. We don't want to surrender or release our own precious points of view. And yet, they can and do "cast our whole being into oblivion" or turmoil. We think and act like "being right" is all that's important, even defending the point of view that this demand to "be right" is not the way "we" really are, that we are really open to receiving the ideas and opinions of others. All of this is the strategy of the mind to survive.

Can you release *all* the past, all points of view, all your relationships and experiences, beliefs, and opinions in order to be happy? Most would find this very difficult if not impossible. Why? Because they actually believe the past has real existence, and therefore they live almost entirely *"in* it," or so they believe. Or they "live in the future," again so they believe, and which they believe is affected by the past. They are not capable of living here and now in this present instant; which paradoxically, this presence, and present moment, is the only reality. The past is entirely conceptual, it does not even exist, it is only a memory, a non-existing concept!

Are you ready and willing to abide in the true state of freedom, which is freedom from the past, with a clear mind in the present moment where life is actually occurring, and which is always a present new adventure? Defending and enforcing a point of view is always dealing with the past, which is not real, it is a false concept. It is a major cause of personal conflict in which there is little or no peace or joy.

Prior to and *free from all thought,* in this infinite and eternal Presence, the Self (I AM, Pure Being, Pure Awareness) abides as non-positioning, non-seeking *being,* the One Reality, in the Heart. Since Reality is *prior to* thought, *beyond* thought, and therefore *free of thought,* it cannot be "known" by thought. So "being right," which is a product of thought, serves no beneficial purpose.

How then is one to contemplate or know and experience this Reality? Bhagavan Sri Ramana Maharshi says, "To simply abide *in It, as It is,* in the Heart (in thoughtless Awareness) *is* its contemplation and experience."

This is the direct insight and experience of this writer as well. The peace, freedom, and joy It reveals and directly releases *as* one's very being are not possible to be shared in words alone. This is possible only by *actually* Awakening *to* It, or *as* It, or by being with one who *has* fully awakened.

FEELING "NOT ENOUGH" AND SEEKING "ENOUGH"

IN THIS UNREAL, YET BELIEVED TO BE "ordinary consciousness" of daily life, where one is identified with the body-mind as being a separate individual "self," he or she must ever deal with *this* and *that* appearing as "other-than-self" or "not-self." There is, particularly in American society (and other similar western societies), this compulsive activity and ongoing pursuit of pleasure. It is misbelieved that pleasure provides happiness, freedom from lack, or contentment. There is an ever-escalating compulsion, even a social competition centered around "more, better, and different" ways for producing ego-gratification. Most people today are seeking and striving with intense effort in what is called "The American Dream," trying to attain the feeling of "enough" – i.e., *enough* security, *enough* sensation or pleasure, *enough* knowledge, *enough* money, and *enough* power, pride, prestige, possessions, fame or recognition, respect…and on and on… etc.

Almost everyone is steeped in the feeling of "not enough," with fear or the threat of loss or decline to what one *already* has. There is the constant need to "guard" or "protect" what is already "one's own" from future loss, breakdown or failure.

In this false, yet presently lived sense of separateness from the Source, and from the Allness of being, one must constantly strive to survive. Life is a quest to defend and to increase one's dominion and control over his "space" or "territory." This is felt as necessary in order to satisfy one's gnawing hunger, one's sense of lack and insecurity, one's feeling of "not enough."

Striving for "enough" means always looking for "more," "better" and "different" ways and means or better avenues of "self" expression; or it means increasing one's "net worth" or personal "possessions," or one's "sense of security" or personal power, and satisfying or gratifying   one's desire for sensation.

Ones' daily life usually involves this attempt to ever-increase one's own domain, or "living space," which is one's "personal" sense of well-being, or sense of importance, or one's home and sphere of influence, and the need to know and protect as "better ways and means of personal survival."

If we *really* observe or take note, this craving is what we ordinarily call "life," or it actually is the *very nature* of worldly life. Moreover, if we look at it *candidly*, this craving for "more," based on the feeling of "not enough," is *not* a pleasant feeling. We usually ignore this fact, that it is actually motivated by the underlying or perhaps even chronic sense of insecurity. We don't see that this striving and defending are really unpleasant, because the mind has converted this compulsive activity into the so-called *"adventure* of life." However, this activity is in fact unpleasant, which means that only during dreamless sleep, when there is no mind, no world of persons, places and things, do we experience *real* peace and *true* freedom from this constant, compulsive seeking, pursuing, striving, searching, and defending.

It is when the personal sense of "I," the ego-self that feels "not enough," begins a guileless inquiry into *itself,* in the search for true Awakening and Realization of "Who am I?" until the Source of being *is reached,* that the feeling of seeking, striving and suffering finally ceases. Peace and rest come about, and finally reprieve from this compulsive search for contentment occurs. Completion, satisfaction, and wholeness are realized; dissatisfaction, separateness, and suffering are ended.

To contemplate the Heart (the inner Source) *exclusively* is inclusive of everything else. For, everything *is always, already within the Heart of the Self,* which is pure Awareness. Its very nature is *completion* – i.e., oneness, love, peace, prosperity, wholeness, and real happiness. It is always, already free of *all* seeking, *all* dilemma, *all* conflict or suffering – free of *all* contraction, *all* struggle, and *all* fear.

THE "SEER" IS THE "SEEN" AND THE "SEEN" IS THE "SEER"

EVERY EXPERIENCE "I" HAVE WITH "another person," even if it brings peace, love and well-being, nonetheless potentially exposes or opens up an underlying, sense of insecurity. Although this conditioned state is perhaps presently dormant or not active, it is still nevertheless capable of being triggered off. If so, it reveals where in consciousness I may be attached, insecure, hung-up, or potentially at the effect of one or more psycho-physical centers – i.e., conditioned mental-emotional patterns in the body-mind – with its corresponding and perhaps addictive point of view.

Based on my particular level or degree of sensitivity, how I feel in the actual presence of another person registers a corresponding emotional pattern that the presence, energy or "vibrations" of that person emits. I may feel attracted or repelled, threatened or secure, inferior or superior. However, when abiding in the Heart, in the pure Awareness of being while in the presence of "others," which is being entirely free and clear of the mind and ego, and any previous self-image with its conditioned memories, patterns or preferences of the past, there is no longer any fear or threat. I am then able to rest fully in the peace, love, freedom, and simple, easy acceptance of all "others," ever accepting what is, *as it is.*

So-called "other persons" are really appearing in the One Self. They are each a facet of "my" mind or self-image, appearing on the surface of Self. When I am at the effect of the mind and not abiding in the true Self, one or more vibrational patterns of the "other person" may have a corresponding mind-pattern in "my" self-image. These are either lying dormant in the mind, subject to being triggered off, or easily capable or ready for recognition or acknowledgment. These patterns abide at one or more various positions or locations in the body-mind as conditioned tendencies or points of view (centers of pre-patterned consciousness). They are sensed as personal "likes" and "dislikes" projected onto the other person.

These patterns are *seemingly* triggered off *by* the "other person," as though he or she is "doing" it *to* me. However, he or she only "brings up" or calls up into "my" attention those patterns of thought that are in fact *already there*, having been previously programmed in the mind by my ego. "I" see "him" or "her" (all "others") doing or being what and who "they" are, because of *who* and *what* "I (the ego) am"– *which is a pattern of conditioned mental tendencies.*

The object *reveals* the subject, and the subject *conforms to* and *perceives* the object. Consciousness is *both*. It is *both* its own content and its own projection seen in apparently separate "individuals."

The content of mind ("my" patterns, desires and aversions – i.e., what I like and don't like about myself) forms the "entity" I think of as my "self." The believed seer *is* what is seen, and the seen only *reinforces* the seer. All that has ever been or has gone on before in my experience or in "my" learning is the sum and substance of who and what "I" am as a *seeming* "individual self," an apparent "entity," even *now*. I look and see everyone and everything through this filter of the past, this *content* of consciousness.

Therefore, everything and everyone "I" see is only the mirrored image of this filtered concept, or "me." Each and every event, personal encounter and experience only adds itself to the already accumulated or present content and serves to trigger off the previously acquired data or add to it even more information. This is gathered material for ongoing upset or elation, for continued pride or prejudice.

But the truth is, it is not the true Self I AM. I AM the One Being, this pure Awareness, timeless and spaceless. When I become free in the Heart, the Source, or pure Awareness itself (prior to the mind and its collected content, including this seeming separate "self," or ego), then I am free to live and move clearly, happily and freely in the world, in love with one and all and without any further upset, without the opposing pairs of opposites comprising the mind and the self-image.

Realization discloses the Self is *prior to* the seer (the mind) and the seen (the world), and is in Truth the substance and essence of both.

REAL MEDITATION

AS LONG AS THERE IS THE NOTION of an individual "I" or "me," a believed "self" or "person" that is felt or sensed as being separate from "others" and from God and/or the world, and believed to be abiding in the world, then chances are this configuration or situation is not being seen or felt for what it *actually is,* which is the meditation of a separate "self" identity.

Said another way, or seeing it from another perspective: as long as there is the felt belief that you are an individual "self" with the sense of "I," "me," "my," and "mine" and are apparently "separate" from the Source (God) and "others" – that is, are living as a seeming "person" or "entity" – and being the "one" who meditates, then *real meditation* – or its true transcendental nature – *has not yet been realized* or seen *as always, already happening,* or as the true Self we always, already are.

Sri Bhagavan Ramana Maharshi said, *"We all have to return to our source. Every human being is seeking his source and must one day come to it. We came from the Within; we have gone outward and now we must turn inward. What is meditation? It is our natural Self. We have covered ourselves over with thoughts and passions. To throw them off we must concentrate on one thought: the Self.*

"The Self is like a powerful magnet hidden within us. It draws us gradually to Itself, though we imagine we are 'going' to It of our own accord. When we are 'near enough,' It puts an end to our other activities, makes us still, and then swallows up our own personal current, thus killing our personality. It overwhelms the intellect and floods the whole being. We think we are meditating upon It and developing towards It, whereas the truth is, that we are like iron-filings and It is the Self-magnet that is pulling us towards Itself. Thus, the process of finding Self is a form of divine magnetism." ("Conscious Immortality," Sri Ramanasramam, Tiruvannamalai, India.)

The truth is, "Real Meditation" is our Pure Being, the Absolute Awareness of the One Self. It is Conscious Awareness, or the innate feeling-quality of simply being I AM – radiating (shining) in the Heart (pure Awareness) as no-seeking, always, already *prior to* the *thought* "I." Abiding consistently and constantly in and as this pure State is *itself* the state of meditation. This is abidance in stillness and peace, regardless of the nature (or apparent nature) of current events or situations going on in one's life. This is *direct cognition* and *experience;* it is not to be held or believed as a concept; rather, *it is what is.* It is giving *full attention to what is.*

When this is directly *experienced,* or *cognized,* or *directly* known, this understanding *is* seen and known as Real Meditation. The separate "self" or "I"-sense is immediately dissolved, its "meditation" ceases once and for all, and natural, effortless peace, freedom, happiness and love – or pure Now-Oneness with God *and all that is* – are seen, felt, lived, and expressed.

Real and simple meditation is resting as "non-doing" in the Heart. This is "accomplished" by *simply inquiring,* "Who am I," until the sense of "I" returns and *merges in the Heart,* or Self.

On "reaching" the Heart (or pure Awareness, the Source of consciousness) the separate-"I" and the sense of separateness itself (which really never left the Heart or became separated), totally dissolves. There arises in its place a wordless, silent awareness of continuous consciousness, shining as the glowing feeling of "I-I," *which is the Heart.* This is *not* the thought of "I" but is a much superior quality. It is an "I"-less feeling-radiance, a glowing or flowing of conscious-light-energy (or pure Awareness) ever-abiding in, yet not in – more like prior to – the right middle of the chest, where everyone naturally gestures or *points to* when indicating themselves.

Once you "reach" or actually re-awaken to the Heart in this manner (really there is no "reaching" the Heart, there is only the awakened realization that the Self *is* the Heart, or the Heart *is* the Self) then simply rest herein, as you remain or abide with attention in the peace of the Heart. This is, in itself, the "dissolving" of the sense of seeking, or *doing,* or *going,* or *efforting.* Conflict comes to an end and real happiness "rises" or is revealed as already shining *in and as* the living Heart; that is, you experience it as the very nature of the true Self in the

Heart. This awareness is *directly known* as eternal existence, the *only* existence; this "discovery" is joy, bliss and freedom.

In the beginning stages of Self Inquiry, thoughts will rush to the surface of your mind and distract you. If you identify with them, they will detract you from the inquiry. When this happens, *very firmly* hold the mind (or attention) *in the inquiry*. Steadily and intentionally "direct attention" onto the *prior* still awareness and observe "who" is having the thought. You will discover ("see") that the thoughts are occurring to "me." This is the apparent "thinker." Then simply inquire, "Who am I?" and follow this "thinker" or "I"-thought inward to its "place" of origin, its expansiveness of pure Awareness, or pure Being.

Really look for and locate its *actual source* within you. What happens is it *disappears*, and *only pure Awareness* remains, which is the true Self. There really is no separate "I"-thought or "self" center as such. It is only an illusion. Or, it is merely the false "I"-thought that *totally dissolves* when you turn *full attention* onto it, to actually *locate* it, in the intentional quest to *find* it. It is just a habit pattern, the habit of identifying with thought and the believed "thinker" of thought. *It disappears!*

The fact is, each thought *itself* gives rise to a false, yet believed "thinker," a seemingly separate "I," as the incorrectly believed "cause" of the thought. However, this is *not* the case; it is an habitual activity, a conditioned response mechanism, a mechanical motion of the mind, like a robotic entity without consciousness or life of its own. The mind borrows, steals, takes, or gets its light or energy from the Self.

Regardless of the nature or number of thoughts that arise *do not pursue the thoughts themselves*; rather, withdraw attention back, deeply within, in the quest to locate the "source" of the "I"-thought. The thought itself, without giving it attention, will die or eventually fall away. With this practice, over time, the thinker or "I"-thought will dissolve into the *prior* pure Awareness, the Self, and disappear. Pure Being then remains.

Sri Bhagavan Ramana says (paraphrasing), "Like diving to the bottom of a lake to find something dropped into it, you should hold your attention (even the breath) and press onward or inward, penetrating to the *very Source of your own being*, within. With practice, your mind will become stronger *in the pursuit,* and your ability will improve in sustaining the inquiry for longer periods without distraction by thoughts."

With *all* that you do, inquire "Who am 'I' that is doing this?" When driving, walking, working, talking, playing, "sexing" – in everything that is required of "you" to be "done" – inquire, "Who is this 'I' and whence is this awareness of 'I' arising?"

Search *within.* Do NOT try to intellectually *answer* the question "who am I?" for your mind's information or satisfaction. That is *not* the practice or process. You are *not* looking for an answer to the question, such as, "It is from me," "I am the son or daughter of John Smith," "I am pure consciousness," "I am That," or "I am a child of God," etc. It is *not* a mental or intellectual answer you are seeking, but rather the actual *dissolving of the very sense of "I"* into the prior pure Awareness, or Consciousness *itself,* as it is *now* always, already eternally *abiding* (or *shining*) in the very Heart of being – *entirely on its own.*

After sufficient practice, you will be able to easily "drop" *everything* (all thoughts, concepts and experiences) and give your attention to the Heart (the core of being) without even thinking "I," or any other thought. You just *remain* or *rest* in pure Consciousness or simple Awareness. Then, in this quality of non-seeking, non-doing *being,* note that *every* impulse, *every* thought, *every* thing that arises, is an avoidance of the oneness that *already is* in the Heart. So, just *don't* "go there" or identify with what arises in the mind, or from the past.

The ex*clusive* meditation of the Heart (in the Heart as the Heart) is in*clusive of everything else.* ALL is in the Heart, *everything* – the mind, the body, the world. Even the notion of God arises with the "I"-thought appearing on the Awareness that is the Heart, and subsides along with the "I"-thought in the Heart. In due time this is *seen* directly, or becomes everyone's *direct* Realization, not just a concept or belief.

There is neither "I" nor "other" than I, there is only That... the Heart. Rest, as That, in the Heart. Abide in pure Awareness, in the Realization: "There is neither I, nor other than I."

Just watch. Every tendency or thought in the mind, as it rises on the surface of pure Awareness, separates and divides consciousness into the appearance of "I" and "not-I."

GET IT: This very activity of compulsive or habitual think-ing is itself the avoidance of Truth. It is the avoidance of Real-ity, the avoidance of Oneness, the avoidance of the very Self. This identification with body-mind as being one's "self" and with rising thoughts projected as "persons," "places" and "things" comprising "this world" is itself suffering and the cause of all suffering.

Stop identifying with this habitual thought process, and just observe it. As you continue holding attention in or on the Self, or the Heart, and no longer identify with all these thoughts, the process will eventually slow down and you will be free of the mind's apparent forms and distractions. Over time, a re-versal of energy occurs on the field and ground of being; there is a relaxing, releasing and dissolving of the former felt identi-fication with the body-mind. The ego with its self-image, its former habit of forming a "center of being" (a personal sense of "I," or separate point of reference) is seen for what it is – a limitation – and as what divides consciousness into polar op-posites. All former felt sensations or contractions in the body, along the spine, or between the head and solar plexus, etc., are no longer of any concern as the seat of awareness returns to the spiritual Heart felt on the right side of the chest (not actu-ally in the body, but prior to the body), and consciousness simply rests as no-seeking in the Heart. The polarization of conscious-energy reverses itself from its usual former ten-dency to objectify, to now simply resting or abiding in the Heart. If thought arises (any thought), observe its tendency to cause attention to move into separateness and do not go there. Just continue to observe it or *quietly* "stop it" with the simple inquiry, "Avoiding?" Eventually, attention will remain in the Heart *as* the Heart, as the mind looses its usual, former ten-dency to rise and move about with random thoughts of "per-sons," "places" and "things."

This is the *one method* of "seeking Truth" that actually totally *dismantles* all seeking within itself, or in its place, or on the spot. For, paradoxically, it *utilizes* the mind to *dissolve* the mind, or its tendencies, and eventually the very "I"-thought itself (the separate-self sense) is dissolved. Henceforth, the peace, freedom, and joy of the Heart remains as the natural state.

Clear or Complete Your Day *Before* Retiring for Sleep

In addition to this process and to enhance its effectiveness, when you retire for bed clear your day *before* going to sleep. Go to sleep at peace and *loving* yourself. If there is any activity in the mind caused by identifying with thoughts of unfinished business of the day, your brain is not able to rest as well when you do go to sleep. So, bring to mind every unfinished or incomplete event of the day, and mentally and emotionally *feel in yourself* that it is *already* complete. See and feel it completed. Go to sleep feeling what it feels like for everything to be *already* completed *now*. If you don't complete or balance your day in this manner, the mind creates dreams in your sleep. Dreams are nothing more than playing out unfinished, incomplete, unbalanced events of the day (or your life), in order to establish a state of harmony and balance. Then the mind can sleep and rest and you can enjoy the deep, peaceful bliss of the Self in dreamless sleep. This is the desired realm of being – without concepts, without cognition or thought, without the burden of "otherness," without the burden of "I" or "I-am-this-body." As already explained, you can even experience this realm in the waking state as pure Awareness or the flow of clear consciousness from the Heart. Be aware *from* and *as* this Realm *even now* by being Awake or Aware as the Self, abiding in the spiritual Heart.

Consider this: when you say you are "going" to sleep, where *exactly* are you going? Even if you are lying in bed and your mate asks what you are doing, you might say, "I am 'going' to sleep." *Where is sleep?* Actually, sleep is *even now* present. It is always now-present, it is only "covered up" by the subtle and gross thoughts of the mind, and the world. Just as the atmosphere "covers" (or conceals) the stratosphere, and they both "cover" (conceal) the ionosphere, the waking state "covers" the dream state and they both "cover" the deep sleep state.

Gross thought is the "waking state" of ordinary life in the physical body, and its "world" of experience. Subtle or dream thought is the nature of the more subtle dream-body in the "dream state" and its realms and worlds. Thoughtless or mindless consciousness is the nature of the "deep sleep state." All these are interpenetrating each other. If asked, "where is the ionosphere or the stratosphere" you might point to or indicate the far outer realms of space; but both are here present and merely covered over by the atmosphere. You might think of "going" to the ionosphere as in a spacecraft. But, actually, it is present so to speak, being merely covered up by the other two "spheres." Similarly, you might think of "going" to sleep, but sleep is actually here, merely covered up by gross thoughts. When thought stops, you are already "in" sleep.

One who abides consciously and totally in the Living Heart, or the Self, is "awake when asleep," and "asleep when awake." This is the state of Natural Meditation. This is the state of pure Bliss, eternal Peace, Liberation, and freedom from conflict. It is the only true Happiness. It is thoughtless, unchanging, uncaused Awareness. It is the Supreme State of the Absolute Supreme Being. It is conscious Oneness with real God; or, it is God shining as the one and only Self.

Continually inquire and contemplate the Heart *as* the Heart until this supreme state ever abides as your real and true nature. This is the end of all seeking and all suffering. It is the "ultimate goal," being eternal life. It is the dissolving of the ego, the separate-self. It is the Realm of Love. It is Christ.

****

A Vignette

FINDING HAPPINESS AND BEING HAPPY is *not* from seeking pleasure; seeking pleasure does not bring *true* happiness or contentment. So why the need, the motivation for seeking pleasure? When we seek pleasure or experiences believed to bring pleasure, it is to ameliorate or cushion suffering; obviously we are coming from a present basis of unhappiness – i.e., discomfort, upset, unpleasantness or potential threat to our well being. We are not happy, but rather are *seeking* happiness. On realizing the *true nature* of the Self, which *is Real Happiness*, you may end your compulsive quest for pleasure.

THE WAY TO THE SELF IS OBSERVATION, NOT ANALYSIS

THE APPROPRIATE "WAY" OR "MODE" for abiding in pure Truth, the Supreme Absolute Reality, is to contemplate the inner Source of being, which is present-moment Now-Awareness. Do this now – by diving deeply within yourself, into the very Heart and Essence of Being *You Are*. This is the very Heart or Core of Being and Pure Awareness (or Is-ness) itself – ever abiding in you *as* the very Self. Do this NOW, rather than analyzing all thoughts or concepts *about* it, none of which are IT.

Analyzing is thinking. Analyzing requires thought and is objectivity or "outwardness" of the mind or attention. The inner essence of one's Consciousness (or very Being itself) is unceasing, steady, absolutely still-light or pure Awareness as Universal Intelligence, *prior to* the thinking mind (or thought itself) and even *prior to the sense of "I"* as a seemingly, separate-thinking-self a believed self-image.

Self is experienced *in the Heart* as the very Ground of Being. It is the steady, ceaseless motion of pure Light showing or revealing all creation, it being the Heart-felt Radiance of absolute Stillness and Silence, which is infinite and eternal in nature, thus "now-here" and "here-now" present. This is so *this very moment* as the heartfelt Radiance of the Self, ever shining or glowing as "I-I" in the right center of the chest. It is eternal and infinite peace, love and joy. This is the Heart of being.

In Sanskrit it is called *"Hridayam,"* the Heart, the originating primary, spiritual center, the Source and Light-essence that gives rise to the waves or rays of spiritual Light-energy. It is the vital Substance of the mind out of which the body-idea and form of the body are fashioned and maintained. It is the Light that supports the mind and thus the entire objective world in its apparent existence.

Do not think about all these word or any of this! Simply let the words point attention inward into a quiet relaxed experience

of their actual meaning. Simply feel.... I AM. Not "I am this,"
or "I am that".... just I AM.... Simply float in the Heart *as* the
Heart, felt in the right chest where you normally point when
indicating yourself or when referring to yourself. Just abide in
the stillness and peace of your own pure Awareness.

The logic is very simple. Rather than analyzing the not-Self,
which is the mind and all its content of the past (none of
which is presently real and thus cannot be the *present* Self),
simply ever abide *here* and *now* in the stillness of the Heart, the
Self. On finally "arriving" or "fully awakening" in the Heart,
the very Self, what more is there to do? Ultimately, all identification with thought ceases. Known thereafter is the Self-
radiance or pure Awareness in the Heart, as freedom and
bliss. It eventually dissolves the mind's tendencies to separateness, and random thoughts stop completely; eternal and
infinite Peace remains. When this occurs with effort, it is
called spiritual practice; when it occurs naturally, without effort, it is called Realization.

With this awakening of the Self comes the radical and absolute removal of the fear of death. As the Self is realized and
lived from this ground of Being – this Eternal Now – all body-
identification as "I" is totally dissolved. One transcends the illusion of time and realizes non-difference from, or true Oneness with, *all that is*. This is the very Principle of Life itself.

You "see" and realize the apparently objective world as being the nature of a dream. At first, just as some people wake
slowly from deep sleep, it may take you a little while to stir
fully awake from this long identified-with dream of mortality,
as the Self has apparently lived out patterns or processes of
time-space manifestations for the equivalent of millions of
years, in thousands of lifetimes. Therefore, it may take effort
to shake off the "dregs of drowsiness" or end your strong belief that this "waking dream" is real, and let go the strong, unconscious pull of desire that may still draw you into continued
indulgence in the so-called pleasures of this world. This is the
strong pull of your ordinary pursuit of worldly life, which you
believe to be happiness, and your long-held but false assumption that the "waking state" is the standard of "reality."

All of this apparent "reality of the physical world" you may believe and assume "along with everyone else" is true because of having forgotten that the true Self is infinite and eternal, existing *beyond* or *prior to* time. It is that pure Consciousness in which the "I-am-the-body" notion and the belief in the solidity of this physical world are now occurring as this dream.

Ultimately, when "you" awaken to and abide in the spiritual Heart, or true Self, realization discloses your body as an apparent object in Consciousness, and that the mind and self-image are also only reflections of this light of Consciousness, like objective patterns of energy, and are not the Self. So, the appropriate process for successful results in the realization of Truth is to stop assuming and identifying with your body-mind as having solid "reality," and dive into the Heart of being, the Self. To the best of your ability, simply go to the very end – even *now* or to begin with – *and just stay there!*

Bhagavan Sri Ramana Maharshi said,
"Just as you don't analyze your garbage before throwing it out, since you know already that it is garbage, why bother yourself and waste time analyzing your body and your mind, with all their functions and contents, when in the end you are going to discard them both as not-Self?"

Directly awaken, even NOW, to the Self we all are – before birth and beyond death. This is the Truth, the Self, the Heart. The Heart is *prior to* mind or body. It is the very-present, infinite and eternal NOW-reality, the *only* Reality, which is temporarily covered by this dream of objective reality, just as the illusion of a snake "seen" in the twilight is really only a coil of rope. It is falsely believed to be a snake until someone "reveals" the illusion by pointing it out.

Again, do not analyze or give extra thought to these words. If you are willing to do so, *just accept them* and let them direct your attention or awareness *back into the Heart* and quietly abide in the stillness of the pure Self (the Heart) as your *here* and *now* felt Experience!

ON "TRUTH"

TRUTH (CAPITAL "T") is *what's so*. What is *now so* is the Truth. You can't reason, change or compare Truth.

Truth *is*. It is its *own* standard. Truth supports and allows for comparison of itself with all that it is not, but it doesn't change with any or all its apparent comparisons.

Truth *just is*.

*   *   *   *   *

To know the Truth, I must empty my mind of all that I think I now know. When the mind is totally emptied of all my held concepts about the Truth, Truth is what remains. This is then the ability for unobstructed *direct insight* into the Truth to occur.

Any definition of Truth is not the Truth it defines. It only points to or indicates the Truth, which is not definable. Truth believed is a lie.

Truth can be realized only subjectively. It cannot be known in any objective sense. Yet, actually, Truth is prior to *both* objectivity *and* subjectivity. Truth is what is left when all objectivity and subjectivity, all non-Truth, is removed. Concepts, beliefs, definitions and opinions are all non-Truth. They are the past. Truth is now.

Truth abides in and as eternity. All descriptions, beliefs and definitions are in the dimension of time. Truth is prior to time, prior to mind or thought. Descriptions, beliefs and definitions are all thoughts or concepts in the mind, which is in time. Therefore, what I *believe* or know *about*, is not the Truth.

Truth is one; descriptions, beliefs and definitions are many. Truth is Source. Out of Source (Truth) all seeming "truth" arises, moves and returns, but Truth is not affected. Truth can neither be added to nor subtracted from. That which can be added to or subtracted from is not Truth, for Truth doesn't change.

Truth is Reality.   Reality does not change.   That which changes is only relative; it is not Truth or Reality.

Relative "truth" (small "t") is being responsible. Being responsible is "being with" whatever is occurring (whatever is at hand) and "owning it" as one's own. It is the willingness to realize and know that I AM (we all are) the Source, the Cause of everything that occurs on the screen of Awareness.

So, Truth is knowing that nothing "I" am aware *of* occurs outside of Consciousness. The Truth being, I AM *is* Consciousness. Therefore, everything that occurs in my perception is occurring in the Self by means of "my" perception of it, which includes my apparent "bodily self."   This is true, but not *the* Truth, not the totality of Truth.

There is no objective reality to the world outside of or independent of consciousness itself. Since all I am aware of, as occurring in "my" world, is occurring in this Consciousness, and since Consciousness is the Self that I AM, then I am the Source and Cause of everything, whether it is occurring or not occurring in "my" space. In Truth, I am even the cause and source of what appears to happen to someone else, since it is apparently occurring in this space that is "the world" as I perceive it.

It is the "I"-thought or ego that gives rise to all that is occurring in "my" space *as it appears to be.* But the "I"-thought or ego cannot arise apart from the Self, which is its Source and Cause. Therefore, I am the source and cause of all that appears in my space, including that which occurs to "others." But this does not mean that I am "to blame" for everything negative or unpleasant that occurs in "my" space to others; nor am I "to be appreciated and congratulated" for everything positive that occurs in "my" space to others. What is occurring is just what is occurring – *as it is apparently occurring.* And *it is occurring in "my" world,* but only as *I* see it occurring. It is *also* occurring in the world of everyone, *as they are seeing it as occurring.*

We see the world as *we* are, not necessarily as it is seen to be by "others."

When I *fully realize* this, IT is the Truth that sets me free from the circumstances of life. Jesus said, *"You will know the Truth and the Truth will make you free."* (John 8:32) This realization may not include removal or change of the events of life themselves, but their effect on "me" is changed. Events no longer upset, pain or hinder "me" as they may have in the past. Instead, they become merely events to be lived out, lived through, or understood and to be replaced in time by other events in the ordinary, everyday process of life.

Truly *realizing* "who" or "what" I am is realizing Self (the absolute Self) as the one creative, causative power, the source of all that appears in "my" world.

Failure to assume responsibility for all of the events occurring in "my" life is unconsciousness and ignorance. Ignorance is not "bad" or "wrong"; it is simply not knowing or understanding the Truth; it is being unenlightened. The result is that my life does not work easily and efficiently and I experience pain, confusion and conflict, rather than continuously, effortlessly enjoying the peace, compassion, humor and joy of the true and real Self-nature. In this ignorance, we are forever *seeking* happiness, peace and freedom, rather than living in present peace, happiness and freedom.

* * * * *

Bhagavan Sri Ramana Maharshi once said (in effect), even if one has several university degrees, but does not know the *true Self*, or one's true nature, the sum of his acquired knowledge is the equivalent to "learned ignorance."

To pretend or feign erudition, knowledge, understanding, wisdom, or enlightenment, etc., in order to appear "right" or "knowledgeable" or "intelligent" in the eyes of others, without having real or *intelligent* Insight or Understanding, is in fact ignorance and suffering compounded and prolonged. It is justifying and defending ignorance while acting as if knowledgeable. Why defend ignorance? It is better to acknowledge one's ignorance and clear the space in Consciousness to Awaken to Truth and thereby live free in real and true understanding. To think you "know" anything, without *really knowing* the knowing Self, is knowing nothing. Acknowledging your ignorance, or that you really *don't know*, is in fact wisdom.

"Non-Self" knowledge does not exist, for there is no true knowledge in the non-Self. The mind does not know; it is only recorded memory data of the past, that is presented as real or true knowledge. The ego calls up the mind's data and pretends it is real knowledge, but it is *not direct knowing*. Like a computer, its data are merely stored records, the relationship of current events to older records, or other data of the past, which in fact are now dead.

When properly known and used correctly, the mind *is* a marvelous mechanism of memory data, being a somewhat total record of the past as sensory thought patterns stored in the cells of the brain. But a record of thought patterns does not *know*. The concept-filled mind can only produce its system of beliefs, its recorded data to *represent* or *emulate* knowledge. Not only is the representation *not* true knowledge, it in fact veils and conceals the Truth or current facts. It is only information without Self-conscious intelligence.

Only Self-consciousness or the intelligence of Self-existence can *know*. Therefore, only the Self knows – not books, the ego, the mind and its recorded data, or *anything* "other." Only Consciousness *knows*, and Consciousness is the Self. Only the Self *knows*.

Truth comes out of no thing (no-thing-ness) or pure Being. This no-thing-ness is not a "void" but is the pure light and energy of Intelligence itself, or Consciousness itself, which is unchanging, eternal, infinite, and total Existence. This pure Consciousness-Existence is the fullness of Pure Being (the Self) and is Pure Knowing.

Truth is Pure Knowing, and this Pure Knowing (as explained above) also comes out of the clear space of no thing. To further explain, the dictionary defines "nothing" as "not a thing," meaning a "thing" that is not any thing as we are normally accustomed to things or would define *as* a thing. This "no thing" exists nowhere. The dictionary defines "nowhere" as "not any place," meaning a "place" that is not any place as we are normally accustomed to places, or would define as a "place"; and thus it is *everywhere*. So, Pure Knowing comes out of *nothing*, which is *nowhere*, meaning that *everything known* comes out of no *thing*. Being nowhere, it is thus *every-*

where – meaning, Pure Knowing is *inclusive of everything.*

*   *   *   *   *

That which is everything and everywhere is the Source. Source is God; it is Self. Since I AM *is* the source of everything in life, I must be the Self. Self is God; God is Self. I am Self and Self is God. This means "my" I AM – or the "I am" that I AM – is God.

This means, metaphorically, the wave is the ocean and the ocean is the wave; and, of course, even though the entire wave is ocean, the wave is not the entire ocean. The radical Realization and Understanding of this is *knowing* the Truth. It is no different from Moses' enlightenment as recorded in the Bible at Exodus 3:14.

It was Jesus who said, *"You will know the Truth, and the Truth will make you free."* This conscious understanding frees "me" and anyone from the conflict and confusion of ordinary daily life. It awakens the present happiness and joy of true Self-existence, which is the One eternal Reality, the Truth.

Everything is the undifferentiated Absolute Supreme Being, which is not different from the Self, or God, which is Infinite and Eternal Intelligence, or Awareness and I am *is* that I AM.

But there is no separate "I" that is it or knows it. For such a separate "I" does not know or even exist.

ISN'T "HAPPINESS ALL THE TIME" BORING?

WITH SOME, WHO FIND IT DIFFICULT to grasp the Truth that we are *not* the body-mind, and that the world is *not* permanent or *real* apart from our consciousness if it, the question occasionally comes up, "If I were happy all the time, wouldn't that be boring? Isn't happiness all the time boredom?"

Only the mind would ask this question, not the Self. The mind *must* ask this question. For to the mind, the only *real* happiness is when the mind with all its accumulated content or the past, has ceased functioning in its old ordinary or usual way.

After experiencing an extended period of pleasure, the mind *thinks* or *fears*, "It is about time for some unhappy or unforeseen upset or setback. You had better be careful now and take heed, for that's the way it's always been. *So watch out!*"

If you are *truly* concerned about boredom or unhappiness being the sequel to happiness, just ask yourself: "Why do I continually seek or even strive for happiness? And try for the things I believe, think, or know will make me happy?" "Is it so I can intentionally feel unhappy when they are gone or lost, or have ended, and no longer arouse in me a sense of joy or pleasure?"

Actually it is *pleasure*, not happiness, which eventually results in boredom or displeasure. It is an honest mistake. The notion that pleasure is *actually happiness* is a basic misconception with the majority of people. In fact, pleasure is the *only* expression or form of happiness that most people are familiar with, particularly during one's usual life, or the ordinary waking state. This statement refers to the waking or dream state only, because *everyone* experiences the state of *true happiness* when resting in dreamless sleep. In fact, this is the *only* time they *actually* experience happiness – even though they may not realize it, or have not really considered this. Moreover, this true and natural state of happiness is *not* "boring" for anyone. In fact, if we are not able to fully sleep or get enough sleep, we become quite disturbed, even taking sleeping remedies to solve the problem. And, if that does not work, we'll go to our doctor, to a specialist, or even to the extreme of taking drugs that numb the brain, just to help us sleep. These drugs are even regularly advertised in western countries.

There is a *major difference* between pleasure and happiness. Pleasure is dependent on or is the result of something else, which is usually something or someone gained *outside* oneself. It is usually dependent on some object – like some person, place, thing or event. Often it's the result of attaining some preexisting desire.

When something desired has been attained or something despised or undesirable has been removed, we say we are "happy." But, we really mean that this has brought us pleasure. For once the desired object, item, or experience is attained, it is then replaced with the desire for something else, something more or better or different. To continue to look for pleasure from "the same old thing" – over and over again – *is* boredom. This is the ordinary method or process of life with most people. They mistake pleasure for happiness (or vice versa) and seek what they call "happiness" from objects, or from the things, persons or experiences outside themselves.

Real happiness is natural to the Self. It is *already* present as the very nature of the Self; only this is not usually seen or realized. Being *non*-dependent on anything or anyone outside the Self, it is *not* boring. Rather it is Bliss; it is *real* Joy.

It is, in fact, our very pursuit or action of *seeking* happiness – from people, places and things – that is *itself* pain producing; for such so-called "happiness" so "attained" will not survive; it will soon wane and eventually die.

However, Real Happiness, when realized and consciously lived, being the very nature of the Self, is infinite and eternal and is the delight of Being, the very nature of Existence Itself!

DISAGREEMENT IS FIRST AGREEMENT

OUR MUTUAL AGREEMENT – knowingly or unknowingly – is the actual basis of ordinary physical reality, as it (reality) appears to be in the world. Consequently, only what we agree to be real, is real. And even to disagree on its reality, we must first acknowledge that it is apparently real.

(Let's be very clear: *in this instance,* what is termed "real" is what *appears* to be real *phenomenally,* or "real" to our physical senses or in our perception. It does *not* mean *actual* Reality, or Truth explained earlier in previous chapters. Thus, Reality is *always, already* true and real just *as it is,* without change, without variation or modification, whether we agree on it or not. Truth or Reality is *beyond* the mind, while sensory perception of phenomena always occurs *in* and *with* the mind and in fact *is* the mind.)

So again, to disagree is to agree. How can you disagree without first *acknowledging,* "being with," or perceiving the *very thing* or *position* with which you disagree? It must first appear to be, at least as a concept, in order for you to disagree; must it not? What is it that you are disagreeing with? Is it there; does it appear to you or your senses, or as a thought, or not? Is the idea or notion of it present in your mind or not? Of course it is there, it is present in your mind as a concept or mental image.

For example, can you disagree that you exist or have existence? Of course, you can say, "I don't exist"; but your denial is not actually *proving* your nonexistence. To deny that you exist requires your very presence or existence in order to raise the idea or speak the words, "I don't exist." So, you cannot actually deny that you exist even though you may be uncertain about the *true nature* of what you are. (This logic is useful when considering whether you exist or not during dreamless sleep).

You may believe that "you" exist as the body-mind. Or you may say "you" exist as a "soul" or "spirit," whatever you think a "soul" or "spirit" may be. However, even to disagree on what "you" really are or exist *as*, first requires that you acknowledge yourself *as an actuality*, as either a concept or some "thing" or a *non*-thing that exists, in order for you to disagree with it.

Therefore, again, to disagree is to first agree.

To be aware of this – that disagreement is based on prior agreement (even if you are unfamiliar with or unconscious about it) – can free you from a lot of unnecessary conflict, sorrow, and even disagreement itself, or within yourself.

THE *"HRIDAYAM"* OR HOLY SPIRIT

JESUS SAID, *"I will pray the Father and He will give you a Comforter."* (John 14:16) The Comforter, or Holy Spirit, promised by Jesus is the Awakening to or Realization of the *eternal* nature of the Current of Conscious Energy, the pure Intelligence, or the very Consciousness-Awareness ever radiating in and as the spiritual Heart, or the very Self.

It *is* possible to "know" or subtly feel this in relation to the body on the *right* in the chest (not in it, but *prior to* it) shining as pure, eternal Awareness or thoughtless I-AM-ness. This eternal light, shining in the Heart as the Self, reflects into the center of the head, illuminating the mind, is reflected down the spine into the body centers, particularly the solar plexus and below, where the thought-feeling "I-am-this-body" is felt. It continues its flow back up the spine to the crown of the head and back down to the Heart *on the right*. In this same form or manner, it recycles continuously, sustaining life in the body and the mental vision of the world until the death of the body.

This Comforter or Holy Spirit is the Supreme Self. The spiritual seat or the throne of power of the very Self is already intuitively known and felt by *everyone* as being in the right center of the chest. No one fails to point to this location when referring to or indicating himself or herself. This sign is universal, it being natural or automatic with *everyone* from early childhood. Among the very *earliest*, naturally coordinated bodily movements, pertaining to one's sense of being – using thoughts, words and hands – it is intuitively demonstrated. It is *not even* taught, for it is *already* known, and continues until death. And yet, this simple fact is seldom if ever considered.

In India, it is mentioned by a few wise ones who know. There is even a word in Sanskrit that describes this seat of spiritual Consciousness that has no true equivalent in English or (probably) in any other language. It is *hridayam*. It means "heart" and stands for this heart-center. Another approximate meaning is "the center that sucks in or draws to it everything." Bhagavan Sri Ramana Maharshi said it means the Self. It is the *apparent* "bodily location" of Universal Being. In truth, it is not located in the body; rather the body is located *in it*. But, as long as the body-idea is superimposed on the Self and is identified with as being the Self, it is experienced or felt like a "psychic or metaphysical sun" shining in this region of the chest to the right of the center of the body. At first one "notices" or "senses" it as a simple glow, or flutter or flow of awareness. It may be felt as emptiness or a knot in the chest. Then, finally, it shines as absolute stillness and silence and as fullness, love and great peace in the Heart, with no direct sense of a separate-self or "I"-thought associated with the body. The body is more *indirectly* felt or sensed, associated with the spine and blood pumping heart on the left. From this transcendental Awareness, the body and the "I" thought are both experienced as objects, which finally merge in this Awareness – the one Truth, Existence, or existing Reality.

The body "floats" (or is immersed) in this pure Awareness as a sponge is in the ocean. The sponge is in the ocean and the ocean is in the sponge – the body is in the Self and the Self is in the body. The Self is the ocean (pure I AM); the body-mind and self-image (personal sense of "I") is the sponge.

When Jesus referred to the Kingdom of God being *within us* (Luke 17:21), he was referring to the spiritual Heart. When he said, *"Lo, I am with you always, even to the end of the world"* (Matthew 28:20), he again meant that the spiritual Heart, the Self, or pure I AM, being infinite and eternal, is always present, *prior to* the mind and thought, which are the world and/or the cause of the world. These (mind and thought) are also the cause of suffering.

When a true devotee or disciple of Christ awakens to the inner-Christ (of his own being), then the Heart – real God – becomes the central focus of his life. He awakens as "I-I" in the Heart. Even though it feels like "I," it is not the ego or "I"-thought but the very Self or Christ Consciousness which Jesus realized and lived as his own awareness.

With this spiritual Awakening, one realizes that Christ was not only living two thousand years ago, but is living NOW in the very Heart of being. Christ is not *outside* the Self, but *is* the very Self. This is the one Self we *all* are. This is "the Comforter" (the Holy Spirit) which Jesus promised to have "the Father" (God) *reveal* to his disciples. (John 14:16-17)

"CONSCIOUS OBSERVATION" AS A PROCESS FOR MEDITATION

THE CONSCIOUS PROCESS OF OBSERVATION is to inquire: "Who is perceiving an 'other,' a 'not-I'?" *Observe* "who" or "what" answers. *Feel* "who" answers. Inwardly *locate* the subjective self or the very point or "place" where you *feel* the energy of thoughts/feelings (or feelings/thoughts) and the very-sense of being "me" or "I," the inquiring entity or self itself. Observe or "feel" who or what is cognizant or is inquiring? Observe the conscious process of cognition or perception *itself*. Observe how, *right now,* you feel the whole body-being and/or the subjective self as "I."

Your observation ultimately discloses that feeling the "location" of the "I"-sense is a contraction or pinch or knot *in* your body, *as your body.* The body itself is a contraction on the field of consciousness or in your range of awareness. You often feel this sense of "I" as a polarization between the head and the solar plexus in your body with perhaps also a reflected sense of discomfort in other centers or areas in your body, or in or along the spine. Simply observe *in your own experience* the pattern or configuration of your own body as being "I," and how it is the *necessary* prerequisite for your observation, cognizance or feeling of the very sense of "other" or "not-I."

Now, observe and re-cognize (know again) that this "I" is the body rising as a thought-feeling originating from or out of the past. It appears as a reflection on the pure Awareness of Being, the Heart-radiance felt in the right chest. So, let the presence of the Heart-radiance now become the *very basis* of your awareness, your only interest and identification. You then feel this as a radiance or deep peace in the right chest, extending throughout your entire being and beyond – to infinity.

Very simply, the Heart-radiance, or pure Awareness, is the One Reality *always, already* behind or *prior to* the body and to *all experience appearing in and as the world.* Yet, it is also that which most easily escapes our attention. Habitually, attention usually goes instead to the body and/or all that *it* experiences.

Simple awareness, although its nature is infinite and eternal, is seldom considered and is very easily overlooked. "Attention" and "simple awareness" are not the same. Awareness is like space, always there making room for the body, but attention goes primarily to the body, overlooking the preexisting space. Awareness is like a floodlight, lighting up everything; attention is like a spot light, focusing in on specific things or objects.

As you identify *only* with the Heart, the I AM, experience the *release* of identification with the thought "I-am-the-body," and *let go completely* of all compulsive identification with the body. Instead, feel the *prior* peace, the feeling of simply being I AM, which has no knot, pinch or contraction in it, as does the body. For its peace is *totally free* and is at all times *everywhere!*

Observe that the tendency for attention to rise in identification with the body-mind and the process of perception as "I" and "not-I" is *itself* separation and division, and is avoiding relationship with Truth, the One Reality, the true Self. It carries with it the *desire* for relative happiness in the world, all of which is itself *seeking* and *suffering*.

So, *don't go there!* Instead, *stay* in the Self, this pure Awareness! Rest in identification with pure Awareness, this Light-Radiance of the Heart, which is Peace. Abide in the ceaseless Peace and Presence of Absolute Stillness found only in the Heart. This is abiding in the Self, as High Indifference, or non-seeking, pure Being – experienced here and now as deep bliss.

Observe and re-cognize this structural mechanism of desire and fear, the opposing polarity of "I" and "not-I," to "link" or "separate" – to unite with or run away from. Mind itself is the tendency to rise in identification with the polarity and duality of "I" and "not-I." This is the basis of all suffering. *Don't do it.*

Observe the process of perception as the rising up of the cognizing "I" with its habitual attachment to identification with the body-mind or ego as being "I." See its dual sense of difference/sameness, separation/togetherness, competitiveness/supportiveness, rivalry/camaraderie, etc., with all "others" or those appearing in the multifaceted phenomena we see in the world as "not-I." Observe this compulsion to balance, rectify, neutralize or avoid this apparent "separation" or "difference." Just watch all this, that is all. *Don't succumb to it.*

Observe all this as a witness from and *as* the non-seeking Heart, resting in the stillness of High Indifference, the now-radiance of the eternal and infinite Self or Heart. Observe that the *exclusive* contemplation of the Heart is itself *inclusive* of all process and creativity. All is the very Self... All is I AM.

As thoughts and tendencies rise, observe the Truth: that there is neither "I" nor "other-than-I" – and simply rest in the Heart-radiance, the Self. Witness what rises, with *High Indifference*, allowing it to occur without effort or opposition and without there being any modification or alteration in your present state of eternal happiness. This is *acceptance* of it all.

No matter what arises, if there is even the slightest potential to identify with it or change it, *don't!* To do so is an activity that brings suffering or avoidance of one's oneness with pure Being. It only contributes to seeking or suffering. Cease *all* identification with what arises and abide in this *always, already presence* of Oneness and Wholeness that is pure Relationship with the Heart. Life will go on as you simply rest, *without a separate sense of "I,"* in this ever-present peace and happiness. Remain as the indifferent humorous, Witness or the nonparticipating "support" to all that is; not as an "I" relating to a "not-I" but as the *observer* of the whole process, without conflict, dilemma, suffering or seeking. When *any* thought or tendency rises, simply observe it. Or, if a tendency is still there to leave this peaceful Relationship with Self, the Heart, and identify with it, then *really see this* and *inquire*: "Avoiding peace and freedom?" and *quickly drop it!*

See if you *really* want to "go there" or get involved; for to do so will only be a *disturbance* to your natural state of transcendental peace. When your peace is disturbed you are not free, and if you are not free you are not happy. *Just see this in its simplicity!* It is somewhat like an older, well-trained dog that is resting peacefully by its master's chair. On hearing another dog, barking in the distance, it instinctively raises its ears as though about to stir from its rest. Its master says simply and quietly: "Be still; do you *really* want to move from your rest?" And the pet, without moving, closes its eyes and settles back into its peaceful stillness and silence. Yet, it is still alert to what could or might occur if action *is* required.

ASSOCIATION WITH A MAN OF UNDERSTANDING

A MAN OF ENLIGHTENMENT (one who is awake *as* the Self, abiding in Realization and Conscious Understanding of the true Self), consciously assumes the enlightenment of his friends. He lives *in* and *from* Conscious Relationship, in all his contacts and dealings with everyone. This allows his friends to partake of and experience *for themselves* this same pure quality and understanding of Truth that *already is* his ordinary and natural state. But this is only if they *choose* to. He does not force this on anyone; it just occurs by living in close proximity to him, to those living in or near his physical presence and are closely associated with him and open to him.

The potential and benefit of this occurring is *always* there, whether others actually know and assume this conscious relationship with the Man of Understanding, or understand it to be in fact occurring for them in his presence, or not. If they do, and choose to remain friends in association with him, they will very likely come to recognize and "see" for themselves their own conditioned limitations and how this close proximity to the Man of Understanding is silently working like by osmosis. It clears the blocks and obstructions to one's own natural and steady abidance in real happiness, the true Self, and passively (if not actively) releases and dissolves them.

Thus, living in the Presence of a Man of Enlightenment is healing to the entire world. It serves to reveal and help remove all limiting "personal" characteristics that obstruct the vision of the Self in everyone. Jesus said, *"And I, if I be lifted up from the earth* (i.e., body-mind identification), *draw all men unto me."* (John 12:32)

In India this association with a Man of Understanding is called *"Sat Sanga."* When it is available, it is the easiest Way to Self-realization for a true spiritual aspirant. To remain in *Sat Sanga* or Association with a Man of Understanding requires spiritual advancement or maturity on the part of the seeker. For the energy of *Sat Sanga*, though blissful to his devotees, is too intense and intimidating to the ego of the ordinary person not truly inclined toward a genuine spiritual quest or pursuit.

A pretentious or "halfhearted seeker" (one who is not actually willing to release all in his or her ego-mind that is contrary to the Truth) will find *Sat Sanga* threatening, frustrating and even offensive, and therefore intolerable for very long. This is why the biblical Pharisees, filled with ego and all their conventional, orthodox *beliefs* and *concepts* of Truth and/or pseudo spirituality, were responsible for Jesus' crucifixion.

Living with a Man of Enlightenment or Conscious Understanding brings up and reveals – in the Light of Truth – all in oneself that is *not* the Truth, all that is conceptual. Therefore, if you are stuck in your mind's conditioned beliefs or patterns of behavior, this could be very threatening to your ego and perhaps be in direct conflict with and a threat to your current ways of "seeing" and "doing" things. Thus, there will be fear.

Living in *true* conscious Awareness and in Association with a Man of Enlightenment, requires you to genuinely question your mind and motives and ask yourself, "Am I here and now willing to drop all my conditioned beliefs and patterns of thought?" "Am I willing and ready to undergo the momentary yet necessary reaction and conflict going on in me, and the threat that it seems to be to my ego?" "Am I *truly ready* to release *all* my accumulated opinions and conditioned attitudes of the past?" "Am I ready to realize and eternally abide in the steadfastness of peace, love, and happiness *without* conflict, that *living* in Conscious Company promises?"

Relatively, the last question above should be easier to answer when compared with the first three. However, the other three are *required*, along with your commitment to carry them all the way through to their total completion, before the promise of the fourth question can be realized.

The mind, which is your memory and conditioned record of all the "what," "whys," and "how's" that you have learned or accumulated in the past, for dealing with life's issues, *will* come up and want to assert itself in the present, with the arising or current issues. It wants to control things, to change, alter or modify the present to conform to *your* more familiar past.

The Man of Understanding lives always *in* and *as* the *present moment*, without being at the effect of the past. He lives in the *omnipresence* of pure Being, which sees everything *just as it is*. His apparent actions from this presence are always free. The past, in fact, is not real; only the present is real, being clear and free just as it is.

If, to you, there is anything appearing to be needed, it is to this "me," or sense of "I," this point of reference in consciousness that is identified with time and space, past and future. This sense of "I" or centering point is the problem. It is the "target" or "center of gravity" around which everything in the world of "time and space" appears to be revolving.

Whereas, with the Man of Understanding, everything happens naturally *in the moment* not based on the past or necessarily related to the past. His apparent actions are free of the past or doership; although to onlookers, they often appear to be from the past and based on the past; or, they also may be entirely different than, in opposition to, in direct conflict with, and a contradiction to how he acted (or appeared to act) in the past. This is often confusing, conflicting and at odds with the onlooker stuck in the mind, or in the past and being a "doer."

Paradoxically, the actions of the Man of Understanding are not "his" actions as a "doer." It is the action of the Totality of Being, the total functioning of manifestation occurring in this moment and not from the past. This can be threatening to the mind, which thinks and measures things entirely from the past.

Just see this. And in the presence of a Man of Understanding, just let the past go. Remember, the "self" you *think* you are – based on your past, or memory, or history – is *not* the Self you *really* are.

Live with the Man of Understanding *in the present*, seeing that everything is always, already complete *just as it is*.

Being *with* him and learning *from* him, you can tune in with what it means to *just let go* into his wisdom and love. Be willing to Awaken to his higher understanding and be happy, free and at peace – always!

PART V

CLEARING THE MIND
FOR ACCEPTANCE,
UNCONDITIONAL LOVE,
AND BLISS

[NOTE: In Absolute Truth there is no need to "clear the mind" for there really is no such entity as "mind"; there is no "thing" to be accepted or rejected; what is called "mind" is only a concept, a record of past experiences that once appeared or occurred in consciousness, pertaining to the body and self-image and its apparent adventures in time and space which are mere concepts. All is the Self, I AM, pure Awareness, the One Reality shining in this infinite, eternal NOW, or this present moment. Some processes in this section (as are a few others in the book) are for those still identified with the body-mind as being the "self" and still perceiving the world as having solid objective reality independent of simple consciousness or Awareness.

[In like manner, there is no past to be revised nor future in which to improve or be improved. There is only the pure Awareness of Being, the one Self and only Reality shining in this Moment, in this infinite and eternal Presence, this Omnipresence, Omnipotence and Omniscience that is Real God.]

DIRECT UNDERSTANDING OF THE MIND

IT IS BETTER TO UNDERSTAND and transcend the mind, than to use it to create *philosophy* about it. Most ordinary seekers of Truth are gathering all sorts of philosophical concepts *about* the mind. These concepts then become the mind's very strategy against being *actually seen* and *understood*.

Closely observe the mind. Learn to *understand* it rather than continually unconsciously using or indulging in it to build elaborate belief systems about how you "think" it works. Observing it *from* pure Awareness, directly see its strategy, its apparent mechanism. This is the only significant spiritual work to be done. Everything else is only commentary or propaganda created by the mind itself.

Basically, the mind is a reflection, a pattern of intelligence-energy; it is an image in consciousness of the pure Awareness of the Self, being an accumulated record of experiences undergone by the Self (or pure Intelligence-energy) in the meditation of a "separate-self-identity" apparently living in time and space. It is identified with the form of the physical body, its own "personally" created and functional vehicle dwelling in time and space. It is an apparent reference point, a seeming center or starting point in consciousness, which in fact has no center, no originating point in itself. This false notion is due to its identification with the body as being the "self."

You can see this (it reveals itself) when, by Self-Inquiry or by effective meditation on the Self or pure I AMness, you significantly slow down the mind and its activity of thinking. Eventually you stop the mind from its perpetual movement in time and space by continuously and successfully holding it in the present moment. Then you may have *direct insight* into the pure Self, ever abiding *prior* to the mind or thought, and from which the self-image appears to rise. From this vantage you can actually observe the working of the mind. In Truth, the pure Self is always, already present, *as it is*, prior to the mind.

Even though the Self is like the nature of space, being indiscernible, it in truth exists as pure, uncaused, unqualified, infinite and eternal Awareness, the very consciousness in which everything appears. Only from this prior "location" of pure Awareness, or pure Being, can we "perceive," "know" or understand the mind that records all that is occurring, or appearing in the consciousness of time and space.

More simply stated (or hopefully so): Mind is thought. The movement of mind is thinking. Prior to the mind and its thoughts is this pure Conscious Awareness, independent of the thinking process. When the mind actually stops (by intentionally slowing it down until there is not the least ripple of thought and it is no longer actively "showing" itself), you may realize the prior pure Awareness or true Self radiating in or as the Heart of Being. This is Awakening to the light-radiance of Eternal Being as the quality of pure Consciousness. It is the very Being of pure Existence, the Supreme Self of all selves, which is real God. This High Place is the only vantage point from which genuine insight and true understanding of the mind and its apparent functioning is "knowable."

The purpose and function of the mind is the survival of itself: that is, the survival of the so-called entity, the seemingly separate individual self (which is one's ego or body-mind identification) and everything with which the ego has become identified – meaning this seeming individual self or entity and its body, its vehicle for continued life or intentional expression as an entity, a "person," an ego-self in this dimension.

This configuration is not directly known or even knowable from the realm of the body or the ego-mind itself, just as a wave cannot know itself as being the ocean.

However (in a manner of speaking) it is *already* known *in* and *from* the Heart. How and why? Very simply, the Spiritual Heart *is* the Self and the mind apparently dwelling in it is *already known* as the ever-radiant sense of "I." This "I" being one-with I AM makes Awakening to this dream of mortality (or time and space) possible by the *consistent practice* of Self-inquiry – i.e., *with each and every arising thought* as already explained and instructed in this book. However, it is the only way that it can "happen." Great and benevolent is the grace of Bhagavan Sri Ramana Maharshi for sharing this tremendous boon with those ready, willing and *capable of hearing it!*

A PROCESS FOR REVISING THE PAST
(OR FORGIVENESS OF SINS)

ACH NIGHT BEFORE YOU GO TO SLEEP, it is *very beneficial* to "revise" all the negative events that occurred during the day. This frees your mind of all negativity *before* you go to sleep. You will sleep better, your dreams (if any) will be fewer and more pleasant, and you will feel more rested and rejuvenated from your sleep. More important, it creates a happier daily life and a more positive "future" for you. This is briefly or partially explained on page 151.

[NOTE: In Absolute Truth there is no past to be revised or future to improve. There is only the pure Awareness of Being, the one Self and only Reality shining in this infinite and eternal present moment, which is NOW. However, if you are still identified with the body-mind and stuck in this habitual configuration as being "real," this process may assist you in getting free of conditioned patterns of limitation and suffering.]

Sit quietly with eyes closed and body relaxed. Sit in an easy chair or on the side of your bed. *But be alert and careful not to go to sleep before completing the process.*

Recall to mind the last event occurring just before sitting down. Then the event just prior to that, and the event just prior to that one, and so on back throughout the entire day. It is easier in this way to recall the last thing you did, since it is more recent than the previous or earlier events and is linked to *each* previous event back through the day. The process is to "play your day backwards" as though the day's events are on motion picture film and you are the editor viewing "the film" of your day in order to edit it.

While running the "film" of the day backwards, when you come to some event that was not agreeable or was negative or upsetting, one you would prefer to have been more pleasing or positive, mentally "tag" that scene or event as one to come back to later for its revision. Don't get caught up in it at this point – just "tag" it for later. Continue going backwards to the next prior event, then the next, etc. (mentally tagging those needing revision) until you come to the start of your day.

Also, if you wish, mentally "note" and tag the pleasant and happy events for recalling and enjoying later. The primary purpose of this part of the process is to play the day backwards and tag pleasant and unpleasant events for later replay.

Also, playing the day backwards has the added benefit of loosening and releasing the mind's attachment to body-mind identification and past conditioning (the self-image) and thus easing the effect these have on concealing the true Self.

On arriving at where you woke up and started the day, now start "playing the film" forward. Quickly run the day forward but don't get caught in any of the scenes; just scan them quickly. When getting to a scene you tagged as a positive event, you may wish to briefly relive and partake fully of its joy being grateful for it. If it was a negative event, recreate that event in your consciousness as though it had occurred *the way you would have wanted or preferred*, with *everyone concerned* being happy and benefited as a true "win-win" situation!

Hold in consciousness how it would feel if *everyone* concerned *was* happy and in agreement with you and everyone else involved. Even though the event didn't *actually* occur that way, imagine that *it did* and how you would feel *if it had*. Hold and repeat the scene in your mind until you have a good strong feeling about it. Firmly imagine it the way it would be *if it were actually positive*. Then continue forward to the next tagged event. Revise it also the same way. If it was positive, briefly play and enjoy it again, as explained above.

In this manner, *replay the* entire *day in consciousness*. "Relive" the positive scenes, briefly enjoying them, and *revise* the negative scenes until they feel *naturally positive and complete* – with *everyone* involved winning and happily benefiting in his or her own way.

Then before going to sleep, meditate and retire in the pure Awareness and simple feeling of just being I AM. Make sure that your consciousness is clear and complete regarding all the events of the day. Always go to sleep feeling complete and contented. If there is anything disturbing in your consciousness, use this revision process to clear it before going to sleep.

Never go to sleep with troubling thoughts or emotions; clear them before you retire.

Use this same revision technique as a "forgiveness process" to clear and complete any and all negative, regretful thoughts, feelings, actions perpetrated and attitudes remembered from the distant past, including all your former relationships or associations. It doesn't matter how long ago an event occurred or how disturbing it was, if it is still remembered in the mind it can be revised. Just as it doesn't matter how long ago an audio or videocassette recording was made, it can be erased at anytime and easily recorded over it by placing it in a recorder and putting another message over the old one. Likewise, this process will work similarly for playing over a mind record. Just awaken the feeling in consciousness of *what is truly wanted* or *preferred* by repeating it *until it feels natural and OK* – and *as now being so* – and it is thereby revised in the mind.

When this process is used *correctly*, it is very effective for releasing *all* past wrongs or believed wrongs – regardless of to whom they occurred, by whom they were committed or when, even if the "other person" is no longer available to either *receive or give* forgiveness or personally accept *your* forgiveness.

Your real Self, being pure Consciousness, is the Source and Cause of your experiences. This process can and will remove the pain, suffering or regret from consciousness and free everyone, including yourself, from its crippling effect. Even if the person in question is no longer living (such as a parent, relative, close friend, or even an enemy or adversary), this process will work to give the mind closure, i.e., bring about peace, completion, release and freedom.

Here is one final and important point: The fact is there is *no* past, it does not exist except as a thought or concept or memory, and the memory of a thing is not that thing. Then to continue thinking about "what occurred in the past," is the *one* and *only* reason for its *seeming* existence, or for the upsets believed to be "coming from the past." Just consider this: Is there any past if you didn't think about it? Then why think about it? Simply don't think about it and there is no longer any disturbance or upset from there. How can there be? *It does not exist!*

CONSCIOUSLY DEALING WITH ANGER AND RESENTMENT

A NGER IS THE FEELING OF SUBTLE OR STRONG dissatisfaction or displeasure directed toward another person or situation, or even oneself. It is measured by the degree of its intensity, being a feeling of antagonism toward some believed wrong or "wrongdoer," usually for some felt injury or loss occurring against someone. Or, the anger may be toward yourself for some wrong attitude or action expressed by you toward another person. To "anger," as a verb, is to enrage: to *make* angry, to intentionally cause another person displeasure.

To want someone else to suffer or feel displeasure is the intention to harm. This is an evil intention, especially if it is arbitrary, that is, *not* acting in defense of either yourself, a friend, or loved one, to avoid harm occurring to you or them. If the intent to do harm is directed toward the would be evil perpetrator *after* the evil event is passed (even if it is believed to be justified), it still falls into the category of a wrong intention or action, since it is thinking and acting in retaliation. Angry actions can or will bring about the equivalent or even a greater degree of evil, loss, difficulty or trouble in the life or experience of the one intentionally perpetrating the action.

All of this about "angry actions" and their consequences is *of course* very basic and is probably (or should be) known by everyone. What is *not* usually known, or realized however (or in all probability), is that even if the anger is seen to be caused by another person, it really actually stems from the *prior* false sense or belief that the so-called "victim" is himself "separate" from the Source of being, the One Reality, or Self. It is coming from a believed reference point in consciousness felt as "*this seeming individual self*" or "*me*," which is in fact the ego.

This subtle feeling of anger or resentment *is always, already present* – without any other outside effort or outer cause – because of this false inner sense of being an "entity" or "person" "*cut off from God*," the Source. In our spiritual ignorance, we are continually meditating a separate-self-existence or identity.

This really means that the intention to "do harm" to anyone, which is in fact a thought-feeling of "non-love," is actually coming from the prior wish to get free from, to end, remove, to react against, or destroy what now is unconsciously and wrongly felt to be the "outer cause" of this primal discomfort. It is the mistaken belief that the actual discomfort (felt inside due to this body-mind identification) is an action that is going on *outside* oneself. It is projecting onto something or someone else the false belief that "it" is, or "they" are threatening or harmfully disturbing "me," or "my" well-being.

So ordinarily, conceptually, the intention to do harm to another is the wish to retaliate, remove, or destroy what is believed and blamed for having caused harm to oneself, or believed to be threatening to or intending to threaten oneself. It is a form of "getting even with" *what is believed to have brought us harm* – what we hate or don't like, *which is entirely conceptual*. In some cases it is taken to the extreme desire, the intention to kill.

We don't realize that what is hated is actually *within our own consciousness* and is due to *our own mind* – being in the first place a result of our misidentification with the body-mind as being our "self." Then, as we willfully *desire* that loss, pain or suffering befall a seeming "other person," (which in truth is only an extension of our *very self*), we are *unknowingly* magnifying and prolonging our own suffering. We are *unconsciously,* ignorantly, indulging in hatred, continued discomfort, and non-acceptance *of our very self.* We are blocking our own ability to experience real and lasting love and happiness.

What happens is we unconsciously and unknowingly punish ourselves. We do not allow ourselves the feeling of being worthy, of being capable of accepting and receiving love and happiness. We do not allow the feeling of lasting peace, prosperity, or good health into our awareness, or the lasting enjoyment of these qualities when they *do* happen to occur momentarily. We unconsciously block our own creative abilities and/or accomplishments. When we fail at something that we want, or have long desired, or see one of our faults, we blow it out of proportion and are unable to forgive ourselves and accept the failure or fault. Instead we feel incapable, helpless, frustrated, guilty, fearful, unloved, upset, unhappy and resentful. We feel suspicious of other people and their intentions, even when they really *want* to help us or make our lives easier or more comfortable.

Anger is the sensation of inflammation in the body felt in the brain and central nervous system or radiating in the spine or focused in the "gut" (solar plexus) and extending throughout the body. It is accompanied by the increased sense of bondage and limitation felt like a knot in the body, much like when you crimp a water-hose to stop or restrict the flow of water passing through it. It is a pinching or tightening up of the contraction of body-mind identification intensifying its sense of restriction or limitation and sense of suffering. It is a scorching sensation *plus* the anguish of being bound. It is like being "tied to and burned at the stake."

So, when the sense of anger is projected – as being caused by someone outside oneself – it is felt like "they" are burning "me," inflaming "me," binding "me." But it is what *you* are *doing to yourself,* and within yourself.

The added reaction occurring in the ordinary person is *resentment,* often with a corresponding thought of *revenge,* the desire to cause "them" injury, suffering or grief to the same extent or worse, as their deserved "punishment." The "other" may be either intentionally accosted, or deliberately isolated and avoided, with strong resentment attached to the action.

When observed with or from conscious insight, anger is the direct experience of one's feeling of separateness, of being cut off from the love of God. Anger is "hell" because it is the primary cause of the "fall of man" from the natural state, the peace, love and joy of the true Self. One who is angry or easily angered has *already* "fallen from grace" which, as biblically stated, "is cast into *Gehenna,* or hell." (Luke 12:5) He will feel this for as long as he continues in this sense of separation from the Source – from love of Self (God) and fellowman.

Forgiveness is the direct way of "return" to the Self – i.e., back into peace, freedom, love, and joy. Otherwise, resentment usually turns to wrath. Desire to do injury or harm to another, to the one who "causes" you injury, even if reciprocal or seemingly justified, only plunges you, the angry perpetrator, into deeper, prolonged unhappiness. There are no winners in the foul game of "getting even."

Absolute or total acceptance is the *one and only way of release.* You cannot "arrive" at this state of true peace, freedom and love by *trying* to "change things" or change "what's so." And certainly "getting even" is a far cry from acceptance.

Any sense of *wanting to* "change what is" implies that *what is, is* either disagreeable or unacceptable the way it is. Instead of "trying to change what is," *completely releasing* or letting go of any and all sense of "wanting" or "trying" is the *key* to ending the dilemma of acceptance. When all sense of "trying" or "wanting" is gone, you are *already there* in the natural state of acceptance. In order to allow what's so to be *truly* accepted – *as it is!* – simply drop all resistance to it, all thoughts, tendencies or reactions surrounding it.

And in this regard, acceptance is *not* "toleration," nor is it "putting up with." Rather, it means *no longer being angry* or being at the effect of the situation (or what's so) *in any way.* It is total, unconditional love, felt and expressed toward everyone involved in the situation, both now and in the past.

This entire process of anger and resentment is the avoidance of relationship with real God and the denial of the Truth. It is the refusal to take responsibility for being the very cause of anger or resentment, which is the meditation of being a separate entity, and remaining stuck or identified with this false position in consciousness.

* * * * *

In Truth, the actual cause of the feelings of emotion (any emotion or any reaction to what is occurring) is not outside the Self, or "myself," but is entirely in *me* and is *mine.* Refusal to accept this Truth, or "my" ignorance of it, is the "fall" from alignment with the true and natural flow of events *as they are occurring in the moment.* Anger is always self-centered and self-caused as there is actually nothing "outside" the Self to cause anger.

There is no upset in *any* event. Upset is projected or "taken to" the event by the one *feeling* the upset. The mind reacted angrily to the event by maintaining a position that is in opposition to the situation, or to the "person," or to "his" position. Then, defending the strong sense of being "right" in the position the mind is holding, or maintaining, it has forced or reinforced the opposition to "my" mind's position and this has caused anger. It *always* begins and ends in "me," or the "self" I *think* I am. Even the so-called "other person" and the event are appearing in the one Self, and are merely a reflection in Consciousness, or I AM.

*   *   *   *   *

In truth, all angry "people" want the same thing – freedom or peace. However, in their ignorance they inflict all sorts of misery on themselves and others, creating their own sense of anger, bondage, and the tendency to cause anger, thus even further binding themselves in or by their separation. It is much like the ignorance of an unruly animal tethered to a pole that, while angrily trying to free itself, only binds itself tighter to the pole.

As we awaken to the spiritual Heart, anger is replaced by humor and compassion, which loosens the knot of contraction and frees us from the qualities of the "lower self-nature" that reinforce the sense of being restrained and bound. On Awakening, we are capable of love and forgiveness to one and all alike. Being compassion, we take no offense at another's anger but allow him or her the space to "be angry" without feeling criticism or projecting a sense of wrong. By fully accepting and approving of everyone even as they continue caught in their anger, any remaining tendencies of anger in the mind are dissolved, leaving inner peace and love as our natural state, and manifesting in our life and affairs. This is felt as deep bliss in the whole body being.

When we dissolve anger and any tendency to wish another person grief or suffering (i.e., when these qualities are no longer present in us, and are not even capable of being activated), we are now Living Free in the Heart. Then our very presence is healing to the environment and to one and all appearing in the space of our environment.

A PROCESS FOR REVISING OR RELEASING ANGER

WHEN EXPERIENCING SOMETHING causing me anger, the process for consciously dealing with it is to FIRST *accept the fact that "I" am angry*. Denial only prolongs the suffering. Telling the truth to myself is *accepting* anger as being *what's so* in the moment, and as my present experience. Also, I accept *myself* in the moment of anger. I love myself *and* accept that *I am the cause of my anger*, for it is *in me*, not in the event itself, or in the other person even if they too are angry. Their anger is "theirs," and my anger is "mine." It is "*my*" anger even if it is triggered off by another person.

Anger is the result of me *first* holding a position that "I am a separate individual." Then it is the position that *I* am "right" and the *other person* or *event* is "wrong." It is due to *my position* that what the other person did or didn't do was in opposition to "me" or "my position" and is "*not right*." I may feel quite justified in my present position and have "the entire world's" agreement that *I* am "right" and *they* are "wrong." But *my* "being right" is no consolation or solution to the resulting suffering. It is *in fact* a dried up ointment for the wound of anger, which is *actually* an irritant rather than a healing balm.

I can be free of the suffering *only* when I accept that the anger is coming from *my own position*, established by *my own past actions and experiences*, and enforced by my *present* emotional demands or preferences, or how "I" think it *should be now*. When I am at least *willing to accept* that the upset is due to my own conditioning, and is out of my forgotten past, I can experience an inner release of tension, and the anger be transformed into compassion. I *must* be *willing* to consciously process my anger *in this manner!* I need to admit that I have done or said things in the past, perhaps of the same or similar nature, that caused someone else to be upset. So I need to be willing *now* to forgive my perceived offender for being *no different from me*, and to *forgive* him and myself for being upset.

* * * * *

Then, if appropriate (meaning it will not further inflame or cause a negative reaction in the other person), openly communicate with the one with whom there is anger, *taking full responsibility* for your anger as *being yours, or in you.* You say to the other person, "What you said (or did), *I let cause me* to be angry. I accept that the anger is *mine,* that *it is going on in me* and *not* in what you said or did. I *am* having to deal with the anger *in me in reaction to what was said or done,* and I just want you to know what I am feeling; but, I am not blaming you."

You explain your anger about what they have done or said – *without making him or her wrong in the situation!* The anger is *in you,* and *not* in the situation. So, *you* take responsibility for it being *in you* by being open and honest about it and *not projecting it* onto the other person or persons. You *don't lie about it* – i.e., feeling anger but *saying* you are *not* angry. *You tell the truth about it!* This process is both for *not* causing them more upset or anger, and relieving the anger *for both of you.* If the situation is still tense, and the other person's emotions are still strained, so that approaching him or her soon after the incident will only trigger further reaction, then wait for the situation to cool down before going to him or her in this manner.

Understand *both* the principle and the truth here and in *every* situation like this: *There is no upset in **any** event or in what a person says or does to you!* The upset is in *you,* as *your mind's reaction* to what is said or done. It is *you* that "takes the upset *to the event.*" It does not come into you "from out of the event."

Get it! The upset (or potential to be upset) was *already there in you,* in your conditioned past. This event has nothing to do with your already conditioned past. *Also, get it:* If the upset were in the event, then *everyone* conscious of the same event would be upset *in the same way* by the event, not one person feeling one way and another feeling another way about it. This is *never* the case, however. In *any* event in which people are upset, there are often different positions or points of view about what is going on. And it is the position or point of view *each one* is taking or holding that triggers or brings up the feelings of "OK" or "not OK" with regard to the event. The anger *is in the persons involved,* NOT in the event. The event is like a switch that turns on a light. The light is *not* in the switch but is in the light-bulb. The "bulb" of anger is in *each person feeling it,* not in the switch, not in the event.

When you are responsible for your anger and tell the truth about it, that it is *actually* coming out of your *conditioned past* – chances are it has very little to do with the present event – the resulting experience of release is very healing to *both yourself and to the world.* And, eventually, all would-be angering experiences are automatically transformed, averted or neutralized without any further effort from you. They just don't come up in the mind or your world. Or if some event *does* arise that would have upset you in the past, you now feel compassion for all persons involved, rather than anger, and you are able to lend a balancing and harmonizing influence to the situation.

Just a word about "hurt" feelings. Hurt feelings are often the result of someone being unable to openly express his or her anger, so anger is shifted or subjugated into the feeling of hurt. Perhaps you as a child (or the person) was not allowed or given the space to be openly angry. The upset was then expressed as the feeling of hurt, that being a *more acceptable* or *agreeable* emotion to those around him, one he was at the time *allowed* to feel *inside* without showing or expressing it outside. Or, you (or the person) may have felt it was wrong or inappropriate to be angry *at* the person who triggered the upset. Yet, the anger was there, only transposed or subjugated into the more "acceptable" emotion or the "allowed" feeling of hurt whenever anger arose. Either way, really look at the sense of hurt or upset and "get it." *It is your own feeling.* It is not in the current situation or in the actions of the one who is apparently causing the feeling in you. *You* are the one causing it *in you.* Inquire, "Whose upset is this?" Feel the "I" or "me" that is feeling the upset. Trace this "I"-feeling inward to the Source, the Heart. Somewhere along the way in the Inquiry, the upset *itself* (regardless of its type or nature) will subside, leaving only the "I"-sense. Continue to trace the "I"-sense inward to its origin or its Source, and it too will eventually subside or disappear, leaving only the clear space of pure Awareness, the true Self. Do this with *all* thoughts and feelings.

There is no reason or need to further hold the feeling of hurt or *any* upsetting thoughts. Dissolve such feelings with this simple yet powerful process, which is pure Self-Inquiry!

This is the Enlightened Way, the Way of Happiness-NOW!

HUMILITY

HUMILITY IS MOST BENEFICIAL, *even necessary* for true, radical or in-depth understanding of a subject or situation.   One cannot perceive the subtleties of *true* spirituality, or effectively live or apply its fine-tuned revelations without having or acquiring simple, genuine humility. Humility is surrendering all sense of intellectual knowing or "already knowing" and the so-called "knowing self" to the *open honesty* of *not* knowing.   Humility is *not-knowing*; it is knowing or confessing that "I really *don't* know." It is "teachability." It is true Wisdom. This opens the door of Intuition.

To read or hear this message while thinking, *"I already know this,"* is not allowing you to actually, *fully* comprehend it, to *truly* hear it or *really* know it. Instead, it is knowing or hearing only the past, your concepts and beliefs, your conditioned mind's earlier programming. You are listening to your mind and ego tell you what *it* knows, which is *not* knowing what is *now* being presented or offered; rather it is your opinion, your concept or belief *about* it. If there is a sense of "I" that is thinking or "knowing" this, then such so-called knowledge is based entirely on the past, not on this *here* and *now* communication. This is a very subtle point of fine-tuned precision, or veracity.

Humility is being open and receptive to what is occurring or being offered, without the inclination to debate, defend, enforce or change it with *one's own* position or point of view about it, with one's accumulated concepts, beliefs, opinions or theories of the past. It is to be open and receptive to what is *presently so*, without trying to adapt or interpret it to some "other" preconceived notion, standard of belief, or theory held about it – either for or against it. Humility is holding *no position* with regard to what is presently occurring or being presented, but is being open and allowing it to occur or be presented in its own natural way, *as it is.*

*   *   *   *   *

How often have I sought the advice of others when I have

been confused, troubled, upset or suffering? And then, when they suggest letting go of something in order to be free of dilemma, I *defend* the very position I am holding that is causing my upset? This is not humility, but arrogance, or defending "my" position and need or desire to "look good" or "be right."

When asking another person for guidance or advice, if I am not *already willing* to admit *that I don't know,* or that what I know *is not adequate or sufficient,* do I listen to the advice I requested, or continually weigh and evaluate what is being offered against my own concepts, ideas and beliefs of the past?

I must be willing to admit that my present knowledge or beliefs are insufficient, inadequate, or incapable; or otherwise I would not need to ask another for advice.

Of course, it is wisdom to ask for advice from someone with more practical knowledge or experience of a situation than myself; but it is wiser still to know just *who* to ask, that is, the one that can be trusted, as to their accuracy and integrity, with regard to any advice given on an important issue or situation.

In the long run, humility (or the openness of "not-knowing") may reveal just who I am able to trust, for true humility is very close to the Self, or the Highest Wisdom. It often draws to the one seeking advice those who are honest, trustworthy and genuinely helpful. This comes from the grace of the Self, the spiritual Heart shining as the Source of being. It even reveals on the surface what is needed, when humility is genuine.

People are usually much more interested in "being right" than in really learning or hearing the truth, or *what's so* regarding a thing, event, situation, or issue. This is the usual, ordinary strategy of the ego-mind with its conditioned content of mental patterns of the past, which ceaselessly functions to assure and maintain its own survival and the survival of everything with which it has become identified.

This means one must be willing to release or reject the mind's beliefs of the past, and even eventually let go of the mind itself in order to know the Highest Truth, the pure Awareness of the very Self now shining as the Heart of Being.

GETTING CLEAR OF OPPOSITION
IN RELATIONSHIPS

WHEN YOU FIND YOURSELF STUCK in a position, in conflict with another person's position, here is a simple process for getting free and clear of opposition. *First,* try to establish with the person a mutual agreement *to be in accord* – that is, that you *both* would like to *agree* and be mutually clear and free of upset in the matter.

Then communicate with the person by asking questions that he or she *can easily answer;* do not make assertions he or she would be inclined to feel need defending, or that make him wrong. The purpose of your questions should be to help you *truly* determine and actually *understand* his position, to see the actual *basis* for the current point(s) of view he has, or is holding and defending in the present dispute or difference of opinion between you. Your attempts to learn and *truly understand* his position must be *genuine.* That is, *not* be coming from a feeling in you that he or she "is wrong." Your questions should be coming from your *honest* wish to know and understand *why* he is thinking and feeling the way he does. Ask questions you feel *truly* convey and *confirm his* point of view. In this way, you avoid taking a position that would only create an opposing position, a position which if he took it would make him wrong in your perception.

After all, if you *truly* wish to *have agreement,* then it is *what* is right rather *who* is right, that really matters. So, allow the other person to "be right" by you never taking an obvious opposing position and insisting on *its* rightness. If you cannot be right without making him or her wrong, then allow him at least to *feel* right, and *you both win.*

Say, "Yes, I can see that from your position this is the way it appears to be. If that was also *my position,* I can see that it is the way I too would see it. But, from my position, it appears quite differently. So, from our different perspectives we are *both* right as to how we are each now seeing it. Now, if either of us changed our positions only a little bit, things would appear quite differently. I am willing to consider a compromise?"

Then look and see if you *really* are. Are you? You must be, in order to bring *true* harmony.

If you are stuck with someone in a position/opposition stalemate and if you *both* would *really* like to be free and clear about it, then a helpful option is to be willing to do a conscious "role reversal" process. Actually exchange positions and *each* argue *from the other's* position *against* your own position, letting it temporarily become your "current" position. Play this out *genuinely* until you are clear enough to take *both* positions equally well, and to see them both with *equal clarity*.

Now you will both be unstuck and be flowing in a clear space, the Heart – in agreement, cooperation and love.

Of course, if either of you is stuck in the position of "being right," then you will not be willing to even consider this "role reversal." It will reveal that you are "more stuck" in your position and insisting on "being right" than *being happy, free and clear*. Remember, to one who is *not* stuck, *what's* "right" is of more importance than *who* is right and insisting on "being right."

If a person is willing, do this process each time you are stuck with someone whose position is in opposition to yours. If not, then attempt to move into his or her shoes, or position, and see the situation from where he or she is seeing it. This is the purpose of asking him questions, as explained. If he is unwilling to play the Role Reversal process with you, just *"agree with your adversary quickly, while you are in the way with him,"* as Jesus said. (Matthew 5:25) Let the other person "be right" without argument and you *both* win. *You* win in your *understanding* and living the Truth regarding "positions and oppositions"; he "wins" what he *thinks* is "an argument." Jesus said, *"What does it profit a man to win the whole world and lose his soul* (his peace of mind, true being, or higher nature)?" (Matthew 16:26)

He might even think you are weak, because you won't or don't *"get* mad," and apparently "loose face" in surrendering your position. However, *he* is actually weak for *"getting* mad," and for "remaining stuck" in the dream, and the childish argument of "right and wrong." You are actually being *truly* "mad" – i.e., unreasonably happy, and *not at effect* – by *consciously staying contented, free* and *clear* in the face of what is otherwise apparently upsetting conditions or circumstances. This is living in the humor and compassion or always being able to live free and clear of upset.

You are living free in the Heart as the Heart, with no positions *for* or *against* anyone or anything, which is unconditional love and acceptance of what's so, just as it is, without upset.

By willingly moving into such a state of mental clarity, you can go beyond any condition of a stalemate. By taking and holding no position in opposition or disagreement with another, simply being willing to totally release your position or adjust it slightly into alignment with the another person or his or her position, you can always be more cooperative, that is more in alignment with, or in support of all seeming "others," where they are not made to feel "wrong," and with you also being "not wrong."

When you establish or develop a sense of agreement with regard to having a common or more positive "intention or purpose" with your otherwise would be "adversary," you may very well bring peace between you. Thus you are able to mutually support any issue at hand, which is far better than both of you walking away from what is or could be an opportunity to benefit not only *each other*, but the world in general, and perhaps an entire group, or a special endeavor in which you both truly belong and have something worthwhile to contribute.

GOD'S PRESENT LOVE

IF GOD IS NOT LOVING ONE AND ALL *RIGHT NOW,* in this present moment, then God has never loved, nor will He ever love "me" or any "other" being or person. The Truth is, God *is* love, *itself.* Therefore, God is *always* loving. Otherwise, God would have to cease being Himself (which is absurd). That which is the Truth is not true one moment and untrue the next. Truth is *ever* true, *eternally* true, even NOW. Facts change but not the Truth. And the Truth is, God *is* Love. Therefore, He is loving *"me"* and *"everyone"* NOW, even when we appear to be wicked, naughty, mean, ugly and unlovable.

It may be a fact that it is very difficult for "me" to accept another "person" as he or she is presenting or expressing himself or herself in a given moment or situation. However, the person's behavior does not in the least affect God's love and acceptance of "him." My understanding and acceptance of this fact (which is the Truth) will set me free from guilt about my own unloving, unlovely and unlovable attitudes, actions and behavior of the past.

It is important that "I" accept that no matter how unloving, unlovely or unlovable "I" or "anyone" else may ever be, God is *always* loving – even here and now – and when "we" least "deserve" it, or expect it!

GET THIS: The paradox of God's Love is His pure Presence, which is the very *sense* of Presence *itself.* God's Presence is the *here* and *now* sense of Presence, which is simply the state of *our own* pure presence, without or beyond thought. It is our being present NOW *as* pure Being, or pure Consciousness. It is abiding in the Power and *pure sense* of NOW – meaning *this moment, this instant!* In fact, there is no separate-self or "person."

When we abide *as* the thoughtless Awareness of pure Being *in this here-and-now instant moment* – ever prior to (or beyond) time and space, free of or transcending past and future – we are abiding in what is in fact the Realm of Love, which *is* True and Real God. So, the Truth is, God is *ever present* as pure Love itself, *in this instant.*

A LOVE PROCESS

I ACCEPT THAT GOD (the Source, the Creative Cause, the Supreme Absolute Being, Very Truth, Very Reality, the Very Self of Real-God) loves "me" and unconditionally accepts "me" and approves of "me" *this very moment,* just as I am. *(And remember, there is not separate-self needing love.)*

I receive confirmation of True Love and the One Reality as I willingly release and let go of the past with all its concepts of right and wrong, truth and non-truth. I now release the past and its concepts – all opinions, beliefs, memories of good and bad, right and wrong, pleasure and pain, desires unfulfilled – and rest in the present-now-acceptance that God, the One Reality and Divine Being, loves and approves of "me" just as I am.

I am willingly and joyously glad that God loves and accepts *everyone* just as they are. Since this is the Truth – that God, being Love Itself, must eternally love *everyone* and *everything* – if I see myself or anyone as being undeserving of love this is *my own ignorance,* and I now release that ignorance. I now accept the Truth that God loves all beings and myself *equally.* I now realize God *always* loves *unconditionally* even those I have not considered worthy of love. Therefore, I cease withholding my acceptance and approval of anyone and allow God's love to be felt in me, to totally fill me and everyone with His present-moment Radiance in the Heart of my Heart. I allow it to be my experience NOW – strongly felt in the right center of my chest radiating *with fullness* to everyone. I rest in the Radiance of the Heart. I rest in Love.

I consciously realize that this personal connection with God, the Supreme Being radiating in the Heart as I AM, is steady, certain and strong enough to supply all needs and comforts, to solve all problems and fill "me" with everlasting love, peace, safety, security and happiness – *which now radiates to Infinity.*

From this Conscious Awareness of Oneness with God, I radiate the Light of this realization to all parts of "my" being. I radiate the Light-Energy of Love to all beings everywhere, to all places, and to all things. All persons, places and things rest in the Light and Love of the Heart (I AM) and all beings receive, share, and exchange this Love as Peace and Joy.

I see no offense, receive no offense nor intentionally give offense to anyone. I accept, love and receive all beings equally in the Heart of "my" heart. That which is harmful or hurtful to anyone is here and now released, once and for all, and I rest in the Power, Presence and Protection of the Radiant Heart that, like the Sun, is never touched by anything or anyone on the earth, yet gives light and life to all.

I release all judgment and criticism and forgive everyone and everything that has ever caused pain and upset in my life; and I forgive myself for all my ignorance and unloving ways.

With love and forgiveness I release all past wrongs and create a Clear Space that allows for all people to come and go in Peace, Freedom and Joy as I accept them just as they are.

From this Clear Space of Unconditional Love and Acceptance, I witness life's events with Humor and Compassion, allowing all "people" to be themselves and express themselves with no projected or identified thoughts or feelings of resentment, envy, jealousy, anger or criticism.

This Clear Space now allows total acceptance of life *just as it is*. As I accept what's so, I am at peace with all that arises or appears. And if it should happen that life presents me with unfriendly or uninvited pain-producing experiences, I am capable of quickly clearing the space to allow for more agreeable things or experiences to occur in their place by loving and accepting *what's so* about those that are presently occurring. My resistance to what is happening only strengthens and prolongs its stay in my experience. My unconditional Love and Acceptance of what is occurring allows even the unfriendly events to pass freely on, without any resistance that would increase or prolong them.

When I am friendly to everyone and everything, everyone and everything is friendly to me, aiding me rather than harming, delaying or limiting me.

In this Openness of Acceptance and Love I am at Peace. I am Happy! I am Free!

A PROCESS FOR ABIDING IN GOD

(This is a Conscious Process. It is Consciousness speaking to Consciousness, not just data to read. Take time with every word, each of which is "pointing to" or indicating a "quality of being" and is not itself the main point. Take time to pause between the words and phrases in the quality of "pure Being" they indicate. Go slowly, allowing a full second for each word and the dots between words.)

ABIDING IN GOD..... IS ABIDING IN THAT..... Pure Consciousness..... which..... when scrutinized..... shows no duality..... not even in the form.....or the appearance.....of these various objects.....nor.....the least trace.....or sense.....of cause and effect.... It is abiding.....in the heart-felt Radiance.....which.....when the mind is absorbed in IT.....there is no thing..... no fear..... none at all..... No desire arises from the Heart..... for ..... in this quality..... all is seen as THAT.... the true Self..... and THAT.....is seen as ALL..... or Everything.

God.... the true Self.....is all.... The true Self... is God.... God .... the true Self.... is playing all the roles..... All are expressions of God.... God.....is seeking God..... It is God....Who questions ..... and..... God.....Who answers..... God is apparently forgetting.....His/Her own true nature.....and looking for....God.... It is God....who worships.....God..... It is God.....meditating.....on God.....and praying.....to God..... It is God..... apparently trying.....to find.....God..... This is the divine comedy.... or perhaps .... the apparent tradegy.... It is only a play.....

Since God is all selves.....and all selves.....are God.....then there is only.....One Self.....and THAT.....is the VERY SELF..... which is.....GOD! The name.....of the Very Self.....of God.....is recorded in scripture.....in Exodus 3:14-15.....as being...."I AM" ..... It refers to Selfhood.....as the very Existence.....of Existence Itself.... and..... which is always.... and forever..... "I AM"..... It says: "I AM is my name..... It has always been my name .....forever..... and it shall always be my name ..... unto all generations" .....which is forever ..... which is even now..... and now.... and Now..... AND NOW..... forever.... without end....

The heart-felt free feeling..... of simply being..... I AM..... as non-separate.....non-seeking.....Being..... is gently.....lovingly.....

and.... joyously.... resting.... and relaxing.... in This Light... of my own real nature.... is always.... already.... being filled ....with the peace.... security.... beauty.... love.... joy.... and abundance.... of all good things.... and good will.... for all mankind. For, all.... and everyone.... is God.... being Himself.... in me.... as me.... lived eternally.... and infinitely.... in this present moment.... and event.... and this present moment.... and event.... and this present moment.... and event.... and this present moment.... to infinity....

Jesus knew his Self....to be relatively....and absolutely....one-with....the Very Self....of God....which he called "Father".... and which.... he also knew.... all other beings.... to be. And.... as he taught.... and lived this truth.... being his conscious message.... and lived example.... he meant for.... the same understanding..... and acceptance.... and example.... of this truth.... to be awakened.... in all people.... he gave it to .... or shared it with. This was *everyone*.... and *is* everyone.... But.... as he also said, ..."only those with spiritual 'ears'.... can hear it.... and.... only those with spiritual 'eyes'.... can see it".... for themselves...

Others.... if they don't understand.... will criticize it.... and condemn it.... as Jesus also said. Even many so-called "Christians".... don't fully understand.... and so condemn this Truth.... by denying that Christ.... abides in the Heart of *all* beings..... as the very *Self* of all beings.... (Matthew 5:11).

This is how.... it has always been.... That God.... plays this game.... of "hide and seek".... with Himself.... of choosing the time.... and place.... and event.... in which He.... as a seeming individual.... and seeming separate-parts.... of Himself.... like "you and me".... becomes again.... consciously.... and eternally Awakened.... in the Heart.... Head.... and Body.... to the Very Truth.... of the Universal Oneness.... of Himself as All.... And as the Very Self.... of all selves.... including this Self.... which is "my" Self.... The First Person.... singular.... of *every* "one"....

"I am That I AM".... as realized by Moses.... And.... "I.... and the Father.... are One".... as realized by Jesus.... and shared by him....

Jesus' level of consciousness.... and quality of being... is the only true level.... and pure quality.... the "only begotten" example.... that I am to be.... and follow.... For I, too.... am One-with.... the Source.... the Father.... And I.... am the Son.... the Daughter.... a living expression of God.... the Supreme Self of all selves.   The Very Self.... or I AM.... is the Self.... we all are....

Yes.... I AM THAT I AM.... now.... and now.... and Now..... AND NOW.... to Infinity.... and Eternally....

There is neither "I".... nor "other-than-I".....there is..... ONLY.....

THE PARADOX OF LOVE

WHAT HAPPENS WHEN the unstoppable force meets the immovable object? The answer: the mind stops!

When always conscious *as* Consciousness, or only as pure Awareness *prior to* the mind, in which there is no separate one, no questioning "I" – no sense of "I," or "me," or a personal sense of "self" experiencing itself as an unknown and unknowing individual, an ignorant seeker of Truth – *you* are already "the absolute answer," the very Truth Itself.

The quality and/or nature of this understanding is bliss. If not yet already known and felt, awakening to and having *radical* Insight and Understanding of this pure Awareness allows intense release from the sense of bondage, which is body-mind identification. It may be simple release, or unspeakably exquisite contentment, peace and unfathomable satisfaction felt up and down the entire spine of the body. This total release from the sense of bondage or body-mind identification is also accompanied by the deep experience of forgiveness and unqualified acceptance of self. It is the radical experience of being OK, "just as I am," and with the world, just as it is.

This deep acceptance, felt analogously as the spiritual Heart on the *right* side of the center of the chest, is awakened to as the presence and experience of Love. It is deep, total Self-acceptance that only inclines to share or express its nature.

In the world of duality, all force creates or calls up its own opposition. Pure Love is uniquely the only force that does not intentionally set in motion its opposition. For love accepts even that which is different, opposite or unlike itself, or not itself. Love sees no difference. Love is the power of unformed, unqualified "undifferentiation," remaining formless, unqualified and undifferentiated. It is the unconditional remaining unconditioned. Absolute Love is remaining absolutely empty of even the slightest whisper of opinion against anything. It is accepting what is, *just as it is!*

Love is "being happy with." Love is the Absolute Power of the Absolute Truth. It is the Universal Fact that *all* is One, and there can never be a second or an "other."

Love lets the *seeming* "other" be right, for love needs no recognition from outside itself to be Itself. Eventually, love draws all that appears other than itself into itself, or into agreement with itself. Love is the Whole Spirit (Holy Spirit) of God shining as Pure Awareness and Intelligence in the Heart of all hearts of all beings.

Love is paradoxical. For how can there be a force that does not trigger or set its own opposition in motion? The law of material creation, as it is confirmed, is that "for every action there is an equal and opposite reaction." Or, by taking a position, any position, you automatically and necessarily create your own opposition. Love, therefore, is beyond all force.

We all can see in ordinary life how love and hate are apparent opposites. In duality – meaning "I" looking at "you" – this is the fact. We experience hate from or toward the same person we experience love from or toward. The object of our love often becomes the object of our hate, and vice versa. We see hateful acts done by loving people, and loving acts done by hateful people. This is the law of ordinary love in the world – it arises from duality.

However, in Absolute Love or Pure Unconditional Love, there is the Supreme Power that comes from surrender. Absolute "forcelessness" is absolute force. When we surrender totally and absolutely to the "force of life," becoming *entirely* free and clear of *all* preferences, the Absolute Love of God fulfills Itself *in us.* The force-field that was formerly generating or moving as separateness is now reversed, redirecting the outward flow of conscious force (that which seemed to separate us), back into the Spiritual Heart (Holy Spirit) thus revealing the Universal Oneness.

We experience this shift in magnetic force as a reversal on the field and ground of Being. Conscious force is refocused in the Heart *as* the Heart, from which it formerly had appeared to have "fallen with Adam and Eve, in the Garden of Eden." Now, it is again focused in, *as* and *from* the eternal Christ, it *being the very Self.* It is the Son of God, or it is Real-God expressing *in* all beings *as* all beings.

This is real Love, the true Nature of the Self.

WHAT DO YOU WORSHIP?

WORSHIP IS GIVING YOUR ATTENTION devotedly to an object, being, or thing. What do you worship? The more you give your attention to anything, the more you are worshipping it. How much time do you spend devoting your thought to the Source of being, or to God, or your oneness with God? How much time do you spend devoting your thinking to that which is fearful, negative, limiting, resentful, upsetting, etc.? The time you spend attending to your fears and miseries is your worship or devotion to misery and misfortune. This is not different from being in hell.

Hell is living in the sense of separateness, or of being cut off from God. It is the feeling of being separate from your good. This is symbolized in the Bible as being under the dominion or influence of the devil, which is actually living from the sense of ego, or the body-mind, as a separate entity apart from God. But this believed and felt notion is a lie. It is not the Truth. However, to continually think about the not-truth as being the truth is to worship the not-truth. Devoting your time, attention, thoughts and feelings to a thing is like worshipping it.

The second Commandment of Moses is, *"You shall not make for yourself any image of anything in the heavens above or the world beneath and worship it"* (paraphrased). This means you (or anyone) should not consider that which is formed or held in your mind as being "cause" in your life – that is, being the cause of either your happiness or your unhappiness.

One's chronic identification with the body-mind as being the Self, resulting in the sense of being separate from God and the assumed belief in the solid objective reality of this world, is the very activity and real meaning of "sin." It is the source and cause of all suffering, and gives rise to all thoughts and feelings, and to the strong mental concepts of lack or limitation. It is itself a violation of the second Commandment.

Two of AHAM's Seven Basic Truths™ (Numbers 3 & 4), which are principles of consciousness *in the world* are: *"What*

you think about grows!" and *"You become what you think about!"*
These two principles bring to mind or into existence the creative law of thought that enforces the Second Commandment.

AHAM Basic Truth number 2 is, *"Thoughts are things."*
Thus, to "see" or look at another as being "separate," "different" and "not-good" is to devote thought and feeling to the not-truth, and violates Jesus' great commandment of Love.

This means we should all follow the biblical injunctions:

> *Beloved, do not imitate evil, but imitate Good. He who does good is of God; he who does evil has not seen God. (3 John 11);*

and:

> *Finally, brethren, whatever is true, whatever is honorable, whatever is just, whatever is pure, whatever is lovely, whatever is gracious, if there is any excellence, if there is anything worthy of praise, think about these things. What you have learned and received and heard and seen in me, do; and the God of peace will be with you.* (Philippians 4: 8-9)

To give your attention *primarily* to the body-mind and the world, results in pain and suffering, and therefore is "evil" or "sin." To give your attention to the things and qualities mentioned in the above scripture is to worship God, or good.

AHAM's Seven Basic Truths™

1. Imagination creates reality. *(i.e., physical or worldly reality)*

2. Thoughts are things.

3. What you think about grows.

4. You become what you think about.

5. Your thoughts or assumptions form your world; therefore keep your mind on what you want, and *off* what you don't want.

6. You can change your world by reforming your assumptions.

7. If you cannot change a situation, you *can* change the effect it is having on you by changing your attitude or assumption about it; and, eventually, you may even be able to change the situation.

EGO – THE CONTENT OF CONSCIOUSNESS

SELF, THE TRUE BEING, ABIDES IN THE ETERNAL and infinite unknown. It is the unknowable Essence of Being, or Pure Being Itself, which is always unknowable as there is nothing outside the Self to "know" the Self. Thus, knowing the Self is simply *being* the Self.

Thought emanating from the mind is from the past, the formerly or previously identified "known." It can only speculate (by means of intellectual comparison) on the present moment, which is in itself unknown. So, thought itself can never know what *any* thing *really is*. Is-ness is always now, and thought is always from the past.

The thinking "I" or "self" (the ego) is itself an object in consciousness, and therefore is in fact not different from the content of consciousness. It being the content of consciousness, i.e., the mind, it perceives things now occurring that it wishes to change. This gives rise to conflict. What is now present is OK as it is, but the mind compares it with the past and wishes to change it to something better or different. The ego or mind looks at all things as separate or different and continues in its dilemma of desiring to change things into something else.

Division of consciousness into the sense of "I" and "other-than-I" ("I" and "not-I," or "self" and "world") is duality. This causes the feeling of isolation and dilemma; it is our *only* suffering. It motivates us to seek happiness in the world, as a relief from this already prior misery or sense of alienation. Identification with the mind and content of consciousness and forgetting that our true nature *is oneness with all that is*, is itself the sum and substance of what in the Bible is called "sin."

The only solution to this sin, or suffering, is realization and abidance in the Self. This is most directly accomplished by the process of Self-Inquiry – asking the question, "Who am I?" and tracing the "I"-thought back to the source from which it rises. On reaching the Source, or pure Awareness (which is the true Self), abide there, or dive deeply into this pure Being and remain in its infinite and eternal peace, freedom and joy.

SEEKING IS SUFFERING

SUFFERING IS THE SENSE OF "SELF" YOU FEEL as a separate individual. It is the very activity you feel in consciousness when *seeking, efforting, doing, going, defending,* etc., in your active, intentional *pursuit* of happiness. It is this very sense of "I," the *very* feeling of *being* the "doer" *by* the "doer" in the compulsive quest for more, better and different forms of experience. It is suffering, because the sense of "I" is itself a contrived state – of being separate or different from the true Self or from a desired object, goal, purpose or intention.

Your emotional need to achieve, accomplish, acquire, gain, improve, defend, etc., – all that goes with desire and ambition, which society ordinarily considers admirable, meaningful and preferable qualities and activities – is in fact the very activity of *avoidance* of the prior, actual Truth or Reality of your always, already *present* and *true* State of Being, which is natural order, balance, harmony, completion, peace, freedom and joy, or being an *already* good, *already* true, *already* beautiful Being.

These preferred qualities are always, already now-present *everywhere* in, as, and for *everyone* and *everything*, only awaiting our seeing, accepting and allowing them into expression in our life. Avoidance of this here-and-now Truth or relationship with Reality *as It really is*, is the Cosmic Joke – the playful adventure-drama of "Forgetfulness of the One Reality." It is like God playing "hide and seek" with Himself.

The Paradox of Life is that, since in Truth the One Self is God, or God is the Self of all, *all* is now in the Self. Therefore, whatever you desire you must first project as separate from you, in order to see it, then come back together with it.

Desiring God is the highest form of separation, and is the biggest joke of all, for it is God desiring Himself – which is divine amnesia. It is the sense of loss of identity. Or it's God meditating a separate-self identity – this "self" that you think of as "me," meaning *yourself*. This separate-sense of "I" is the Cosmic Joke, for there is no "thing" and no "one" actually apart from God, the One Omnipresent, Omnipotent Being. Nor can there ever be. Everything – apparently *good AND* apparently *bad* or evil – is actually from this one and same Essence. Everyone is this One. "I" is this One. "You" are this One. This One is the *only* One appearing as "I" and as "you."

There is no "I" or "other than I" existing apart from this One. This One is *all*, including the very "I" or "me" that may not know itself *as* the One, but *is* nevertheless *only* this One.

To believe and feel "your" being as "other-than" and "separate from" God is the Original Sin. This "sin" is the origin and cause of all present suffering and is the dilemma of life. It keeps the illusion of a separate "individual" existence and its life in the world (or *as* the world) running like a movie projected with "you" and "I" as its light-shadow players or characters.

Seeking has its own qualitative feeling, its own sensation. As a seeker, and during the activity of seeking, you feel the sensation of dilemma, which is its nature, regardless of what you seek – high or low. For it is *itself* conflict and suffering.

The energy-vibration you feel as a seeker and in the activity of seeking is the quality of separation from the Source. It is a sense of division, of being alone and divided and desiring to be happy, to be free from this sense of alienation. It is felt in the body like a huge knot or pinch, or a contraction usually in or near the region of the solar plexus, or perhaps elsewhere, like in the "gut." Or, it may be felt in the back somewhere along the spine as a bind or discomfort in or below the shoulders. Some may feel a contraction in the throat, others as a subtle to intense sensation in the forehead or middle of the head, the seat of the conscious mind in the brain. In its final stages before awakening in the Heart as the Heart, one may feel this contraction or knot in the right center of the chest.

With the majority of people, instead of feeling and recognizing this as a chronic discomfort, or as suffering being caused by seeking, their mind enters in and changes, substitutes or "surrogates" it into a more desirable or acceptable state or form of experience, and associates it with "*this adventure called life.*" Nevertheless, when seen clearly and consciously, it is still suffering, appearing as a chronic dissatisfaction or sense of "not enough." It is what motivates everyone to pursue "more," "better," and "different" experiences or adventures in the world. But *all this* is really the desire to be free from this prior contraction that is actually identification with the body-mind as "self." This body-mind identification is the activity always going on as *your ordinary life in the world*. The true Self, that is Consciousness itself (or Pure Being), is always, already complete and whole in itself only needing re-cognition of it.

Seeking entails the activity of perceiving the world and the things in it as "other than" or separate from you, the perceiver, and desiring to "have," "do," and "be" what appears to be apart from you. However, this is all an illusion in Consciousness or true Being.

Seeking is living the lie of separation while remaining identified with the body as being your "self." Only when you fully Awaken as non-seeking Being, in the living Heart of consciousness as the very Self, is freedom from all suffering attained or realized and true Bliss experienced as your true and natural state. This is the *only real* Happiness. This is Salvation or Spiritual Freedom. It is Liberation.

Happiness "born" of the world is not real or true happiness, for it is short-lived, varying, unsteady, uncertain and always changing. It usually ends in disappointment, upset and eventually death. Happiness born of "re-birth" into the very Heart of the very Self (God) is eternal, unwavering and indestructible happiness. This Happiness is experienced as non-seeking Being in the Heart. For it is complete, whole, full, always already Now. It is love, peace, joy and real understanding.

This is the end of all seeking and even the notion to seek. For, apart from pure Being Itself, there is nothing for which to ever seek that is in *any way* more, better, different, greater, or "other than" Itself.

This awakened realization is the only *real* Salvation – where life is everlasting joy, humor and Now-delight. All pain is released and suffering is no more. The Self is complete. I am complete. I am That Now. I AM FREE... I AM THAT I AM.

SECTION III
TRADITIONAL TECHNIQUES

PART VI
METHODS FOR GOING WITHIN

"PREVENTIVENESS OR PERMISSIVENESS" – THE *TRADITIONAL* WAYS OF "RETURNING" TO GOD, OR THE SOURCE

TRADITIONALLY, IN THE EAST, THERE ARE TWO basic approaches to spiritual practice (*sadhana*). Ostensibly, both are designed to free the conditioned body-mind, the illusory ego, of its tendencies, desires and fears that apparently divide, separate and limit one's total abidance in the true Self or Source. These two approaches are the traditional ways of Yoga and Tantra.

First, understand that all traditional methods of practice presuppose (though incorrectly) the existence of an actual separate, individual being, or person, living in time and space apart from the Totality of Being. Ultimately, however, the unequivocal situation is that there is no separate self, even though there still *appears* to be; and the majority of people usually get stuck in this ongoing dilemma of trying to give up or destroy the ego, which in fact doesn't exist in the first place.

You might wish to consider this: To presuppose the actual existence of a separate self identity, and then set out to eliminate or dissolve it by using *any* practice, method or technique, since it in fact doesn't actually exist, is destined in the long run to frustration and probable failure in the desired end result. So why practice any method or process? Well, as the humorous saying goes, "Everyone has got to be somewhere." But more practically, the ancient scriptures and all the sages say the benefit is to purify the mind, to rid it of its pollution due to ignorance, i.e., its conditioned patterns and tendencies that do not allow us to see the real nature of the Self we all really are.

With this in mind, you might consider the two traditional ways. One is that of "prevention," the other is that of "permission." They are entirely different approaches that in their practice actually oppose each other. However, either – when used singularly or exclusively – is designed to contribute to the accomplishment of the final goal, purification of the mind resulting in spiritual awakening. When practicing them *traditionally*, you are supposed to choose *only one* of the "two directions for returning home" and stick with *that one*. To blend or mix the two, going back and forth from one to the other, will just produce conflict, confusion, and contradiction. It delays progress, and results in increased frustration and failure.

Yoga, being more or less the way of "preventive" discipline, limits or restricts desires by not participating in or allowing the body to indulge in sensual pleasures. It is to limit all actions stemming from one's desires in order to *end* desire. Yoga means "union." It is the way of union (or reunion) with God through developing dispassion. Hatha Yoga (simplistically defined) is a system for controlling the body, mind, emotions, etc., by developing proficiency in special exercises or physical postures called *"asanas"* and by controlling the breath with breathing processes called *"pranayama."* Over time, some yogis in the advanced practice of these processes are capable of developing tremendous psycho-physical feats, dispassion and will power. You could say it is the way of "I can't."

By contrast, Tantra is more or less the way of "permissiveness," which (as it is meant here and is again simplistically stated) is the process of intentionally *though consciously* indulging or participating in the body and mind's desires in order to *consciously experience* the experience of an object of desire. The theory and intention is to terminate the "experiencing-subject" by merging "him" or "her" with the object of desire and thus dissolving the cause and source of desire – i.e., the ego or separate-self identity. It is ending desire and all sense of separation by dissolving *their very cause* (the sense of being an individual that is also separate and apart from them). You might say this is the way of "I can." It is more risky.

Ordinarily, the ego will usually gravitate to the method or "way of return" most appealing to *it*. But, the ego's choice is usually for the wrong reason, that being: its own survival. This means (particularly in the West) that one is not as apt to choose the way of *true* Yoga (preventiveness) that requires a strict discipline and may more likely be interested in the method of Tantra, which allows one to be less disciplined and live more permissively, yet many still choose yoga instead.

The discipline of Yoga is intended to ultimately *dissolve* the ego by eliminating the mind's conditioned patterns and tendencies in order to eventually merge the mind in the Self, the Source of being, or God. However most Westerners, including those who affirm or verbally state that they truly want enlightenment, are not in the least bit agreeable with the notion of "dissolving the ego," which is in fact *necessary* for final enlightenment. This is one aspect of spiritual work or discipline most Westerners do not understand, at least not fully. They incorrectly believe enlightenment is attainment of a higher state of consciousness where the ego, the *personal* sense of "I" still survives; they think it remains intact as an expanded personal sense of "self." *This is a widespread misconception!*

Since the ultimate end is enlightenment – being the extinction of the ego or the sense of a separate "self" – then whichever Traditional Way one chooses (that is, the Path of Yoga or of Tantra) – again, when considered *traditionally* – is a legitimate method; but the way must be practiced *exclusively* or *singularly* once the specific choice is made. This is based on the *proper* traditional practice of the way or method. It is important that one practice or use the method one chooses by conforming to it *exactly* or exclusively.

On first consideration or examination, many would-be spiritual aspirants in the West may be naturally inclined to choose the way of Tantra, or intentional "permissiveness." Yet, it is very unwise for Westerners to listen to the inclinations or argument of the ego in choosing Tantra as one's method. For to do so, one is likely to attempt to practice it *only to indulge desires,* which leads to further increasing them rather than consciously and intentionally practicing Tantra to *dissolve them* or their cause, which is the ego.

With either method, logic is often the ego's argument for its choice – being very convincing yet dangerous due to the mixing in of desire with logic, which is the very element we are working to eliminate. This is based on the prior false or incorrect assumption that we are in fact an "entity" or individual "self" living separate and apart from the One Reality or Source of being. There is great resistance, even fear, of letting this false notion go or dissolve.

Here, a mental-emotional dilemma, quandary and questioning may occur as to which of the two traditional ways to choose. Since the ultimate purpose is the radical and absolute dissolving of the sense of "I" in order for this so-called "reunion with God" to occur, the ego may argue for the way of preventiveness. It may look at all that is usually considered to be "sinful" or "nonreligious" or "evil" or "wrong in the world" and deduce that the only possible way to be "accepted by God" is to prevent oneself from acting or indulging in any or all worldly desires or "ungodly" practices. Thus, the way of strict discipline may appear to be the only possible way of "returning to God."

These seekers are very likely affected by guilt and fear and let these feelings become their strict "disciplinarians" in their quest for returning to God. It is the more logical choice and apparently the only "correct" one for those whose moral sense of "right and wrong" is strongly involved in making the choice.

Most orthodox religionists and practically all monks living in monasteries (Christian and/or Buddhist, etc.) choose this preventiveness, or a similar, comparable way of restricting themselves, and consider all indulgences of the senses as inappropriate or even evil. The same is true with the strict yogis in India and other Eastern locales and even practicing yogis in the West.

It takes *tremendous* effort to hold or keep the mind still and let it finally merge in the Source, or God. Ultimately the practitioner of Yoga (the discipline of preventiveness) reduces all desire to *this one desire* (total union or reunion with God). The strategy is to develop mental strength by restricting the mind and senses from engaging in thoughts of worldly pursuits or indulging in tactile gratification. This gives the practitioner (yogi) the mental power of focused energy to introvert his/her mind and attention and hold it steadily on a chosen object of meditation and eventually merge with it in consciousness.

The way of preventiveness for the dedicated beginner or spiritual aspirant may at first appear easier to choose for it is more logical.

But, the power of desire builds. If thoughts are not checked, desire can grow continually stronger over time, making it very difficult for one to maintain a high level of discipline. Usually, temptation for the gratification of the senses grows and one may stumble and fall, fail, or backslide. This usually results in guilt. Fear can plague the novice that is filled with desire and can hinder his progress. And you may see even advanced aspirants of this traditional way "falling off the wagon" or going through periods of "sinful" indulgence, resulting in an interval of mental-emotional "setback" or their mind being filled with guilt and remorse. They sometimes even give up the path of Yoga entirely.

To initially choose the way of Tantra, or conscious permissiveness, also has its own drawbacks and is itself very risky. It could even be more detrimental, because as stated it is usually chosen for the wrong reasons, such as the above example of one who falls from Yoga. It may be chosen by those who are not alert to the subtleties of the ego and who choose the method for the wrong reason or intention, not for the actual purpose of clearing the senses and merging with the Source, or God. Thus, Tantra is or can be even more tricky or dangerous than Yoga, for it is more often intentionally used as a license to indulge the senses. It is considered as a permit to "free living," all for "pleasure's sake" and under the guise of indulgence being OK since one is *practicing a traditional method of spiritual return to God.*

Certain isolated, rare sects of Hinduism and even a few esoteric sects of Tibetan Buddhism (and some Western derivatives of these) actually recognize and give a place to this otherwise uncommon practice of Tantra, or way of Conscious Permissiveness. However, these rare sects are usually criticized by the more orthodox members of the traditional community, and their adherents are even ostracized or considered with suspicion. This is because these sects are often incorrectly thought to be associated with sexual promiscuity.

The basic premise or principle of pure, authentic Tantra is that God has created *everything* for us, and therefore nothing God creates is innately evil, bad or wrong. In the creation story in the Bible it is *all* called "good." This is especially so when the principle and process of Tantra are used and expressed appropriately, in the way or manner for which they are originally intended to be used.

Christians have no comparable method of spiritual practice.

Many Christians even consider sex as "sinful," they overtly suppress their sexual urges, and yet in some instances covertly live a life of depravity while hiding their true sexual desires even from their mates. Others live suppressed lives similar to some yogis.

St. Paul has verified the appropriateness of *everything* provided to us by the grace of God, including sensual pleasure or sexual expression. He said, *"I know and am persuaded in the Lord Jesus that nothing in itself is unclean, but for him who thinks it is unclean, to him it is unclean."* (Romans 14:14) And Proverbs 23:7 says, *"As a man thinks in his heart, so is he."* Therefore, it is our own conception of a thing that makes it evil, bad or wrong; or it is the way we use (or misuse) it. Evil or wrongness is not in the thing itself. It is entirely our own thought about it that matters.

There is nothing innately evil, wrong or immoral about the body or in experiencing and expressing the joy and pleasure of sex in and with the body. You can truthfully say that is what the body is created for. It is a vehicle of transportation, and of individual expression in this world, being an instrument of pleasure and a way for God (or the Self) to experience and express love and enjoyment in time and space.

However, strong attachment or addiction to pleasure that is derived solely from or confined primarily to the body's senses, and overindulgence in sexual pleasures, can become a serious problem. When taken to the extreme this behavior can or will become pain producing. Attachment to the body as being the "self" causes one to remain in a deep amnesia of forgetfulness of one's true nature and relationship with God, or the *true* Self.

Sexual expression as such is not evil, immoral, bad or itself wrong. However, when one is attached to the body and remains strongly attached to it sexually, it can cause an insidious degree of body identification that is eventually painful. Actively seeking and indulging in excessive sexual gratification binds the Self even more tightly to the body.

Sex, like smelling, hearing, or tasting, is very natural. It is not evil. The genitalia or sexual organs are in fact organs of pleasure, as the eyes and ears are organs for seeing and hearing. Of course, genitalia are also instruments of reproduction for the procreation of the species; and the pleasure experienced in sex is nature's way of guaranteeing the perpetuation of the species. It is not evil; it is quite natural. Since sex is for generation, its higher function is also for regeneration or raising one's consciousness to the higher level of pure Being. We must only take care and not use it unwisely in degeneration.

Sexual energy is among the most powerful energies generated in the body being next to the basic energy directed and used for the body's physical survival. Survival of the apparent individual or the sense of "I" and "other" is first, and survival of the species in itself, which is sexual energy, is second. This energy though being lustful is similar to love in its power of attraction. There is self-love, parental love or the love for an offspring, then there is love expressed with a mate and the survival of "I" and "other" which is perpetuation of the species or race. Of course this is not *pure* love, but physical attraction. Pure Love is pure Being, the love of the one Supreme Self.

Sexuality among healthy adults is quite natural, so use sexual energy appropriately – i.e., joyously and freely without guilt, shame or embarrassment. Just use it *wisely*, without compulsion or over-indulgence. Remember to Inquire, and fully observe your sexual play, consciously using it to return your personal sense of awareness to God, the Source, or Universal Awareness. This is the Purpose and Way of Tantra.

A word of caution however: You can easily pretend or fool yourself into saying and believing you are "practicing Tantra" when in fact you are indulging in sexual play only, or primarily for sensual pleasure. This will keep you attached to the body even longer and also more strongly identified. So, it is best to have a guru or Conscious Teacher to guide you in your selection and use of this way – that is, to counsel you in your practice of Tantra so you don't end up falling into a sensual trap of your own making.

BASIC METHODS FOR MEDITATION

B HAGAVAN SRI RAMANA MAHARSHI often said that
meditation is our true and natural state. What is called
"meditation" is usually an intentional mental activity
ironically practiced in an attempt to stop or quiet the mind. It
is practiced because thoughts are now distracting the natural
state of peace and silence. When these thoughts are dispelled,
only *we* (as pure Awareness) remain as we *truly* are – this One
Presence and Reality entirely thought-free. This state of pure
Being – here and now present, free of all thoughts – is Real
Meditation and is the state we are now "trying to gain" by
keeping away all other thoughts. "Such keeping away of all
other thoughts is now called 'meditation' by the ordinary
seeker. But when one's abidance is steady and firm, one's true
nature reveals itself, and this experience is seen, known and
understood as true Meditation," says Sri Bhagavan.

To this writer, this is one of the clearest and best descriptions of true meditation heard or given by anyone.

In the process of ordinary practice, when one attempts meditation techniques or methods, all sorts of thoughts arise. And
this is even more forcibly so when one is intentional about
"arriving" in the true State of one's true Being, the very Self.
Sri Bhagavan says this is only natural and is to be expected. It
is because all that is contained in the mind, all that is lying
dormant, latent or hidden within us, is brought out into the
light of pure Awareness to be released and destroyed. As Sri
Bhagavan says, how else can we release and destroy what is
there unless it is revealed or uncovered? In the process of
practicing truly effective methods of meditation, all thoughts
eventually spontaneously rise up in order to be extinguished,
thereby leaving the mind "stronger" (meaning, more capable
of remaining one pointed) – i.e., focused steadily on oneself or
held on a single thought such as the "I" thought, to the exclusion of all other thoughts.

As you progress, you begin to experience quietness in the
mind. When you "arrive" in pure Consciousness, along with

this quietness of mind, persons and things may take on a rather vague, almost transparent form, as in a dream. One ceases to observe these things as "outside" but rather is passively conscious of their existence, while not actively conscious of any sense of selfhood. There is a deep stillness or quietness in the mind; the observed object appears as bathed or immersed in a radiance or pure light. It may appear as though it is on fire but is not being consumed, or as though it is outlined in a halo of light. This is very possibly the experience Moses had as recorded in the third chapter of Exodus in the Bible. He might very well have been on Mount Sinai meditating and while doing so was possibly looking at a distant or nearby bush in his reverie. When his mind plunged into the Self, or the inner Source of being, the bush might have appeared to burn. In that moment he could have realized his oneness with God and with all creation, which is *prior* to time and space, yet within "one and all" and everywhere.

This is commonly known and described as Moses' experience of the "burning bush" in which it is recorded that "God spoke to him" – or that he realized the Self, by spiritually Awakening to know directly: "*I am* that I AM."

This "I AM THAT I AM" is the unconditioned and unconditional Condition of the Self. In the first stage of re-cognition (knowing again) and re-experiencing this Supreme or true State (since we are now ignorantly or wrongly identified with the body-mind as being "ourselves," and are "approaching" the Self from this apparent yet pseudo-position and distorted perspective, not seeing the true Self as being what is real), our experience of IT is usually unsteady, short-lived, and being glimpsed only for a few moments or so. When this real experience of the true Self *does* occur (in these beginning fleeting moments), we may prolong or intensify this "newly found" abidance by intentionally diving into the inner current of awareness, or plunging with full attention into this inner Consciousness and quietly bathing in its inner Bliss and Peace – the true nature of which is the bliss of pure Being.

Sri Bhagavan Ramana called this "a dip below the surface of externalities." When real quietness of the mind occurs and prevails without obstructing the pure Consciousness, then just remain as you are. There is no need to "dive," for this is the true State of the Self and is real or effortless Being, which is Real Meditation, or thoughtless awareness. It is eternal and infinite Awareness, *prior to* and *beyond* the mind and any and all thought processes.

The mind's constant activity and conditioned content conceals the true Self. When our meditation is successful and stills the mind, we realize the real nature of pure Consciousness Itself on which the mind depends; mind only gives us Its *reflected* light. The mind draws its energy and light *from* pure Consciousness, the Self-radiant or shining Heart, just like the moon draws its light from the sun, and only reflects the sun's light. The moon has no light of its own; and neither does the mind, it simply reflects the light of the Self.

Two Basic Types of Meditation

Basically, meditation methods have two basic or primary emphases, meaning they use one of the two "different directional flows" of the mind. The mind flows *outwardly* onto objects and the objective world, or *inwardly* onto the subject (the thinker) which is the mind and centering point or reference in consciousness, which is its "place of contact" with the Source, or Self. Even the so-called "subjective" inner worlds are themselves actually objects of the perceiving Self. This means that all visualized mental-images, as well as the seeing subject of all these, including all thoughts and the thinker, are actually occurring in or on the Self, thus objective to *pure Seeing* itself.

In this sense, the mind moves only inward and outward. When it is focused on a thought or mental image, it is outward turned. It is inward turned when it is resting in its own nature or formless "form," which is pure Awareness, or formless consciousness alone, being without any form or image in it.

All methods of controlling the mind and making it quiet are called "meditation." These methods or techniques are numerous and varied. There are some methods that are more direct or immediate in principle, process, and effect than others. However, the most effective method for *you* is the one that works the best for you. This depends on your nature. You will know if a method is working for you when you are experiencing a deeper quality of peace and stillness, or steadiness of mind, after using it over a long, consistent period of time.

As already pointed out, in the beginning a really effective method might at first bring stillness of mind and inner peace, and then begin to increase the activity of the mind. So you want to stay with a method for a significant time, at least a few months, *and work consistently with it* before determining whether or not it is truly working for you. You will feel it.

Self-Inquiry is *More* Than Meditation

It has often been said that there is no "one method" of meditation that is best suited for everyone. This is because the mind's conditioning and the various natures of people are different. Therefore, it is usually suggested that you try several methods before you find the one that seems to be the most effective for you. In this regard, using a method requires a true loyalty and diligence to that method on a regular or disciplined basis and not just "hit or miss" sporadic attempts. All methods in their own way will purify and focus the mind and prepare you to control your thoughts. The ultimate or highest purpose of every method is to finally give you the strength to still or quiet the mind, thus turning it inward to merge with the Self, which is real God, the Source, or pure Awareness.

NOW HERE IS A MOST IMPORTANT POINT: all methods of meditation *other than Self-Inquiry* actually utilize the mind in order to practice the method! This is true of *all* methods, *regardless* of the method used. You are actually *reinforcing* the mind, making it in fact stronger or more durable in its believed or assumed appearance and identity by the very use of these other practices or methods.

Therefore, if you can see and understand the true *purpose* of *all* forms or methods of meditation and if you are capable of applying the Self-Inquiry process *from the very start*, then what has been said about there being "no best method" for you *does not apply!* For Self-Inquiry, when you are capable of correctly practicing it, *is the best!* It is the most direct and immediate method for awakening to and abiding in the very Self, which is always, already present *prior to the mind*. It is therefore *the best method* for *everyone* – either in the beginning or if taken up later. The reason for this is quite simple and logical.

See this: You are always, already the one Self and *only* the Self. The Self is the One Reality; it is Real God. As said already, abiding in the true Self is the highest purpose and the ultimate "goal" of all meditation. It is to "bring you back" into your true nature. If you now or at anytime incorrectly assume that you are *not* the Self, but are the body-mind, and are thus thinking and feeling you are "out of the Self," then all methods, other than Self-Inquiry, may serve to reinforce this false or wrongly held notion and sensed or felt belief. Someday, *in the moment*, this false notion must be *totally released and overcome*; so why not use Self-Inquiry *from the very beginning* since all these other methods are, in a manner of speaking, working against this final requirement? Yes, they are somewhat beneficial to start with, being designed to help stop thoughts, purify the mind, and control it. However, these methods *actually reinforce* the false notion that you are a separate individual "self" *living apart from the true Self* – the Self that must ultimately be awakened, "return to," or "attained."

Self-Inquiry *stops* all thoughts *as they arise*, or *even before*. The mind only *appears* to arise. It is actually occurring *on* the prior Awareness that is the Self. Identifying with this "appearing thought" takes attention *away* from pure Awareness, the Source (or Self) and onto the mental ideas or outer objects, including the body-mind. All this gives rise to the false belief that you *are* the body-mind and not the pure Awareness. This is the *very false notion* you are trying to transcend, or end, and remain in the Self that you always, already *are*. Therefore, since this is the "end" that eventually *must be attained*, why not directly achieve this *from the very beginning*? Self-Inquiry takes you *immediately* or *directly* to the truth *from the very beginning!*

Nevertheless the interesting, humorous, and yet sad paradox is, that many spiritual seekers *incorrectly* think and believe they must use what are in fact *less effective methods* in the beginning, in order to "acquire the strength of mind" to hold it in the Self.

Self-Inquiry Is All You Need

Do you acknowledge that you exist? Are you aware of the sense of your own being? as this sense of "I?" When you can, without any effort, identify with or recognize *that you exist*, you can use Self-Inquiry. The sense of "I" is all you need – realizing it as "the thinker" or "feeler" of all thoughts. When you can simply hold on to *it* – with your attention – to the exclusion of other thoughts, at least momentary or for brief periods or intervals, then no other method, process or meditation is really necessary for you, or your spiritual practice.

This *is* the simple yet *primal* Truth. Use it as your practice of Self-Inquiry, which soon reveals to you a relatively quiet mind where you *are already abiding* in the Self (the purpose of all methods) and where all thought can and will eventually, totally stop with the practice of the Inquiry. Just continue to practice the Inquiry; when or as *any* thought rises, simply Inquire, "Who is having this thought?" and continue the process as described below. Or ask: "Avoiding abiding in pure silence and stillness, the Self?" Or, simply say to the mind, "Be still."

As a thought rises ask: "Who is having this thought?" The obvious fact is, "I am." Then simply hold attention *firmly* on this "I," the feeling of "I" that is having the thought. This "I" is *itself* the primal or original thought coexisting *in the moment* along with the rising thought that surrounds or accompanies it. All other thoughts totally depend on this "I"-thought for their existence, while the "I"-thought totally depends on the pure Awareness, or the one Self for its existence.

Deliberately withdraw this "I"-thought (that arises momentarily with other thoughts) back into its Source (the prior Self). Or ask: "Who am I?" and continue holding *only* this question. The rising thought will simply subside or disappear like clouds in the sky, and eventually even the "I"-thought itself will subside or merge in the Source from which it appears to arise. This Source is the Self, pure Awareness. It is real God, the awareness I AM, and is the Location of Peace, which is Real Happiness.

Consider this analogy: an iron rod remaining in a blast furnace becomes white hot. As a cool rod, it has no power to burn things or start a fire and is difficult to bend or reshape into other forms. The iron rod is like the "I"-thought; the blast furnace is like the pure Awareness or Self. The "I"-thought gets its power to form or shape thoughts (consciousness-energy) into the images of this world by way of its direct association with the Self; it does not have this power on its own.

There is a major difference between the "I"-thought (which

is the mind) and *pure* Awareness (which is the Self). The Self is *not* a thought but is *pure* Existence, *pure* Consciousness, *pure* Being, *prior to* the mind or "I"-thought. *You do not have to think to know you exist!* Really get this! Your existence is Self-evident; it cannot be denied. Self-Inquiry makes this important distinction *quickly and easily* – between thought and pure Awareness .

During the practice of other methods of meditation you remain identified with the mind, and also believe you are a separate "self" or "entity" that is "doing" the meditation – even though you may practice the method for years, if not for lifetimes. Most people who use other methods may practice them without *ever* directly knowing or making the subtle distinction between the mind and the Self – i.e., pure Being, or pure Awareness. You see, while other methods use and actually *depend* on the mind in order to even practice the method, Self-Inquiry both transcends and dissolves the mind *in the actual practice* and begins subtly to accomplish this *even from the very start!* Strength in your ability to make this very important distinction grows or increases over time with the proper use of Self-Inquiry, contrary to your practice of other methods.

If you can understand and accept what has been said in this text about traditional meditation methods and Self-Inquiry, and are able to discern and hold on to the "I"-thought or "I"-feeling, then you are ready for Self-Inquiry, it being the highest and most effective method available. It will soon directly result in complete and radical transformation of the mind, or "self" (little "s"), into abidance in the true Self (capital "S").

From all this, if you understand and feel compatible with Self-Inquiry *as your practice*, you need not read the next chapter on "Breathing Processes and Mantras. " However, if it is difficult for you to keep attention firmly on the "I" thought, then using the breath may be easier *in starting out using Self-Inquiry.* So, *just that first part* of the next chapter may help.

Or, the next chapter may be of benefit in better understanding these lesser methods just for knowing what they provide to those who practice them. Its material, however, is *only* for those wanting to *better understand* these subjects, it is *not* to recommend using them as one's primary practice.

THE ESSENCE – I.E., BENEFITS AND LIMITATIONS – OF OTHER METHODS

Using the Breath

There are two ways of working with the mind to control it – working with the mind itself or working with the breath. The breath has a common root or source with the mind. To control the breath helps in controlling the mind, and controlling the mind helps to control or regulate the breath. The breath is actually the gross form of the mind when seen from the point of view of pure Consciousness. They are linked together.

Most people habitually identify with the mind's externalized flow or activity, and its *compulsive* involvement with the objective world. They see everything from the reference point of a conceived and felt separate "self," or individual "me," or "I" thought. They not only see and *believe* in the "solidity of this world," but live *totally at the effect* of the myriad polar opposites this "point of reference" gives rise to and *sustains* in consciousness, such as *outside/inside, past/future, right/wrong, good/evil,* etc. Such people usually have little if any awareness of the subjective quality and power of the ego-mind, and the inner world of the mind. They do not realize it is the source and cause of all they perceive, objectively. This conceived "separate-self-sense," or body-mind identification, is taken for granted and believed to be the basis or "truth" of one's being. This, however, is still usually only inferred or known *about,* instead of being actually *understood* or *known directly* as being in fact the mind. (This limited perception is even true of most psychologists and psychiatrists whose knowledge is mostly theoretical, intellectual, and conceptual, rather than experiential or *direct knowing*).

BELIEVING THE BODY IS THE SELF: Most people adamantly think or believe the body is actually the Self. Some who are more subjectively oriented may have come to accept, at least intellectually, that the body is not in fact the Self. These may, however, be more attached to the equally false notion of the mind being the Self. Those who are objectively oriented defend the outside against the inside. Subjectively oriented persons defend the inside against the outside. The former declare the cause of things to be outside themselves, the latter are usually more often open to accepting that they are the cause of their experiences, or that the cause of things is within themselves. Or they may believe that only *some* things have an inner cause and are in a dilemma as to how to change, correct or deal with situations which appear to be beyond their control.

The truth is that *both* the objective and the subjective are contained in and comprise the whole of that which appears as ordinary life in the world. Like the age-old debate: "Which came first, the chicken or the egg, or the seed or the plant?" the answer is they "arise" and "set" together, being linked and mutually interdependent. They are not two separate elements or "things" but two complementary phases or aspects of one composite whole.

It is easy to see and understand the dual aspects of the breath – its inward and outward nature. This is obvious from the process of breathing itself which is more evident in our consciousness. Everyone knows that when you inhale you breathe in and when you exhale you breathe out. You cannot *only* breathe in or *only* breathe out; they go together. But very few know or understand the source or cause of breath or that breath has a common source or root with the mind. This can be seen with the momentary stoppage of either. When the mind stops – like from a sudden, unexpected shock or surprise – the breath also momentarily stops. Also, when the breath is suddenly knocked out of you (called "winded"), your mind momentarily stops.

The breath is the "gross form" of the mind. It is the objective "side" of the mind, rising with the mind (and the "I-am-the-body" notion) and setting or merging with the mind in the Self at the time of death of the body. But, as Bhagavan Sri Ramana Maharshi explained, it does not set or cease during sleep (which he called the short death) due to God's will that life remain conspicuous in the body so that those observing the sleeping body will not mistake it for a corpse.

In India, the system or practice of Yoga utilizes this knowledge and understanding. It has, since ancient times, developed elaborate techniques for both quieting the mind and refining the breath. Some of these methods are very strenuous for most people and are even unsafe for those not thoroughly trained in their proper use. They require the direct supervision and guidance of an accomplished master teacher, or guru, who has himself either transcended the body by means of the method or has practiced using the method for many years and knows how to guide the student. None of these methods are given here because of the extensive time and unrelenting discipline required for their mastery. And besides, none of them are even needed for enlightenment. For, as explained in the last chapter, Self-Inquiry is an easier and safer method and is in fact the most direct and immediate means of attaining the highest goal of life, and itself contains (within its own form) the very best of all methods.

In Yoga, a method of controlling the vital energy or life force in the body-mind is by controlling or intentionally directing the breath. This process is called *pranayama*. Some very rare yogis are so proficient in advanced methods of breath control that they are able to actually stop the breath for hours and even days at a time, totally unaware of the body and the world while the mind and breath are suspended in a state of deep trance called *nirvikalpa samadhi*. Some are even able to, at will, intentionally stop their heart from beating and then start it again. Others are capable of controlling the temperature in different areas or regions of the body, others the flow of blood in different parts of the body, and some can withstand what would be unbearable pain for the ordinary person, such as allowing their body to be surgically operated on without anesthetics.

This may sound preposterous to those unfamiliar with Yoga or the higher laws of Consciousness and how these laws operate or the extent to which some advanced practitioners are able to utilize these processes to control their body-mind. But, nonetheless, these are feats accomplished by some *yogis* and *fakirs* (Muslim holy men) from their long intentional practice, which has given them control over their mental and bodily processes by using advance controlled breathing exercises.

Mantras

Another method well known in the East for controlling the mind is the use of sound or certain vibration frequencies produced by silently uttering or openly chanting special words or word phrases. In India, this method is called *mantra*, while *japa* is the term used to mean the continued repetition of a particular *mantra*.

Also, early American Indians used similar methods or special sounds for controlling and purifying their minds and to hold their awareness firmly in the Source of being, or the "Great Spirit" as they referred to God. When practiced in unison, this gave them tremendous combined energy and power which they were able to channel or focus and use to fight and conquer their enemies. Some American Indian Medicine Men (Shamans) can even control the weather to produce strong wind, clouds, thunder, lightening and rain. The Hopi Indians in central Arizona once performed Rain Dances in which the entire tribe participated in chanting and dancing to bring rain for growing corn and other crops in the extremely dry desert regions where there is seldom if ever any ordinary rain for the cultivation of their crops.

The Sanskrit word *siddhis* means powers or the special ability to use invisible forces to one's advantage. Those having these *siddhis* are called *Siddhas*. Some *Siddhas* can exercise these powers at will; with others, who have developed even higher states of consciousness than the *yogis*, these phenomena just happen in their presence as a spontaneous manifestation of God dwelling in them. Some High Beings with these special *siddhis* are Sai Baba of Shirdi who lived in the 1800's, and Lahari Mahasaya the guru of Sri Yukteshwar (himself capable of such *siddhis*) who was the guru of Paramahansa Yogananda, the now famous yogi who founded the Self Realization Fellowship near Santa Monica, California. Other *Siddhas* are – Baba Muktananda (known personally by this writer) and his guru Bhagavan Nityananda, as well as Karoli Baba, the guru of Ram Das (Richard Alpert) a former Harvard professor and once head of its psychology department in the early 1960s. All six of these great beings lived in India from the mid 19th through the early to mid 20th centuries. India is commonly known for its many hundreds of *Siddhas* who have flourished there for thousands of years, even before the time of Jesus Christ.

In the West, Jesus is the most famous example of one having the power of *siddhis*. He is known for having "performed miracles" both as intentional acts for the grace and benefit of others and unintentionally as those occurring in his mere presence. It is recorded in Matthew 9:20 that a woman was healed of a hemorrhage she had had for twelve years by simply touching, without his foreknowledge, the hem of Jesus' garment. He afterwards knew that she had been healed by her own faith in the power she felt emanating from him.

Among the countless numbers of such Beings in India's long spiritual history, Jesus is considered a *Siddha* of the highest order and degree. Among the Hindus, he is widely respected and even worshipped as an *avatar* (an incarnation of God). This is a far contrast from the non-acceptance, hostile attitude and ill treatment perpetrated against him at the hands of the local orthodox religionists of his own day, who accused him of blasphemy for calling himself a "Son of God" and of drawing his healing powers from the devil, or an "evil" source. Today, there are similar allegations made by so-called "good" Christians and other orthodox religionists against similarly accomplished High Beings as these mentioned. Although, historically, there are and have been many among the ranks of Christians capable of performing "miraculous" healing, very few among them accept the fact there are *now* and, throughout history, have been *many* in the non-Christian world who rank *equally high* with Jesus – i.e., in both their level of spirituality and their ability to manifest spiritual powers.

None of these physio-mental feats, whether from *mantra* or breath control, are necessary for real or true spiritual advancement or Self-realization. In fact, when these rare or unusual feats begin to manifest in the experience of seekers, they are strongly discouraged by true Spiritual Teachers as being both distractions and detours from the one primary Goal, true Self or God-Realization. For all such feats or powers can easily detract from the true work and higher purpose of dissolving all tendencies of the mind. Such powers tend to cause the mind to remain strong in its functioning, as the mind's activity itself must be kept intact in order to perform such feats of phenomena. The only exception is a *Jnani* (an Enlightened Being) like Jesus or the other great Beings mentioned above.

Mentioning these unusual, supernatural powers is brought up here *only* to acquaint readers with the fact of the existence of these actual higher powers awakened in some exceptional beings. These powers are beyond the ordinary intellect and its field of operation but they may occur with some. It is also to discourage or even caution anyone already awakened to such "mind powers" from pursuing them or further indulging in them. These are really pitfalls to be avoided, for they actually delay true spiritual practice or progress. They *do not* lead to enlightenment which is accomplished or demonstrated *only* by a quiet or still mind unaffected by such attachments.

There *are* some simple and safe methods in both *pranayama* and *mantra* being used by practitioners in both the East and the West which are often helpful to them for quieting, stilling and purifying the mind and as an aid in gaining temporary control of it. A strong minded person, as we are using the term here, is one capable of controlling the direction, nature and flow of his thoughts. When you are incapable of controlling or quieting the mind, you have very little inner or outer peace or control over the events of your life and their effect on you. However, the practical ability to control or quiet the mind is developed even more quickly, easily and safely with the consistent practice of Self-Inquiry

One word of advise however: Using a *mantra* or *pranayama* actually externalizes or objectifies the mind, for both the sound of the *mantra* and the breath and the breathing exercise, are themselves objects in the mind. They are each objective in relation to the subjective user of the methods. Even though one may say these practices are going on "within," they are still going on in the mind or the body and therefore are "objective" to pure Awareness, the Real Being, if not to the apparent "person" practicing the methods. This means that the mind, even though being focused or controlled in the process, is still being reinforced in its objective mode in the "person."

Ultimately, for enlightenment, the mind must be fully tuned inward or withdrawn and merged in the source of the "I"

thought or pure Awareness Itself. This may become even
more difficult for the mind that has been long conditioned to
being externalized by the practice of *mantra* or *pranayama*.
This happened with Ganapati Muni, a highly mature devotee
of Sri Bhagavan Ramana who was an advanced user of *mantra*
(even a Mantra Master with hundreds of devoted followers of
his own) before coming to Sri Bhagavan. He once exclaimed,
"I have done countless crores (millions) of *mantra*. I've developed the skill or ability to compose and recite extemporane-
ously from memory thousands of verses; and I can remember
what has been stated by those I hear speaking and can even
write it down later word-for-word *exactly* as stated. I can even
travel to the world of the gods and converse with Indra, their
king, and with all the other gods; but I am unable to take even
one required step backward, out of the mind, into the Self."

Therefore, if enlightenment is your primary interest and
purpose, it is better to immediately start practicing Inquiry. If
you are presently practicing either of these above-mentioned
(or any other) methods that use the mind for its practice, then
begin to inquire, "Who is saying or hearing this *mantra*," or
"Who is observing or controlling the breath?" Then turn attention inward, back into the Self, the Source of the "I"
thought or the "me" who is practicing the method.

Never forget, the *mantra* and the breathing are both in the
mind of the "meditator" and in the body-mind of the practitioner of *pranayama*. Without the mind, you would be unaware of either of the practices being used to quiet or control
the mind. The Self is *prior to* the "I," prior to the actual practice of the method, and prior to the mind of the practitioner of
these or any other methods of meditation.

Realization of the Self occurs *only* when the mind is totally
merged or dissolved in the Source, Self, or One Reality, not
when it rises in thought as it does when you practice methods
of meditation other than Self-Inquiry.

METHODS ARE MANY – THE ULTIMATE RESULT IS ONE

ALTHOUGH THERE ARE NUMEROUS METHODS or practices for achieving purification and strength of mind, all of them in the end – if one is *competent* to take them to the ultimate or final *completion* – actually achieve the same purpose and result. It will be seen that when one concentrates (i.e., steadily, intently focuses mind on any *one object* to the *exclusion* of any other thought), he will ultimately remain *in a state of oneness with* that object, with cessation of all distractions and/or other mental concepts. This is the ultimate power of concentration or successful meditation.

Bhagavan Sri Ramana Maharshi explained that turning the mind *inward* and pursuing the Source of the mind with one-pointed inquiry (practicing Self-Inquiry) is the focusing of the mind on Consciousness *itself*. Those who follow this method realize that the simple, pure Awareness that remains at the end of the Inquiry is the One Reality, or Real God, without a second. Those following the practice of *outer* concentration realize at the peak or high point of their meditation, the object of their meditation is also pure Being, or real God. Since the final goal or result is the same in either case – inwardness (Self-Inquiry) or outwardness (concentration-meditation) – it is therefore the duty of all sincere spiritual aspirants to continuously practice whichever of these methods is easier for them or whichever feels natural or appropriate, *until final completion.*

The result is usually called "God-realization" when the quest is outer-directed and realized, or "Self-realization" when inner-directed and realized. The actual *experience* is the same for both approaches or points of view. God is the Self, the Self is God; they are One and not different.

The Self, realized by inner Inquiry, is the Supreme Self of all selves, the one Universal Being or Supreme Self that is God. When God is realized in the way of outer concentration or meditation, It is the one Universal Supreme Being of *all that is,*

– all beings, including the very Self of the devotee or aspirant.

God is the one Universal Awareness that not only *contains* all, but *is* all. All major religions expound this simple truth in various ways. God in *all* traditions is acclaimed as: omnipresent (everywhere present) Being, and Omnipresence (all-presence, everywhere simultaneously); omnipotent (all-powerful) Being, and Omnipotence (all the power there is, everywhere); and omniscient (all-knowing) Being, or Omniscience (the sum of all knowledge and intelligence).

This being the declared Truth of all major religions, where does this leave room for "you" and/or "me" or any "other" being or *thing*? God being Infinite and Eternal Being "takes up all the room," and performs all actions and functions. God is all and everything, including all time and space and beyond. As God is the one Absolute all-inclusive Self, there can be no thing or no one but That. This is the *absolute* and *final* Truth, the one and only Realization.

*   *   *   *   *

The actual realization is always already the *same*, only the way of approach or methods differ. There is only one God, one Universal Being, and "I am" ("I AM") That I AM. This is the Truth for all – for all is this One Being.

Since the One Being is infinite and eternal there is no separate self, or individual being.

There in neither "I," nor "other than I," there in Only...

SELF INQUIRY

A S HAS ALREADY BEEN STATED AND EXPLAINED, for final spiritual revelation you don't need any method of meditation or way of mind control if you are capable of effectively practicing the *direct process* of Self-Inquiry. Simply feeling and following the current of your own conscious awareness or sense of "I" back in (upstream) to its inner Source, the Heart, and abiding therein is enough, while meditation actually *is* and *requires* duality for its practice – i.e., both the one who meditates *and* that on which he meditates.

In fact, *there is no way of dissolving the ego* – which actually is only a concept, a false notion – *using methods of meditation.* Why? Because *with all methods of meditation* you are actually affirming and reinforcing the very notion of the mind and ego's existence *as a separate entity* when you use these methods. You have to, in order to practice these methods. Self-Inquiry is a stealthy way of transcending the mind or dissolving the false notion that the mind or ego exists as a separate entity. It Awakens you directly from this dream of ignorance.

Also, this single method actually contains or provides the benefits of *all other methods.* It is the highest and very best for focusing awareness in the Heart and dissolving the felt sense of contraction, the "separate-self-sense" long identified with the body-mind. Of all methods of spiritual practice, it is the most *direct* and *immediate* for "attaining" Self-realization or God-realization, the always, already Truth, or One Reality.

Once you awaken to the living Heart-current (the radiance of the Self) and abide in the Heart *as* the Heart and steadily feel, understand and recognize it for what it is, then you have *already arrived* where all other methods are attempting to take you. You then have no further need for *mantra,* or *pranayama* (controlled breathing) or any other form of spiritual practice.

Thinking is the apparent separation of consciousness into the sense of "I" and "other-than-I." It is meditating a separate-self identity, or felt separate existence, or giving rise to a non-existent "self." This is sin and suffering. Pure, unbroken Awareness is the natural state of the Self. Thinking disrupts this natural state of being.

"The Self-conscious being of 'I'-lessness is the That which is one's true State realized by destroying the ego through Self-Inquiry.

"With breath and speech controlled and with one-pointed mind, one should dive within and reach the Source whence rises the 'I'.

"To dive thus within is alone Self-Inquiry. Meditation on a precept concerning the nature of the 'I' is merely an aid thereto.

"On reaching the Heart, by Self-Inquiry, the one continuous Self-awareness or 'I-AMness' reveals itself as the perfect Being, whereupon the 'I' subsides and is lost.

"For one who has realized that State of perfect Being which is verily the inherent Bliss indescribable of the Self absolute, nothing else remains to be accomplished."

– Bhagavan Sri Ramana Maharshi, from *Truth Revealed*

The usual question most people have is, "How will I get any work done?" and/or "How can I be responsible for anything if I don't think?" These questions, which are seemingly logical and reasonable to the mind, are themselves posed by the mind, not the Self. The mind which believes itself to be the "doer" is never really the true Doer but only a "recording" or the accumulated record of "what has been done before." The real Doer of all that is done is God, the very Self, the One Supreme Conscious Awareness. Nothing whatsoever can be done without the power of this Supreme Lord, *which does all.* With revelation comes direct understanding of this fact. God, the great I AM, is the Doer of all actions, being the very present Power and Intelligence that allows all things to be done, and is the Understanding itself of how to do them.

"If one considers oneself as the doer, one has to reap also the fruits of three-fold karma (good and bad fruits of past deeds). When the ego is destroyed through Self-Inquiry, there is neither the doer nor the three-fold karma. The ever-present State of Liberation alone remains." – Bhagavan Sri Ramana Maharshi, from *Truth Revealed*

Consider this: no one ordinarily gives conscious attention to every step he or she takes while walking or to every function performed while driving an automobile. Yet one moves about from place to place easily and responsibly without thinking about it. In a similar manner, all work is done without effort when you abide as you are – as thoughtless Awareness – in the Self, or in the spiritual Heart *as* the Heart.

Sri Bhagavan used to say, "While riding on the train, you don't carry your luggage on your head or in your lap to your discomfort. You put it down and let the train carry it. In the same manner, give all your cares and burdens to the Lord. He who created this universe is capable of carrying all loads, just as the train carries the entire load of passengers and all their baggage."

In the same manner, while abiding in the pure Awareness of the Self – the Heart, which is pure Intelligence – one is just as capable of getting done what is required or expected of you; in fact, even more so, and with far less effort, doubt, or fatigue.

Part VII

In Conclusion

FOREWORD AND FORWARD

IN THE DICTIONARY, THE WORD "FORWARD" means, "being up front, first, foremost, and also onward," while the word "foreword" means "a preface or an introductory note to a book."

This chapter, "Foreword and Forward," is intentionally placed at the end of this book for three reasons. *First*, many people never read the Foreword to a book, but once they start reading the book, they like to read its ending. So this Foreword, located at the end, may be more likely to be read. *Second*, it is also placed at the end to encourage you the reader onward or "forward" with the practice of what it contains, to strongly urge you to make these principles and processes *first and foremost in importance in your life!* And also, it is to suggest that you read the book *again*, in this regard!

The *third* reason is to graphically illustrate that in apparent time and space *all* beginnings innately contain their endings; and, conversely, *all* endings are new beginnings. Therefore, as the reader of this book, you are now in the somewhat unique position of A NEW BEGINNING! It could also be "the beginning of the end" of all further seeking, and therefore *the end of all suffering!*

If you are like the vast majority of spiritual aspirants, prior to reading this book (and even what you may *still feel* to be your experience, or *still* a very strong long-held belief), or perhaps your continued, felt concept of yourself – i.e., "who and what you are" and your resultant point of view – is that you are "a separate individual-being," *one among many* multiple "selves" or "persons" born into this preexisting "solid objective world." That you are now living apart from or different from all these "others" whom you can "see moving about" and around you "in bodies," and living their daily lives "in time and space" in a similar manner *as you appear* to be.

If this is so, it means that you have been (or perhaps still are) considering yourself as being the actual individual "doer of" and/or "recipient of" these very actions "now going on or occurring around you" in the world, and called "life's situations." However, as this text has been attempting to explain in rather extensive (though perhaps still not fully adequate) detail, this is *an enormous misconception about yourself* or the true Self you *actually are*, and is the very cause of all your present suffering in life.

If your primary purpose in life is the "search" for the highest understanding of Truth, or Awakening to Reality, that is, for you to "have this as a factual Realization," (which is usually considered to be spiritual Enlightenment or direct Revelation of the Self), then are you now consciously realizing you are *already* That which you seek? There is no "special" realization apart from the simple, basic everyday awareness you are presently now shining *in and as*. In other words, *this is It*. You are *already* "home free." Quit looking for *another* awareness.

This *is* what's so, now and always, and is only awaiting your immediate, present re-cognition (again knowing it). This book is a direct invitation, a strong urge for you to simply *drop*, or *totally let go*, of all seeking and all the mind's conditioned beliefs causing you to seek, and here and now abide *absolutely* in the ever-present Truth of Being, which is the one Self we all are. If you are thinking otherwise, then re-read this book.

If you are still not directly *realizing* this pure Self, then are you ready to use this preconditioned tendency for "seeking" the Truth (which prolongs your suffering) in a more constructive and life transforming way? If so, turn it into the conscious, intentional practice of Self-Inquiry! That is, begin *now* to *directly* Inquire into the very essence of this "self" you think you are, the one who is now "seeking and doing?" If you do so (by following the instructions contained herein), it will ultimately Awaken you from this dream of mortality into the true Self. It will bring you into the very Heart of your Heart, which is the non-seeking, non-doing, non-dual Infinite and Eternal Self, which is Always, Already Free, Always, Already Peace, Always, Already the Truth and Always, Already Pure Happiness. But you must *stay* with this practice, *constantly!*

Of course, a book cannot "give" you Enlightenment. But a book written *from* Enlightenment can indicate appropriate directions which, when conscientiously followed and applied *within yourself,* can produce results that align your mind with the non-thinking, non-seeking Awareness of the Heart, the very Self, where true Enlightenment is *already happening* in you. If you will recognize it, this text is pointing you in the correct "direction" for applying or "practicing" for yourself the correct processes that *will* bring you *certain success!*

If you are open and receptive to what you have read, are already beginning to apply these principles and precepts in your life, and are using the Self-Inquiry process, then this is already beginning to occur with you from reading this text. If this is not yet your experience, it can and will be as you again read the text and study more deeply the material it contains. Hundreds of people, who have read the book's first printing, have reported this to already be the case for them.

When you read a textbook and open yourself to the quality of realization and understanding that the author is experiencing, you allow that quality to Awaken as *your own* qualitative experience, even if only at very subtle depths of your being. You may "re-discover" that same quality in your own nature by reading often, again and again, their written words, or by hearing their spoken words. This is especially so when they are spiritually Awakened teachers who are *already consciously abiding* in the state of pure Awareness.

Conversely, this principle or process at work in the written or spoken works of those who are merely "seekers-of-enlightenment" (not already living from the enlightened state) keeps you *continuing in your seeking.* Therefore, you are truly fortunate when you can associate with one who is *already* spiritually Awakened, and can study his or her written or spoken messages on spiritual Truth.

There really can never be "enough said" about the Truth, for the real Truth cannot be "said" anyway. Yet, paradoxically, everything an "Enlightened Person" says regarding the Truth is the Truth, even though the Truth cannot be said. So, any amount of reading or listening directly to the statements of Truth of someone who is Awakened can produce good results such as triggering enlightenment in a sincere seeker.

In this context, all that can be said about the Truth is said in this book. Yet, neither this nor any other book can possibly *say* all that can be said about the Truth, or itself *awaken* you.

An immediate example and demonstration of the problem and the paradox of "speaking" about enlightenment is seen in the second paragraph above, which speaks of one who is enlightened as being an "enlightened person." The Truth is, there is no enlightened "person," for this is a contradiction in terms. Enlightenment brings about the realization that there is no person, as such, nor has there ever been a "person" or individual being, per se. All is the Self, the One Absolute Being.

However, when you come to the place in your life, through suffering the frustration and futility of seeking after the Truth (or Real Happiness) and are ready (due to your frustration and suffering from your unfruitful seeking) to truly "hear" and understand that *all* seeking after Truth and Happiness is in fact really *avoiding* rather than abiding in the Truth and Happiness, you should then be ready to stop seeking and simply be quiet and abide in the true Self *that you always, already are.*

If you *are* ready, and you *truly understand* what has been said about the mind and Self-Inquiry, you will see that this very simple, yet powerful and paradoxical method or process is a conscious strategy to trick the ever-seeking mind and bring the search to an end.

Then you should be willing to apply Self-Inquiry and this teaching *to end all further seeking!* For now, if you do understand, you have a *new weapon* and *a new-direction* or *a new strategy* of "specialized seeking *that ends all seeking.*" This means the non-seeking *abidance* in the true Self, the Location of Real Happiness.

Consciously understand: Even though this "inner quest," which is *a method of seeking that ends all seeking* (by "seeking the source of seeking") appears to be a contradiction in terms, it is nonetheless the Truth, AND IT WORKS! However, you must be intelligent, diligently dedicated, and steadily alert in your effort.

[Since the four previous paragraphs beginning with, *"However, when you come to the place in your life..."* are exceptionally long and perhaps not easy to read and grasp, you should read them again to make sure you get their true and real meaning].

The purpose of this text is to provide you with a procedural means for clearing a space in the mind or Consciousness that allows you to directly *experience* the real nature and essence of your very Being, which is always, already Present Happiness – not dependent on anyone or anything for its existence; for it *is* Existence, itself. This means the end of all further seeking and suffering.

"Purpose," as meant here, is defined as an aim, direction or intention. It is the reason a thing exists. Though it is *not* your goal, it is the reason you are willing to set a goal and work toward its achievement. You may have the goal of going from New York to Los Angeles. West would be your purpose; Los Angeles would be your goal. On arriving at your goal you would still have more "west" (or purpose) that is not yet completed. As it is meant here, you never really end a purpose unless you intentionally choose to withdraw from it, for "purpose" is the actual *context* – in which or from which you function or operate.

Even if your goal is only the reading of this book, don't let that end your purpose. If the book's purpose (Enlightenment NOW, or in this lifetime) is truly *your own* purpose, then you should continue reading it and set goals to read and re-read it again and again – thoroughly and often – especially those chapters and parts that strongly appeal to you; but also, include those chapters or parts where you feel resistance, doubt, opposing views or disagreement. Then soon, the realization of the book's conscious purpose will be your own. For it is *even now* only waiting to be awakened, uncovered and revealed to you from within your own Heart!

Use the "Notes and Personal Index" (on page 253) to index material for easily finding it again and to make your own notes, personal insights, experiences, and even disagreements. Also, it is recommended you write down the dates and page numbers for the notes or comments you list, for future reference and comparison, e.g., new considerations, changes of outlook, and revised or new thoughts, insights or ideas, etc. This can be a big help. It is beneficial to see your progress and observe the development of your spiritual insights and understanding when you read and consider the same principles, processes or ideas in the coming months ahead, or even years from now.

During my years of seeking I used to underline material in all the books I read and write notes to myself in the margins with insights, questions and disagreements, and the dates of these. As I advanced in spiritual understanding and experience and again read these books, it became very interesting. I could easily recognize my own progress or development. Material I didn't fully understand or agree with during earlier readings was often clear and even informative or enlightening on subsequent occasions. In some cases, what I had thought to be true earlier was later seen to be only partly true or even completely false, based on my increased understanding over time. I sometimes wrote to authors who were still living and questioned or challenged their concepts, positions or points of view or complimented them on their significant insights or thanked them for their explanations. This became very beneficial to me and even on occasions to them as well.

It is recommended that you do this with this book and also write if you have any difficulty or disagreements with what you have read. I am open to hearing your insights or points of view if different, as they can perhaps lend a deeper meaning to what is being stated or herein explained.

ABOUT RAMANA

STARTING AT A VERY EARLY AGE, RAMANA intentionally sought a deeper understanding of God, the true source and cause of things, of Self, and the real meaning and Purpose of Life. Born in El Paso, Texas on November 1, 1929, he was named Dee Wayne Ray by his unmarried mother. At 13 months, foster parents adopted him, giving him their surname, Trammell. They had no children of their own and loved him as their own son. They were ordinary people, not very well educated, and of only modest means. During the years of the 1930s Depression and after, they made many personal sacrifices just to meet his needs, often before their own. And on occasion, within reason, some of his childhood wishes or needs were met even before their own, though they were careful to never spoil him. They did not tell him he was adopted but secretly concealed the fact from him until age 16 at which time he legally chose their family name as his own. The shock of the unforeseen disclosure of his held-in-secret adoption brought to light in consciousness the cause of a great deal of long suppressed feelings of confusion, doubt and mistrust he had always had and never quite understood. This began releasing pent up conflicts that took years to complete.

Yet, there was a short period in Ramana's early childhood years that were nevertheless lived from a unique consciousness of being one with all life. He was either born awake to this oneness with all being, or it came about as the result of a serious accident when he was about 5 years old. During what were really hard times in which his parents were having to temporally live in a one room tent, he was accidentally seriously burned when a pot of boiling water toppled into his lap. The town doctor was not available, and so to calm his screams and soothe his pain his parents at the suggestion of nearby neighbors sent some older boys deep into a nearby woods to the small shack of a hermit living there, to ask him to please come and use his reputed healing powers.

The old hermit was called "Uncle Billy." He was considered strange and mysterious by most of the local community for he always remained alone and isolated from the world, he hardly if ever spoke to anyone and no one knew much about him. He willingly responded, walking the distance through a freezing rain to where Ramana was still writhing and screaming in pain. With a silent gesture, he ran everyone out of the small enclosed tent. The boys had gone for him on horseback and had already explained the situation. Without saying anything, not even a word to anyone, he sat down on a box beside the cot on which Ramana was lying that also served as his bed. Uncle Billy moved his left hand back and forth about an inch above the major area of the burn which covered the entire area of the top side of Ramana's left thigh, leg and ankle. The other hand alternated between Ramana's head or rested gently on the area of his heart. Ramana remembers that Uncle Billy silently whispered a few non-perceptible words, some of them into his ear. Everyone else was outside the tent waiting anxiously. Almost immediately, Ramana became disassociated from or unidentified with his body, stopped crying, and total silence filled the entire space around and about Ramana and Uncle Billy. Without saying a word, Uncle Billy left the tent and returned to his shack. *Everyone was amazed!* For the longest time everyone remained subdued, then talking hurriedly resumed as all recollected the event and speculated on what had just occurred, *but no one knew for sure what really happened!*

Ramana recollects that his consciousness was taken temporarily out of and beyond his body that was itself still undergoing pain. However it was happening only *to his body* and not to him, as he then recognized awareness to be what he was, and *not* his body. Following this incident, he remained clearly aware that he *as awareness* was one with all life, and existing as simple perception prior to all life as it was appearing in all its many forms. This state of freedom from body-mind identification continued for a good while after that.

Ramana's recognition of this "prior-to-the-body-awareness" remained with him (on and off) for about three or four years. It would come and go, usually in the morning on awakening from sleep, but subside when he became active. It would sporadically return at various intervals during the day when he was quiet, which he could usually induce. This was usually at meal time, or when walking or playing alone in the nearby woods, or when sitting or lying quietly in his favorite spot under the shade of his favorite tree.

This state might have been there to some degree before the accident, but Ramana is not really certain about this since it was a very long time ago. He believes it was perhaps his destiny, was brought about by the accident and by Uncle Billy's intervention and compassion. However, Ramana's destiny did cause this highest insight to be eventually totally lost from his experience. While it lasted, he was aware that this experience of oneness was not shared by others around him. This fact and early traumas eventually brought about the loss of this awareness, subsiding like a thick veil was now concealing it, when at about the age of eight or nine years he again "fell into the soup" or "the amnesia of Self-forgetfulness" along with everyone else. Nonetheless, he never fully forgot this early cognition even though it moved to the background of his memory, much like the declining memory of a vivid dream that gradually fades as the years go by. But it was always there, beckoning him back again into it.

During Ramana's young adult to middle years, there was the compulsive quest to again finally return to the full consciousness of this transcendental Awareness. He was driven by this quest, although few around him during these years knew this was his primary concern. He took up most of the usual, traditional paths and methods of spiritual seeking. He studied the Bible and other sacred scriptures, along with the methods, teachings and philosophies of both West and East. His earlier years were spent in the life and practice of traditional Christianity. But each gain in traditional knowledge only left him as incomplete and as identified with the body-mind as before. Intuition of the underlying pure Awareness always remained present, though trapped deep within him, along with the "knowing" that seeking after what one *already* is, is futile. Yet he was always compelled to keep seeking, for he had not yet again found the state of natural abidance that he sought. It was like a thick veil was concealing it.

His ordinary adult life has included the various roles of husband (in four marriages) and father of three children, with the deep pain of loss of his first daughter drowning in the family swimming pool at the age of eighteen months. [Since the first edition of this book, his 42 year old son died in May

2001]. Ramana founded two successful businesses. He spent a number of years as a clergyman, a counselor, and as a self-improvement instructor. His life has been both full and interesting, in his words "having experienced just about everything a person *can* experience in one lifetime." He has lived from coast to coast in the United States and for a short time in the Orient while in the U.S. Army.

In the summer of 1973, his spiritual search was brought to completion and conclusion when he discovered his real and ultimate Teacher (guru) Bhagavan Sri Ramana Maharshi. By means of a mystical experience, Ramana's body was forcefully "taken" to a bookstore in Houston, Texas, where his hand and eye were simultaneously "guided" to a specific book of Sri Bhagavan's teachings. As he opened the book, it opened immediately to a picture of the gentle Sage and his eyes fell upon the picture. As he peered into the intense compassion, beauty and wisdom radiating from the Sage's eyes, Ramana experienced again the immediate radical transformation in his total being, reawakening him once and for all to that former awareness lost during his childhood, which he now learned or realized was the true Self. Thereafter, with the spiritual Heart fully re-Awakened, when any thought arose, Ramana simply used the newly discovered Self-Inquiry process of Sri Bhagavan and settled back into the Self, or the Heart.

He found Self-Inquiry to be the end of all seeking. For those just starting to use it, it is the "beginning of the end" of their seeking and *the only true method of ending all methods of seeking.*

Bhagavan's grace transcended time and space, awakening Ramana spiritually and leaving him abiding free and clear in the Heart of the Self.

In the early spring and summer of 1974, Ramana underwent a series of experiences that produced an even more radical, stabilizing and final Transformation. This resulted in part from his regular use of this simple yet powerful process of Self-Inquiry. It was, however, further magnified and intensified and his spiritual state formally and finally confirmed by a significant meeting with the renowned Swami Muktananda Paramahansa (affectionately called, "Baba"), from Ganeshpuri, India, who was then visiting America. Baba, a God-realized Indian yogi saint (being a *Siddha* Yogi [Perfected Being]) immediately recognized Ramana's spiritual state and gave him the spiritual name "Ramana" after his beloved guru.

The name Ramana means, "one who plays (or revels) in God." "Ram" and "Rama" both mean "God" in Sanskrit. Ramana now "revels in God," for he lives and plays in the awakened Heart or Self as his natural state.

In 1978, in Greensboro, North Carolina, where he was living at the time, Ramana founded AHAM – The Association of Happiness for All Mankind. He was joined in this major endeavor by Elizabeth MacDonald, his first sincerely dedicated student in Greensboro. AHAM now serves thousands of spiritual aspirants, with students of its Conscious Teaching all over the world. There are AHAM graduates living on all five major continents. Ramana now serves as AHAM's spiritual director.

AHAM now owns and operates a beautiful 35-acre Meditation Retreat and Spiritual Training Center located at the edge of the Uwharrie National Forest, 10 miles south of Asheboro in the very heart of North Carolina on the east coast of the United States. It also owns and operates ARUNACHALA RAMANA AHAM ASHRAM, a new modern ashram in South India, located in Tiruvannamalai near the holy hill, Arunachala, and the ashram of Bhagavan Sri Ramana Maharshi. Ramana now makes annual visits to South India during the winter season where he spends from three to four months a year. Both there and in America he receives and redirects sincere students from all over the world back into the true Self.

Students and visitors to both of AHAM's facilities are guided by Ramana and AHAM's dedicated staff (all Ramana's students) in the Way of Enlightened Happiness, or in living the Conscious Way of Happiness-NOW – rather than seeking happiness in some future experience, time or state. The influence of his conscious presence has a profound and peaceful effect on those around him, especially those who approach him with an openness to receive a higher insight and understanding of Self or God. This openness really means having a genuine willingness to let go of all that is blocking one's abidance in the very Self – one's own true and natural state.

There is nothing mysterious or "other worldly" about Ramana. He is a very ordinary man who for years has had a daily work schedule (often putting in from 6 to 8 hours a day on the computer in the AHAM office) alongside everyone else living and working at the AHAM Center or Ashram. However, due to the effect on his body of a stroke in late December, 2000, he has been progressively less physically active.

Ramana is usually easily available or accessible (although now this is more by advanced appointment), talks very openly and plainly, and jokes and laughs with those who come to visit the center or ashram, or to study AHAM's Teaching.

Over the years, he developed the majority of AHAM's Conscious Curriculum for Awakening to the Self. Most of which he personally wrote, or compiled from the teaching of Sri Ramana Maharshi, and from a few other recognized Conscious Teachers some of which served him in his earlier spiritual practice. Much in the AHAM teaching is taken from transcripts of his talks to students of various AHAM programs.

Most portions of AHAM's programs, even in later years contributed by Elizabeth MacDonald, AHAM's executive director and senior trainer, were overseen and verified by him, as to their conscious authenticity, accuracy and purity.

EPILOGUE
(From the First Edition)

A S STATED IN THE PREFACE TO THE FIRST printing, this book was written in January 1979, in Greensboro, NC. At the time, AHAM was an idea that was only beginning to manifest. It had hardly begun as an outreach.

The original idea of AHAM was revealed to Ramana in a vision during meditation in the early morning of August 28, 1978, in which the very strong Presence of Sri Bhagavan Ramana Maharshi was felt in the room. During this period, Ramana was in a state of transition, looking for an indication of the next significant step for him to take following the radical spiritual transformation that had occurred just five years earlier by the profound grace of Sri Bhagavan. He was temporarily residing with a friend in Greensboro. The living room where he was meditating when the vision occurred seemed to radiate or glow with Sri Bhagavan's Presence. It totally overcame Ramana and remained in the environment hours afterward. Elizabeth MacDonald, Ramana's first dedicated student in Greensboro, visited him later that day and was herself noticeably affected by the Peace, Presence and Power that were still present in the room a few hours afterwards. They talked about it and Ramana told her about the vision and how he had been given the idea and the name of AHAM (Association of Happiness for All Mankind) during the vision. AHAM was revealed as being a conscious instrument of Sri Bhagavan's pure Teaching that would one day extend across America and eventually around the world, bringing Sri Bhagavan's Presence and His Conscious Transformational Process of Self-Inquiry to millions of awaiting seekers everywhere.

On that day Elizabeth agreed to join Ramana in the context of AHAM and holding it in consciousness as "an idea whose time has come." A few weeks later, Elizabeth met Patricia Thompson and introduced her to Ramana. She too, a sincere spiritual seeker, became one of Ramana's first students. When Ramana told her about AHAM and shared its world vision, she offered him a permanent home in her new townhouse. It also became the first official address for AHAM.

Ramana wrote this original Epilogue twenty years, three months and nine days later, while visiting Sri Ramanasramam in India. This was as final arrangements for this book's first printing, in its first hard cover edition, were being completed.

Here is the remainder of the first Epilogue as written *at that time* by Ramana, in first person:

Both Elizabeth and Patricia [mentioned above] are also here at the ashram with me, and today [1998] we have a few thousand graduates of AHAM's Conscious Teaching. We now visit Sri Ramanasramam annually, bringing AHAM graduates and students who are now devotees of Sri Bhagavan; they all have been introduced to Him by the spiritual work of AHAM and its growing staff of dedicated people. All who make this annual group pilgrimage with us do so to be in the close physical proximity and environment of the Holy Hill, Sri Arunachala, where Sri Bhagavan lived for over fifty years sharing the highest spiritual Truth. Also, AHAM now owns a few acres of property viewing the western slope of the Holy Hill, where it plans to build its own center, providing a place for AHAM people to stay when visiting Sri Bhagavan's ashram and the Holy Hill. It will also serve as a focus for charitable services to the less fortunate in the local community.

[**NOTE:** *AHAM now owns a beautiful, modern ashram with all Western amenities at a different location, as well as the property mentioned here. Plans are for building additional living accommodations on it, for devotees visiting from the West.*]

AHAM's Conscious Curriculum has grown from the transformation programs I alone was conducting in the early days of AHAM, to now having qualified Trainers trained by me who are giving a full schedule of courses designed to awaken students who diligently live the Teaching to the Self. Also other programs have been designed solely for living consciously and effectively *in* the world, but *not of* the world.

Letters are received daily from scores of graduates expressing their heartfelt gratitude for this spiritual Awakening and/or the radical improvement that has occurred in their lives, especially in their relationships with family, friends and coworkers, based entirely on what they have learned at AHAM. But even more significant are those who, with the Grace of Sri Bhagavan Ramana and AHAM's presentation of His Conscious Teaching, have discovered and Awakened to the true Self and live steadily and happily in the Heart of pure Being. Today, the primary purpose and message of AHAM is being realized and lived, as more and more seekers are learning about us.

Our simple message of the Truth, as realized: Consciousness *must* be, before anything else can be; if Consciousness is *not*, nothing else is. We are *all* this Consciousness, whether we realize what Consciousness *is* and the significance of it – or not. If we are not conscious, we cannot be aware of anything – of the mind and thoughts, of the body, of this world or of anyone or any thing in it. Consciousness *JUST IS, prior to* thoughts, *prior to* the mind. We do not have to think in order to know that we exist, or that we *are*.

Consciousness is God; God is pure Consciousness. This Consciousness in its purity is omnipresent, omniscient, and omnipotent. It is not individual. It is Universal, being without divisions, parts or limitations, without beginning or ending; it is always, already the One Presence and Reality – infinite and eternal.

So, God (being Consciousness itself) dwells *in* us, *as* us, and we don't have to "do" anything to *be* the Self (this pure Consciousness) or to be God-realized; for this is always, already the One Reality and our true and natural state. We are all the one Self, like waves on the one Ocean of being.

Just stop seeking outside and look within. Turn your attention inward, dive deep into the Self – without thought – and make this awareness absolute; surrender to the Absolute Consciousness within. The Real Self is ever-radiating in the Heart of "your own being." For this to be "your" ever-present *lived* experience, Self-Inquiry is the One *direct* and *immediate* Way.

A great aid to quickening or knowing this Conscious Process is abiding in *Sat Sanga* (Conscious Company) – that is, "hanging out" in the Conscious Radiance, the transforming environment that pervades the AHAM Center – which is lived and shared by the staff and all who abide in its proximity. Also, it radiates in the presence of members of AHAM's Community at Large. This includes many participating in regular AHAM "Association In Consciousness" meditation sessions held in many major cities along the East Coast of America, at a few locations in the mid-west and on the West Coast, and in Canada and Europe. Also, it is present at our ashram in India.

Today, by the grace of Sri Bhagavan, by the extension of His Presence and His Divine Will – for those who are open and ready to receive it – **AHAM (The Association of Happiness for All Mankind)** is *"An Idea Whose Time Has Come!"*

There are people living on all the major continents of the world who now know how to abide in Real Happiness-NOW as a results of AHAM – from its existence, or living presence, and its teaching efforts.

AN INVITATION

IF YOU HAVE ANY DIFFICULTY UNDERSTANDING or fully accepting *anything* contained in this text, or any special problem or question regarding your spiritual quest or practice of Self-Inquiry, please feel free to contact us. Also, if you would like information about AHAM's Conscious Curriculum based on the teachings of Sri Bhagavan Ramana Maharshi, Non-duality, Spiritual Enlightenment, or living in the Self and the State of True Happiness-NOW, contact us.

AHAM is the only established organization in the world that actually teaches Self-Inquiry, the Conscious Transformational Process for the Realization and Abidance in the True Self as introduced to the world by Bhagavan Sri Ramana Maharshi. In your early practice, an advanced graduate-student is assigned to be your Buddy, answer your questions, and assist you in the correct practice of the process. This is a great benefit! Our buddies often become life-long friends. You may also have an AHAM Sponsor to stay free of addictive body-mind thoughts!

AHAM also offers a *free* weekly telecommunication program called "Heart-Line." Do participate in these *free* seminars, and have a *direct experience* of the Self in Conscious Company (*Sat Sanga*) with the Awakened Heart. The only cost to you is your one hour long-distance phone call. *A reservation is necessary!* If living abroad, we know of special rate telephone services. Just email us for the Heart-Line number and for full information.

If you wish guidance in your own quest of the Self – based on the Teachings of Bhagavan Sri Ramana Maharshi – call, write or email AHAM at either location below:

AHAM Meditation Retreat and Spiritual Training Center
4368 NC Hwy. 134
Asheboro, NC 27205-1117 – USA
Phone: (336) 381-3988 • Fax: (336) 381-3881
Email: ahamcntr@asheboro.com

Arunachala Ramana AHAM Ashram – India
India telephone: 04175-237283
India email: arunaham@vsnl.com

Visit our web site: www.aham.com

NOTES AND PERSONAL INDEX

Date	Subject or Key Idea:	Page

Notes and Personal Index (Continued)

Date	Subject or Key Idea:	Page